# FROM MORALITY TO VIRTUE

# FROM MORALITY
# TO VIRTUE

MICHAEL SLOTE

New York   Oxford
OXFORD UNIVERSITY PRESS
1992

## Oxford University Press

Oxford   New York   Toronto
Delhi   Bombay   Calcutta   Madras   Karachi
Petaling Jaya   Singapore   Hong Kong   Tokyo
Nairobi   Dar es Salaam   Cape Town
Melbourne   Auckland

and associated companies in
Berlin   Ibadan

## Copyright © 1992 by Michael Slote

Published by Oxford University Press, Inc.
200 Madison Avenue, New York, NY 10016

Oxford is a registered trademark of Oxford University Press

Library of Congress Cataloging-in-Publication Data
Slote, Michael A.
From morality to virtue / Michael Slote.
p. cm.   Includes index.
ISBN 0-19-507562-5
1. Ethics.
2. Virtue.
3. Kant, Immanuel, 1724–1804—Ethics.
4. Common sense.
5. Utilitarianism.   I. Title.
BJ1012.S5165   1992   170—dc20   91-38853

1 3 5 7 9 8 6 4 2

Printed in the United States of America
on acid-free paper

This sharp distinction of virtue and morality as co-ordinate and independent forms of goodness will explain a fact which otherwise it is difficult to account for. If we turn from books on Moral Philosophy to any vivid account of human life and action such as we find in Shakespeare, nothing strikes us more than the comparative remoteness of the discussions of Moral Philosophy from the facts of actual life.

H. A. Prichard in "*Does Moral Philosophy Rest on a Mistake?*"

*For David Lewis*
*and*
*Derek Parfit*

# ACKNOWLEDGMENTS

This book has accumulated many debts on the path to completion. Portions of Chapters 1 and 3 have previously appeared in Owen Flanagan and Amelie Rorty, eds., *Identity, Character, and Morality: Essays in Moral Psychology* (Bradford/MIT, 1990). For helpful criticisms and suggestions, I would like to thank Marcia Baron, Larry Blum, Keith Campbell, Louis Pojman, Georges Rey, Amélie Rorty, Ernie Schlaretzki, Jerry Schneewind, Nancy Sherman, Peter Simpson, and, especially, Derek Parfit and two readers for Oxford University Press. I am also grateful to Terry Mackey for secretarial assistance.

# Contents

# Introduction

In recent years there has been a resurgence of interest among philosophers in the ethics of virtue. For a long time, ethics has been dominated by a concern with right and wrong—a concern central to the ethics of Kant, utilitarianism, and common-sense moral intuitionism. But lately there have been numerous attempts to account for the nature of one or another particular (moral) virtue, to interrelate various of the different virtues, and even to characterize the notion of virtue generally, that is, to say what virtue is or what it is to be a virtue. Others have urged that the whole subject of ethics is best introduced through discussion of (the) virtue(s), and still others have called for an ethics of virtue that does away with considerations of right and wrong action or that at least gives such concerns a minor or secondary place in an overall theoretical account of ethical phenomena.

However, it is as yet unclear whether there will or can be any plausible positive response to these calls for another approach. Dissatisfaction, for one reason or another, with the ruling theories of contemporary ethics, theories more fundamentally concerned with right and wrong than with any other substantive ethical topic, has so far failed to elicit a systematic alternative to those approaches. What has been offered has mostly been ways to supplement one or another view of right and wrong with an account, more or less systematic, of how dispositions toward the right or toward the good are essential to the moral life. But virtue and particular virtues understood as dispositions of this kind clearly have a secondary or derivative role in ethics, and although others have gestured more strongly in the direction of a truly independent ethics of virtue, no one has offered a specific enough foundational or non-derivative account of (the) virtue(s) to enable us to see how such a positive ethical conception fares against the standard conceptions of ethics—Kantianism, utilitarianism, common-sense moral intuitionism, for example—that represent the most obvious and inevitable competitors of any new and systematic ethics of virtue. Until such an ethics is articulated with sufficient breadth and specificity so as to be able to take its place among the live options of systematic ethical theory, until, moreover, the sorts of conceptual and theoretical issues that have been raised among utilitarianism, intuitionism, and Kantianism are also raised in connection with a virtue ethics possessing enough structure to make such issues relevant to its own validity, the idea of a fundamentally virtue-ethical approach will remain a merely speculative possibility.

In *From Morality to Virtue* I offer foundations for a general account of a specific form of virtue ethics, one that is sufficiently oriented to conceptual/structural issues and specific about what counts as a virtue to enable us to compare its merits with those of currently dominant approaches to ethics. Our discussion will not be dominated either by purely theoretical considerations or by an attempt to offer intuitively adequate descriptions of particular virtues and their instances; we will operate at varying levels of generality and attempt to indicate how the claims made at different levels cohere within a single and fairly systematic view of ethical phenomena. And I will argue that there are reasons for preferring the particular version of virtue ethics introduced here to the various general conceptions of ethics we are nowadays most familiar with.

Those who have spoken of what is or could be distinctive in a genuinely virtue-theoretical approach to ethics, in an ethics in which virtue plays a fundamental, rather than secondary or derivative, role, have often focused on two features that might differentiate a total virtue ethics from more familiar theories like Kantianism, utilitarianism, and commonsense intuitionism. They have said that such an ethics will be more interested in the virtuous character of virtuous individuals than in the actions of such individuals, and they have also claimed that virtue ethics should be grounded in aretaic concepts of goodness and excellence (and their opposites) rather than in deontic notions like "ought," "right," "wrong," and "obligatory." There is a troublesome but interesting ambiguity in the first mentioned of these criteria that will occupy us at a later point in this book, but for the present I can say that the approach taken here will meet both these criteria.

However, since all the ethical views under serious consideration today give an important or central role to deontic notions, it seems almost unimaginable that a proper ethics should make no use of them. We might grant that an ethics without deontic concepts could represent an important *fragment* of the ethics we ultimately seek, but we can't imagine a complete ethics doing without such notions altogether. And I might, therefore, just mention at this point that I hope to be able to show you how deontic concepts can be derived from aretaic ones and used in ethical rules and precepts. Of course, one might wonder whether derivative deontic notions can possibly have the force of such notions conceived as fundamental or as independent of the aretaic, but I will argue that an adequate objective account of ethical phenomena doesn't need judgments possessing such greater force, and base that argument in part on the idea—familiar from utilitarianism—of a split between theoretically valid ethical standards and judgments, on the one hand, and the practically useful and perhaps more forceful ethical principles/rules/advice that serve to govern everyday life, on the other.

Although there is obviously something attractive, at least to some people, about the idea of a distinctive ethics of virtue, I believe the case for developing such an ethics becomes stronger, even becomes pressing, in the light of the criticisms that can be made of presently dominant general approaches to ethics. A great deal of recent work in ethics, has focused, for example, on paradoxical features of our common-sense moral thinking, and I have in mind here both Nagel's and Williams's treatment of "moral luck" and Scheffler's discussion of the quirks and difficulties of ordinary deontology, as well as work of my own on the odd and even paradoxical consequences of the self-other asymmetry that attaches to common-sense morality. In the light of recent discussions and other considerations mentioned, for the first time, in this book, I believe it can be shown that common-sense morality—and any total ethical view that includes the latter as a part—faces serious, if not insuperable, difficulties, and I shall also attempt to show in what follows that rather similar considerations also threaten Kantian ethics. The upshot, after the argument of Part I, will be that we need to improve upon Kantian and common-sense ethical/moral ideas, but that both act-utilitarianism and one kind (at least) of virtue ethics are not touched by these criticisms and, remaining as it were intact, deserve to be further explored and evaluated to determine their relative merits and demerits. (Of course, one could also try radically revising common-sense morality and/or Kantian ethics, but some of the obstacles to doing so are pointed out in Part I.)

One thing that utilitarianism and the virtue ethics I wish to propose have in common is self-other *symmetry* of a sort precisely absent from common-sense and Kantian morality. According to both the latter, failures to help others may be wrong in a way it doesn't intuitively seem wrong to fail to help oneself, and one of one's acts may be morally better than another because it produces more happiness for other people, but an act is not morally better because it produces more happiness for its agent. However, both utilitarianism and my proposed version of virtue ethics treat benefits and harms to the agent as relevant to the evaluation of actions in the same way, basically, as benefits and harms to other people are relevant to their ethical evaluations of actions, and it turns out that their common avoidance of asymmetry allows utilitarianism and virtue ethics to go forward securely in a manner that, as I argue, is not possible for either Kantianism or common-sense (intuitionistic) morality.

But what kind of virtue ethics can escape self-other asymmetry if such asymmetry, as I have suggested, pervades common-sense moral thinking in a general way? For if it does, then (as I think we should assume) both common-sense deontic and common-sense aretaic moral judgments are subject to debilitating forms of self-other asymmetry, and that presumably means that a common-sense ethics of virtue that uses common-sense ideas about what is morally virtuous or morally good will be open to criticism in the same way that common-sense deontic judgments (as a class) are. Does that then mean that virtue ethics should abandon common-sense for some other possible approach?

In a sense, yes; but, as we shall see, in another sense, certainly not. An ethics of virtue should, in light of the criticisms referred to—though hardly explored—above, abandon common-sense aretaic moral judgments, but it is also important to recognize that our common-sense ethical thinking *makes use of certain aretaic notions that are not specifically moral.*

Consider the notion of a virtue and that of an admirable act, person, or trait of character. All these ethical notions are *aretaic*, but none is tied to *moral* evaluation in particular. An act useful or beneficial to its agent may not thereby count as morally good or as having moral merit or value, but we may admire such an act, regard it as admirable, and think of it as exemplifying some self-regarding virtue. In other words, even common sense distinguishes between moral virtue, or what counts as *a* moral virtue, and what counts as a virtue *ueberhaupt*. Roughly speaking, only what concerns people other than the agent or trait possessor counts intuitively as a moral virtue or as morally good, but by our common lights both other-benefiting and self-benefiting traits and actions can be admirable or (instances of) virtues. And clearly it is a part of the business of ethics—though perhaps not of morality proper—to describe and evaluate such (largely) self-regarding traits as prudence, fortitude, heedlessness, circumspection, and injudiciousness.

The virtue ethics I will be developing will discard specifically moral aretaic concepts in favor of "neutral" aretaic concepts like admirability and (a) virtue. But since in common-sense terms the latter apply in virtue (excuse me!) of both self-regarding and other-regarding considerations and since, in addition, those aretaic concepts are capable of giving rise to derivatively deontic concepts with self-regarding and other-regarding relevance, our virtue ethics will cover a great deal of the ground covered by our common-sense thinking, but it will do so without falling into the paradoxes and difficulties that can be seen to beset common-sense morality in particular.

But what of utilitarianism, which I want to claim also avoids the problems of common-sense morality (and of Kantian ethics)? Clearly, we must consider utilitarianism and, if virtue ethics is to be defended, show why the latter is superior to utilitarianism (and/or consequentialism more generally). To that end, I shall consider utilitarianism in the final chapter of Part I and begin a mutual comparison of utilitarianism and virtue ethics in Part II of this book. The "agent-neutrality" of utilitarianism entails a fundamental equality of concern for every single individual, and it will turn out, by contrast, that common-sense virtue ethics is committed to (aretaically formulable) principles or rules recommending (merely) a *balance* of concern as between oneself and *other people considered as a class*.

Moreover, in Part III it will emerge that just as virtue ethics is *eliminative* of certain specifically moral concepts that common-sense morality applies in an asymmetrical and consequently paradoxical fashion (I am somewhat simplifying here), utilitarianism tends toward *reduction* of those (and other) concepts. Utilitarianism allows for rationality, prudence, obligation, and justice all to be understood in terms of producing overall good consequences for human well-being, and the latter can then be reduced to empirical and non-ethical terms by equating it with the production of (overall, on balance) happiness, pleasure, or desire-satisfaction.

But the contrast with virtue ethics takes another turn when we consider what the latter may want to say about the relation between virtue and admirability, on the one hand, and personal good or well-being, on the other. For utilitarianism, what counts as excellent or admirable or a virtue counts as such because of its overall consequences for human well-being conceived as reducible to happiness or pleasure. But our virtue ethics eliminates neither the notion of personal well-being or good nor that of admirability or status as a virtue, and for reasons to be explored later it cannot consistently reduce admirability/virtue to personal well-being, even by refusing to allow the latter to be further reduced to pleasure/happiness. Does that then mean that virtue ethics has to retain two independent concepts—that of admirability and that of personal well-being—while utilitarianism has the presumptive advantage of reducing every ethical concept to the single ethical concept of personal good or well-being (and the latter in turn to non-ethical terms)?

Not necessarily. For there is at least one other way of merging or identifying concepts than that offered by reductionism. And as Part III will explore in considerable detail, the contrast between Stoicism and Epicureanism as forms of virtue ethics can enable us to see how this is possible. Like utilitarianism, Epicureanism reduces all virtue to personal well-being understood hedonistically, but it differs from utilitarianism in tying the virtue of any given individual not to the pleasure (or freedom from pain) of mankind generally but, in an egoistic manner, to the pleasure of the individual said to be virtuous. One is virtuous, has virtue, according to Epicureanism, if one acts to ensure one's greatest freedom from pain over the long term. (This may involve helping other people, but such helpfulness is considered only derivatively virtuous by Epicureanism.)

By contrast, Stoicism reverses the direction, as we may put it, of identification or unification, by claiming that virtue is the only intrinsic personal good. Ordinarily, we think of virtue and our capacity for virtue as a higher aspect of ourselves and our lives than (mere) happiness and our capacity for it and/or for well-being. And Epicureanism says that the former, supposedly higher element of human life is reducible to, can be brought down to the level of, mere happiness or well-being. But Stoicism says that our well-being, our human good, is nothing less than (egoistically conceived) virtue or virtuous living. It takes well-being, which is commonly regarded as lower than virtue, and treats it as nothing less—or lower—than virtue. In other words, it identifies all distinctions of well-being or personal good with distinctions of virtue or admirability, and in the terminology we will be adopting later, we can, therefore, say that Stoicism *elevates* (all distinctions in) well-being to (distinctions in) virtue or virtuous living.

Both reduction and elevation are possible ways to bring virtue/admirability and personal good/well-being together, and although the virtue ethics of this book is far from egoistic—arguing, as I mentioned above, for balance as between self-regarding and other-regarding concerns—our virtue ethics can, if it wishes, borrow a page from Stoicism. Even if it cannot reduce the admirable to the personally good in the manner of utilitarianism and Epicureanism, it may attempt to elevate the personally good to the level of the (self-other symmetrically, rather than egoistically) admirable, and this would enable it to bring all its ethical notions under the single concept of the admirable.

Virtue ethics is capable, therefore, of bringing into its apparatus of concepts a unity fully comparable to that which utilitarianism achieves by reduction—doing so by a strategy of seriatim elimination and elevation; but in Part III I will argue that such unity, however theoretically desirable in itself, can only be purchased at the expense of unintuitive consequences that virtue ethics—especially one based in common-sense ideas of admirability and virtue-status—is likely to find unacceptable. We will also see that utilitarianism has a problem justifying its reductionism over an eliminative approach that would claim that nothing is good or right and that all there is is pleasure/happiness and acts (motives, etc.) that are conducive to pleasure/happiness. And, beginning in Part IV, the emphasis will shift from comparison of the methods and results of utilitarianism and virtue ethics to direct criticism of utilitarianism.

Utilitarianism is capable of directly evaluating not only acts, but also motives and traits of character in terms of their consequences for human or sentient happiness, and in Part IV I attempt to show that the utilitarian conception of what is admirable or excellent in people has highly unintuitive implications that (unsurprisingly) do not attach to common-sense virtue ethics. (It turns out that similar criticisms can also be made of consequentialism generally.) In addition, Part IV will argue that all specific forms of utilitarianism are underdetermined relative to the methodological and foundational assumptions utilitarianism typically relies on. Utilitarianism is in fact underdetermined in more than one way relative to its own distinctive forms of justification, and the impossibility of giving such a justification for any specific version of direct (act, or motive, etc.) utilitarianism constitutes, therefore, another reason for discarding utilitarianism and for preferring virtue ethics as an ongoing viable theoretical option.

Because our virtue ethics depends on no specifically moral concepts and all the currently prevalent ethical theories to be discarded in its favor make use of such concepts, it should be clear how distinctive our proposed virtue ethics really is. For in addition to focusing on character and making aretaic concepts fundamental, in the way that genuine virtue ethics is generally supposed to do, it restricts itself to non-moral aretaic and deontic concepts, and in that sense the kind of virtue ethics being developed may be even further from the currently dominant utilitarianism, Kantianism, commonsensism, and the like than advocates of a different, of a new virtue-ethical approach may have anticipated (or desired).

However, our motive for dropping moral notions is not (à la Nietzsche) some general defect that can be pointed to or that one says can be pointed to in every moral view; the rejection of the moral has proceeded, rather, in stages and (in a clearly Rawlsian manner) by the elimination, *seriatim*, of a short list of currently important or viable alternative ethical theories.

(Later I will mention some reasons for not adopting a specifically Platonic or Aristotelian form of virtue ethics and for not discussing the particular views of Rawls, Gauthier, and other recent contractarian theorists.) We have discarded moral notions, not self-righteously or gleefully, like Nietzsche, but reluctantly and in the wake of extended argument. And, also unlike Nietzsche and other putative egoists, we have discarded morality in favor of common-sense views that allow one to place inherent value on other people and on action concerning the wellbeing (or admirability) of others. In all fairness, it might be said that our ethics of virtue is not so much less concerned with others than commonsense morality and Kantianism, as more concerned than both the latter with the happiness of the self/agent who does some action or possesses some admirable trait.

In recent years, it has emerged that utilitarianism is far more regular or symmetrical in its basic assumptions than our ordinary moral thinking can be said to be, and, overall, an approach to ethics that stresses the underlying structures of different ethical or moral views has lately led us, I think, to a much better critical understanding of the differences and similarities among Kantianism, utilitarianism, and common-sense or intuitive morality. However, those who have advocated the development of a distinctive ethics of virtue or who have undertaken analyses of virtue or particular virtues have largely remained aloof from such terms of controversy; and I believe, in fact, that any attempt to provide adequate foundations for a distinct virtue-theoretical approach must consider structural issues and show that an ethics of virtue need not have the structural irregularities, or flaws, that will be shown to be associated with common-sense and Kantian morality. This is the subject that will mainly occupy our attention in Part I and to which we must now turn.

# I

# KANTIAN, UTILITARIAN, AND COMMON-SENSE ETHICS

# 1

## Some Advantages
## of Virtue Ethics

Act-utilitarianism and act-consequentialism more generally are frequently said to require too much of moral agents. Such views standardly demand that one produce the best overall results one can, and if they express a valid conception of morality, then in most individual cases, one will have to sacrifice one's interests or one's deepest personal concerns to comply with the demands of morality. Frequently, defenders of common-sense, intuitive moral thinking criticize consequentialism for making unreasonable demands on moral agents, and it has often been taken to be an advantage of common-sense morality that it treats our most fundamental, our most important form of act-evaluation as in most cases requiring nothing like the kind of self-sacrifice entailed by a utilitarian or consequentialist form of morality. To be sure, there are occasions when even common sense seems to require an agent to sacrifice her deepest concerns, even perhaps her life, but as a rule common-sense moral thinking seems to permit the individual to pursue her own good or well-being as long as she refrains from harming, and does a certain amount on behalf of, other people. And this is precisely what (act-) consequentialism, with its requirement that one always do what, in impersonal terms, is (considered) best (for mankind), seems not to allow.

In this first chapter, however, I want to argue that, for reasons somewhat different from the familiar ones just mentioned, common-sense and Kantian morality can likewise be said to give insufficient weight to the interests or well-being of moral agents, and thus, in an important sense, to slight, devalue, or downgrade such agents. By contrast, a properly conceived virtue ethics does not slight us as moral agents in the way that consequentialism is commonly thought to do or in the less familiar way that ordinary and Kantian morality can, I think, be shown to do. And this constitutes a major advantage of virtue theory that may help to add impetus to the recent revival of virtue ethics. Much of the recent interest in virtue ethics has focused on the analysis and comparison of particular virtues and on the ways in which talk of virtue may importantly supplement what ethics needs to say about the rightness and wrongness of actions. But the virtue-theoretical advantages to be argued for in what follows support virtue ethics in a deeper sense. If (utilitarian) consequentialism, Kantianism, and common-sense morality all give insufficient weight to the interests of the individual agent, then perhaps a virtue-theoretic approach that avoids this sort of difficulty may in fact turn out to offer the best way of *grounding* our ethical thinking.

## Moral Asymmetry

In the past few years, a great deal of energy has been expended on the critical evaluation of so-called common-sense morality, and much of what I have to say in criticism of ordinary and Kantian moral thinking is based on—though in important ways it seeks to go beyond—these recent discussions. It has frequently been pointed out, for example, that common-sense thinking about right and wrong is permissive in the personal sphere in ways and to a degree that act-consequentialism and, most familiarly, act-utilitarianism are not. (Henceforth I use "consequentialism" and "utilitarianism" in place of these longer designations.) Just above, I spoke of our common-sense permission(s) to pursue our own personal projects and concerns even at a cost to overall or impersonally reckoned good. And in recent work the distinction in this respect between consequentialism and ordinary morality has been expressed by saying that the latter grants agents a moral permission to pursue innocent projects and concerns in ways that are not optimific, not productive of the greatest overall balance of good.[1] These moral permissions allow the agent to favor herself, to some extent, over other people: to seek her own good on some occasions when she could do more good by trying to help others, and this, of course, is precisely what standard utilitarianism does not allow one to do. In the present context I shall also refer to such permissions as *agent-favoring* permissions, because I would like to draw a contrast between this familiar category of common-sense moral permission and a less familiar form of moral permission that treats it as morally permissible for agents to neglect their own projects and concerns and even, in fact, to thwart them.

Our intuitive moral thinking seems to regard it as entirely permissible, though of course hardly advisable or rational, for an individual to deny herself the very things she most wants or to cause herself unnecessary pain or damage. (Here common sense diverges from Kantian ethics—criticism of the latter will come in later in our discussion.) Even if no one else stands to benefit from such self-sacrifice, even if there is no reason of moral deontology for it, such an act of self-sacrifice does not seem morally wrong,[2] and it is appropriate to refer this new class of permissions as *agent sacrificing* in order to mark the contrast with the agent-favoring permissions that are already so well-known in the ethics literature. Both sorts of permission allow for non-optimific action, but in addition the agent-sacrificing permissions allow for (non-optimific) behavior that doesn't even serve the interests or concerns of the moral agent. So if, as we might put it, agent-favoring permissions allow the substitution of the agent's good for the larger overall good that consequentialism uses as the standard of right action, then agent-sacrificing permissions morally allow for action that cannot be justified by any appeal to what is good or best, allow, indeed, for action that must inevitably seem stupid, absurd, or irrational by comparison with agent-favoring behavior. However, we should not immediately assume that common-sense morality itself cannot sensibly make moral accommodation to behavior that itself is not sensible, and for the moment at least we need only focus on the fact that common-sense morality does seem to permit such senseless or stupid behavior.

Consider, then, what our ordinary moral thinking seems to allow and to forbid with regard to our treatment of *other people*. Negligently to hurt another person seems, intuitively, to be morally wrong in a way or to a degree that it does not seem wrong through negligence to hurt oneself. (It can be wrong to hurt oneself if one thereby makes it impossible for one to fulfill certain obligations, but I am speaking of less complex situations.) Similarly, if one could easily *prevent* pain to another person, it is typically thought wrong not to do so, but not to avoid similar pain to oneself seems crazy or irrational, not morally wrong. And so given the agent-sacrificing common-sense permissions we have described, we may now also speak of an *agent-sacrificing* (or *other-favoring*) *self-other asymmetry* that attaches to what is commonsensically permissible. Various ways one may permissibly act against one's own interests or well-being are ways one is commonsensically not allowed to act against the interests or well-being of others.[3]

But isn't there another side to this coin in virtue of the familiar agent-favoring permissions that we have also attributed to our common-sense moral thinking? We ordinarily think people have a right to neglect their own interests, but don't we also believe that one may to a certain extent permissibly favor one's own interests over those of other individuals and doesn't this latter give rise to some sort of agent-favoring self-other asymmetry? If so, don't we then also face the considerable problem of explaining how our common-sense permissions can simultaneously yield agent-favoring *and* agent-sacrificing asymmetries?

These difficulties can be avoided, however, if one recognizes that our agent-favoring permissions provide no obvious footing for asymmetry. I may be permitted to act against overall optimality in the pursuit of my own concerns, but this yields an agent-favoring asymmetry only if the analogous claim with respect to *other* people seems commonsensically suspect, and in fact it isn't. Just as one may favor *one's own* interests or special concerns, there seems to be nothing intuitively wrong with helping *another person* in an overall non-optimific fashion.

However, there is a great deal more to be said about the agent-sacrificing self-other asymmetry we have located in common-sense morality. We have thus far largely concentrated on the asymmetry of our common-sense moral permissions, but we have also just briefly indicated that such symmetry is also to be found in our views of (positive or comparative) moral merit, and it is time now to focus our attention on the way self-other asymmetry of an agent-sacrificing kind applies outside the area of permissions. Moral theorists tend to assume that moral evaluation is our most fundamental and/or important form of ethical evaluation. But the aspects of self-other asymmetry we shall now focus on force us to question whether either common-sense or Kantian morality can properly fulfill such a role.

The point I wish to make about both these forms of morality is perhaps best approached by means of a contrast with a well-known aspect of (utilitarian) consequentialism. The latter allows neither for agent-sacrificing nor for agent-favoring permissions of the sort we have described, because it is entirely agent-neutral: no one person may be treated in any fundamentally different way from any other, and this uniformity of treatment crosses the boundary between self and other as well as that between different others. In consequentialism, if something is permitted with respect to one individual, it is acceptable with respect to any other individual as long as the causal-evaluative facts on which moral judgments are based remain otherwise the same. And if, for example, it is wrong for me to hurt another person when, by not doing so, I can create more overall good, then it is wrong for me to hurt myself in similar circumstances. Even if I hurt myself in order to help others, my act will count as wrong, if I could have done more overall good by favoring myself more and benefiting others less.[4] Furthermore, if the agent's sole choice is between helping herself and helping another person to exactly the same extent, the two possible acts are of equal moral value, are equally good morally, according to any recognizable form of consequentialism. But if the agent has to choose between helping herself more and helping another less, or between helping another person more and helping herself less, the morally better action, in consequentialist terms, will always be the one that does the most good.[5] And this also holds for choices exclusively concerned with the good of the agent or exclusively concerned with the good of others. As a result, I think we may say that consequentialism treats the good of the agent and that of any given other as counting equally toward favorable moral assessment.

Note the contrast with egoism. The latter presumably regards what helps the agent more as automatically morally better than what helps the agent less, but makes no similar comparative judgment about effects on other people. It is only when the agent's good is (contingently) tied to that of other people, that effects on others can make a difference to egoistic moral evaluation, and so in respect to its comparative moral judgments, egoism is asymmetric in a way that consequentialism clearly is not. Where does common-sense morality fit into this picture?

Unlike egoism, our ordinary thinking tends to regard it, other things being equal, as morally better, or more meritorious, to give more, rather than less, to another person. But when we turn to situations in which the agent is in a position to affect himself in some way, a different picture emerges. We earlier saw that common-sense morality allows or permits the agent to hurt or fail to help himself. But when comparative moral judgments are at issue, the agent's own good also appears to be irrelevant. If I have to choose between helping myself a little or a great deal, the latter choice would not normally be regarded as morally better: wiser, more rational, more prudent perhaps, just not *morally* better. Here there is a marked contrast with both consequentialism and ethical egoism, but not just here. Where both the agent's and another person's good are at stake, our ordinary moral thinking seems to assign the former no positive weight whatever. It may be more rational to choose a great good for oneself in preference to a lesser good for another person, but in common-sense terms it is not morally preferable to choose one's own greater good, and it even seems morally better to seek the *lesser* good of another in preference to a greater benefit for oneself. Here again, there is a contrast with both egoism and consequentialism.[6]

Of course, what helps the agent would ordinarily be taken to be capable of indirect moral value. It may be morally better for me to be careful about my health than to be indifferent about it, if a family's or a nation's welfare depends on my keeping healthy, but if in order to make a case for the moral value or merit of some agent-beneficial action, we ordinarily have to say something to tie that action and that benefit to the well-being of others, that fact only serves to underscore the asymmetry of comparative evaluations I have just been calling attention to. It is now time to see whether our ordinary understanding of virtue and virtues is subject to any similar asymmetry and whether, if such understanding turns out to be relatively free of such asymmetry, we can use this difference to argue in favor of a virtue-theoretic approach to ethics.

## The Symmetry in Virtue

In her ground-breaking article "Moral Beliefs" Philippa Foot assumes that if a trait of character does not benefit or serve the needs of its possessor, the trait cannot properly be regarded as a virtue. She notes that in the *Republic* Plato takes it for granted "that if justice is not a good to the just man, moralists who recommend it as a virtue are perpetrating a fraud" and she points out that Nietzsche, unlike present-day moral philosophers, seems to accept a similar view.[7]

Foot herself, however, subsequently retracted this assumption. In some of her later work, she has separated the issue of what counts as a virtue from issues concerning what the agent has reason to do and treated it as intuitively unobjectionable to hold that traits that fail to benefit their possessors may properly be regarded as virtues.[8] For present-day common-sense thinking it might be enough, for example, that a trait be one by which *other people* generally benefit. (As Foot herself notes, what counts as a virtue in functional objects like knives doesn't benefit the knives themselves, only those who use them.)

To the extent that Foot's retraction constitutes a concession to our ordinary thought about virtue and virtues, I think Foot was correct to retract her earlier assumption and recognize that virtues may not benefit their possessors. But it would be a mistake to conclude from this that our ordinary thinking about the virtues is subject to self-other asymmetry similar to what we have found in common-sense morality. Our assessment of whether a given character trait counts as a virtue (and of whether a given act, in exemplifying a certain character trait, also exemplifies a virtue) is favorably affected by the consideration that the trait in question benefits people other than its possessor. But no less positively, or favorably, is it affected by the consideration that a given trait benefits, or is useful to, its possessor(s). In our ordinary thinking it may not be *necessary* to status as a virtue that a given trait be beneficial (more or less generally) to its possessors, but it certainly *helps to qualify* any given trait as a virtue that it is useful or beneficial to those who possess it, and in fact I think it is entirely in keeping with common-sense views to suppose that both helpfulness to its possessors and helpfulness to others are independently, and in fairly equal measure, capable of conferring virtue status. To consider the issue first on a fairly abstract level, if I hear that people generally need a given trait of character and benefit from possessing it, I will normally think I have been given excellent reason to regard that trait as a virtue.[9] But by the same token if I learn that a certain character trait is generally useful to people other than its possessors, I will also naturally or normally think I have been given reason to regard that trait as a virtue.

When, furthermore, we look at the whole range of traits commonly recognized as virtues, we once again see that self-regarding and other-regarding considerations are both capable of underlying the kind of high regard that leads us to regard various traits as virtues. Justice, kindness, probity, and generosity are chiefly admired for what they lead those who possess these traits to do in their relations with other people, but prudence, sagacity, circumspection, equanimity, and fortitude are esteemed primarily under their self-regarding aspect, and still other traits—notably self-control, courage, and (perhaps) wisdom in practical affairs—are in substantial measure admired both for what they do for their possessors and for what they lead their possessors to do with regard to other people.[10]

It is also worth noting that traits admired for other-regarding reasons do not have any sort of general precedence over predominantly self-regarding virtues that might be taken to entail a self-other asymmetry of the sort we have discussed in connection with common-sense morality. (I think the opposite problem of precedence for self-regarding virtues need not concern us.) The other-regarding traits mentioned above lack any (implicitly) recognized status as greater or more important virtues than the self-regarding traits also mentioned above, and neither does a "mixed" virtue like courage or self-control or wisdom seem inferior to, or less of a virtue than, such predominantly other-regarding virtues as justice and kindness. We greatly admire probity and fair dealing, but we also have enormous admiration for many self-regarding and mixed virtues, so I think our ordinary thinking in this area gives rise to nothing like the marked or extreme self-other asymmetry that characterizes common-sense morality.

Yet consider the view of Hume, who says that "when a man is called *virtuous*, or is denominated a man of virtue, we chiefly regard his social qualities."[11] I have no wish to deny what Hume is saying here, but I think we must distinguish between virtue and virtuousness, on the one hand, and what constitutes something as *a* virtue, on the other. Both "virtue" (without the qualifying article) and "virtuous" are sometimes used in a restricted sense to refer to certain sorts of sexual conduct, or non-conduct, on the part, especially, of women. But no similar connotation arises when we say that a certain trait is a virtue or speak of various virtues. And even when "virtuous" and (unarticled) "virtue" are used in a more general sense/way, they have a moral significance that doesn't automatically attach to our talk of particular virtues. It has often been pointed out that in its broader usage "virtuous" is roughly equivalent to "morally good," and in a similar way a phrase like "man of virtue" is typically used in rough equivalence with the notion of a (*morally*) *good man.*[12] Hume is certainly right if he assumes that our talk of virtuousness lays a special emphasis on social virtue, on other-regarding traits or dispositions. But that is because these notions are fundamentally moral, even if the word "moral" and its cognates do not always appear when they are employed. (As Ross points out, even "good man" is normally understood to mean "morally good man.")[13] By contrast, the notion of *a virtue* lacks such an automatic connection with morality and other-regarding considerations. When we say patience, circumspection, or prudence is a virtue, we are not committed to saying that it is morally better to have than to lack these traits. Of course, these traits can be useful to morally good individuals and so help such individuals do morally better things than they otherwise could have, but prudence and the other traits we have just mentioned can also be used for morally neutral or nefarious purposes, and (unlike Kant, as we will see) we commonly regard these character traits as virtues independently of any implicit judgment of how selfishly or altruistically they are likely to be used. It is enough that the person with patience or prudence (or fortitude or circumspection) have a trait people need to possess to get on well in life. And so I have quite deliberately, till now, been talking about given virtue*s* and what counts as *a* virtue precisely to avoid the self-other asymmetry that attaches to moral notions and to terms like "man of virtue" and "virtuous" in common usage. Our common understanding of what it is to be or to exemplify a virtue (or an admirable character trait) is unburdened with agent-sacrificing moral connotation, and I hope to show you in what follows how this enables virtue theory to gain an important superiority over the familiar sort of moral view that employs terms like "right," "wrong," and "morally good."

Our ordinary thinking about virtues is symmetric in a way that ordinary thinking about morality is not. But we have also seen that other possibilities exist in the field of morality, with egoism embodying an agent-favoring self-other asymmetric conception of morality and consequentialism a strictly symmetric form of moral thinking. And it turns out that similar variation with respect to self-other symmetry is also possible in the sphere of the virtues. Even if most of us would intuitively reject the notion that there is no virtue in a fundamental concern for the well-being of *other people*, that assumption is arguably common to Stoicism and Epicureanism, and such a fundamentally egoistic understanding of virtue, like egoism about morality, is self-other asymmetric in an agent-favoring manner.

Furthermore, even if our ordinary thinking about virtue(s) fails to exemplify the agent-sacrificing (or other-favoring) asymmetry we find in common-sense morality, such self-other asymmetry is clearly *possible* in the realm of virtue, and in fact I believe we have a good example of such asymmetry in Kant's views about what counts as an estimable character trait. Kant's doctrine of virtue is fundamentally a doctrine of moral virtue, but, more important, in the light of what we said above, his views about what counts as *a* virtue entail the same agent-sacrificing asymmetry we find in his view of morality. In the *Fundamental Principles of the Metaphysics of Morals*, Kant says that character traits like moderation, perseverance, judgment, self-control, courage, and the ability to deliberate calmly have value and are praiseworthy only conditionally. In the absence of a good will, these traits are not estimable and presumably do not count as virtues. Having a good will, in turn, is understood by Kant (roughly) as a form of conscientiousness, of doing one's duty out of respect for the moral law, of doing one's duty because it is one's duty rather than from any other motivation.[14] So the Kantian conception of virtue will turn out to be asymmetrical if Kantian morality is asymmetrical, and in fact Kantian morality is asymmetrical in some of the same ways that common-sense morality is. On Kant's view, for example, we have an obligation to benefit or contribute to the happiness of other people, but no parallel obligation to seek our own well-being or happiness. We have a duty to develop our natural talents, a duty not to *harm* ourselves, and a duty of self-preservation that derives from our other duties, but except insofar as it is necessary to fulfill those other obligations, we have no moral reason to make ourselves *happy* or *well-off*. (Our obligation to seek others' happiness is not derivative in this way.)

But (roughly speaking) if the status of moderation or perseverance as a virtue depends on its being accompanied by a Kantian good will and such a will is fundamentally directed toward concern with the well-being of others rather than toward the well-being of the moral agent, then the agent-sacrificing asymmetry of Kantian moral obligation will translate into similar asymmetry in Kantian views about what properly counts as a good trait of character, as a virtue. Our common-sense views of what counts as a virtue escape this asymmetry, despite the self-other asymmetry of common-sense moral obligation, because, unlike Kant, we ordinarily regard some of the character traits mentioned above as admirable or estimable independently of their accompaniment by moral goodness or virtue. We may have an unfavorable moral opinion of a colleague who mistreats his friends and his family, yet have a high regard for that colleague's devotion to some academic subject, or his coolheadedness, or his fortitude in the face of (deserved or undeserved) personal tragedy.[15]

And so in the area of virtue, the same three possibilities exist as exist in morality, but we find common-sense views occupying a different position among these possibilities. With regard to personal happiness or well-being, common-sense and Kantian morality are agent-sacrificingly self-other asymmetric by contrast with the agent-favoring (other-sacrificing) asymmetry of egoism and the self-other symmetry of (utilitarian) consequentialism. But in the field of the virtues it is common sense that occupies the symmetric position (along with utilitarianism, but I am ignoring some complications here); whereas egoism, once again, is agent-favoringly asymmetric, and only the Kantian view, among those we have mentioned, is agent-sacrificingly asymmetric.

Of course, we have not yet explored the significance, the theoretical implications, of these varying symmetries and asymmetries. To the extent symmetry is a favorable characteristic of an ethical view, we could perhaps on that basis alone argue for the superiority of either consequentialism or a common-sense ethics of the virtues over a common-sense or Kantian ethics of right, wrong, and obligation. But in fact the symmetry in consequentialism and in common-sense virtue ethics has a significance that far outstrips the widely assumed theoretical desirability of symmetry as such. However desirable symmetrical consequentialism may be, it still is subject to the complaint of being too demanding, of requiring too much individual sacrifice. And we are now in a position to show that the agent-sacrificing asymmetry of common-sense and Kantian morality subjects them to the rather similar complaint that they downgrade or deprecate the importance of the moral agent, a charge which, as we will also see, the particular symmetry of our ordinary view of virtue allows the latter to escape.

## How Ordinary and Kantian Morality Devalue Moral Agents

How can common-sense morality be guilty of devaluing or deprecating the importance of the moral agent? After all, it is itself the source of the criticism that consequentialism and utilitarianism ride roughshod over the particular concerns and projects of the individual by demanding that she sacrifice them whenever they interfere with her production of impersonally reckoned best results. Is common-sense, or Kantian, morality perhaps more demanding than its adherents have realized? Is that the basis for the objection I wish to make to such morality?

I do want to claim that these forms of morality downgrade the (actual) importance of moral agents and their individual concerns, projects, even desires. But the argument for this claim will not be that, like consequentialism, the ordinary and/or the Kantian standard of right and wrong make an insufficient concession to the moral agent's welfare. On the contrary, it will involve, rather, the claim that common-sense and Kantian morality *do* make concessions to the well-being and happiness of agents, *but make them only as concessions.*[16]

Common-sense and Kantian ethics permit the moral agent to seek and find her own happiness at the expense, at least to some extent, of overall, or impersonally judged, optimality. But this does not mean that they treat such usefulness to the agent as a source of *positive moral value.* Other things being equal, if an agent has to choose between two actions and one of these would (probably) be more helpful to the agent, then the more helpful action would typically be regarded as one that it is more rational for the agent to perform and, in the appropriate, reasons-related sense, as a better option from the standpoint of the agent. But from the ordinary or Kantian point of view such an act would usually not be considered morally better or morally more praiseworthy or meritorious than the act that would do less good for the agent. The point simply recaptures some of what we were saying earlier: for ordinary or Kantian moral thinking, how morally good or meritorious an act is will depend in part (and especially in the absence of deontological factors) on whether it is directed toward the well-being of other people, but not on whether it is directed toward that of the agent.

So in cases where someone helps herself at the expense of overall best results and of the potential good of other people, common-sense morality may maintain the moral permissibility of what the (utilitarian) consequentialist would standardly regard as a violation of moral obligation, but will nonetheless share with consequentialism the judgment that such action is morally less good than what would have achieved greater overall good and greater good for other people. And in such cases, therefore, common sense makes moral concessions to the agent's personal good, but attributes positive moral value only on the basis of what the agent does for the well-being of others. (Again, I am assuming an absence of deontological considerations.) And if you wish to object that our ordinary thinking here accords positive moral value to what the agent does solely on her own behalf, but simply refuses to assign *greater* moral value to what is *more* self-beneficial, then consider what we think about purely self-regarding cases where someone has to choose between having or not having something nice. Intuitively speaking, if someone on purely prudential grounds decides to have lunch rather than not eating at all, then, other things being equal, what that person does is neither morally better than the alternative nor, intuitively, the sort of action we would praise as morally a good one. And Kant's conception of morality likewise provides no basis for assigning positive moral value to actions to the extent they are directed merely toward the happiness or well-being of their agents.[17] (More on this in Chapter 6.)

By contrast, the utilitarian and the consequentialist more generally (but remember we are talking about act-utilitarianism and act-consequentialism only) will treat the intended or probable preference-satisfaction or well-being of the agent as a basis for positive moral assessment. In self-regarding cases, the consequentialist holds not only that the agent has a moral obligation to do the best she can for herself but, in addition, that it is morally better for her to do so than for her to perform some less self-beneficial alternative action. Moreover, where an agent has to choose between (a) doing $x$ amount of good for others and $y$ amount for himself and (b) simply doing $x$ amount for others, consequentialism regards the former act as morally superior, but our ordinary thinking about morality seems to lack this tendency. We don't normally regard someone who could have benefited himself at the same time he helped others, but who chose only to help the others, as morally less meritorious for having done nothing for himself—indeed there may be some tendency to regard such action as morally better or more praiseworthy precisely because the agent *sought nothing for himself* in the process.[18]

In summary, it would appear that over a wide range of cases our ordinary thinking about morality assigns no positive value to the well-being or happiness of the moral agent of the sort it clearly assigns to the well-being or happiness of *everyone other than the agent*. The fact that an act helps or seeks to help its agent cannot for such thinking provide any sort of ground or basis for the favorable—as opposed to the merely non-unfavorable—evaluation of that action. And harm to the agent seems similarly irrelevant to an act's unfavorable evaluation. I believe that this aspect of common-sense morality is and can be shown to be ethically objectionable.

Defenders, as well as opponents, of an intuitive or intuitionist approach to ethics typically regard morality as the central concern of ethics and treat the moral assessment of acts and agents as our most fundamental, our most important, form of act-evaluation and agent-evaluation. (This fact is reflected, for example, in the familiar use of the expression "moral philosophy" to refer to the area of philosophy people in ethics are interested in.) And I believe it is objectionable to suppose that our most central (or fundamental or important) mode of ethical evaluation treats facts about whether and how an act is (or is intended to be) helpful or harmful to its agent's interests as (at best) irrelevant to favorable and unfavorable evaluation of that act. If at the most fundamental level or in its most central concerns, our ethics is in this way indifferent to whether the agent is helped or hurt by his actions, then our ethics devalues the interests of the agent and the agent himself as agent and imposes or entails a kind of self-abnegation or selflessness in regard to the *agent's own* assessment of the ethical value of what he is doing. And I believe such considerations give us as much reason to be suspicious of common-sense or Kantian morality, considered as our most central or fundamental form of ethical evaluation, as consequentialism's supposedly exorbitant demands for self-sacrifice give us reason to question the validity of the consequentialism.

I should point out, however, that it is hardly objectionable that *some* form of act-evaluation should fail to concern itself with the interests of the agent. The existence of such a mode of evaluation is entirely consistent with a proper concern for the interests of agents as such, because it is entirely consistent with the existence of important forms of evaluation that *do* take the agent's interests positively into account. What seems to deprecate and devalue the moral agent, to rob her of her actual importance, is the assumption, rather, that *at the most fundamental level*, or *in its most central concerns*, substantive ethical thinking gives no positive evaluative weight to the interests of agents as such. Of course, viewed as a recipient of the acts of other agents common-sense and Kantian morality regard the well-being of every person as having a positive and fundamental valuational significance. But at the same time, they assign no such significance to the effects of an act on the well-being of the act's agent, and the latter face lies behind the charge that I am bringing against common-sense and Kantian morality.[19] If morality is to function as the centrally important part of our ethical thinking that most of us think it is, then both common-sense and Kantian morality are unfitted for such a role because of the way they depreciate the interests of moral agents both from the standpoint of those agents' evaluation of their own actions and more generally. They each require the agent to be valuationally selfless or self-abnegating with respect to her own actions—though not with respect to other people's actions—and, in effect, they alienate the agent from her own self-interest or welfare when she evaluates the ethical significance of her own actions. But even from a more general standpoint of evaluation, both views regard all effects on the agent's well-being as fundamentally irrelevant to the favorable or unfavorable evaluation of a given action, whereas that well-being is taken into account when anyone else's actions are being evaluated. Clearly, common-sense and Kantian morality, if seen as concerning themselves with the most central or fundamental questions of ethics, can each be criticized for depreciating or devaluing the welfare interests of the moral agent as such.[20]

Of course the *way* in which these two conceptions of morality can be regarded as devaluing the moral agent and her interests is not precisely the way in which utilitarian consequentialism can be and is commonly thought to devalue agents and their interests. And by the same token, the way ordinary and Kantian moral thinking impose self-abnegation or self-alienation upon moral agents is to some extent different from the way utilitarian consequentialism imposes these constraints. These differences, as I have already mentioned, have something to do with the difference between conditions of permissibility and conditions of (positive or comparative) moral goodness, but even granting that such differences exist—and that more needs to be said about them—it nonetheless seems highly significant that the very same charges may be leveled at consequentialism, Kantianism, and common-sense morality, and ironic, in addition, that common-sense morality, at least, has in recent years been directing such charges at consequentialism and using them in an attempt to demonstrate its own superiority over consequentialism.

However, when we turn to our common-sense views about what counts as a virtue, we get an entirely different picture. Nothing in our usual understanding of (major) virtues like probity, generosity, prudence, benevolence, and courage requires us to assume that the person who has such virtues will invariably act for the greatest good of the greatest number whenever such action importantly conflicts with his own interests. And, furthermore, the fact that a certain trait of character enables its possessor to advance his own well-being is not treated as irrelevant to a positive evaluation of that trait; indeed many of our most significant common-sense virtues—for example, prudence, perseverance, foresight, caution, fortitude, courage, sagacity—are to a considerable extent admired for such usefulness to those who possess them. So our ordinary thinking about the virtues treats both self-regarding and other-regarding usefulness as bases for the favorable evaluation of traits of character and actions (or feelings or thoughts) that exemplify them. And the same, *mutatis mutandis*, holds for traits that harm either their possessors or people other than their possessors.

## A Temporary Respite

For some view or set of views to function adequately as our most fundamental or central form of ethical evaluation, it should not devalue agents by treating their happiness as irrelevant to the positive, or negative, ethical assessment of their own actions. And we have seen that Kantian and common-sense morality both fail to meet this condition of adequacy, in a way that common-sense virtue ethics does not. (By virtue ethics I here mean an ethics that deals with what counts as admirable or as a virtue, but does not speak of moral virtue as such. The latter is part of common-sense morality and shares its problems.) But none of this shows that common-sense or Kantian morality is mistaken or invalid: it may only show that neither can function on its own as the foundation or most central part of our ethical thinking, and this precisely leaves open the possibility that either common-sense or Kantian morality might function *together with* common-sense virtue ethics as the foundational, or most central, part of our substantive ethical thinking. And it also leaves open the alternative possibility that common-sense or Kantian morality might be a valid, but merely superficial part of ethics, with virtue ethics then exclusively taking on the central or foundational role that morality is often assumed to have.

Each of these results would demonstrate the importance of virtue theory and vindicate its recent claims to be taken seriously, rather than shunted to the side, as has so often happened in the past, in favor of an almost exclusive ethical preoccupation with moral right and wrong, with moral obligation, duty, and permission. But all of this fails to take into account another possibility that needs, at the very least, to be considered before we draw any conclusions in favor of virtue ethics.

We earlier saw that certain actions thwarting the well-being or interests of their agent can be regarded as stupid or irrational, even when, in common-sense terms, there seems to be nothing morally wrong with them. And this point surely suggests that our common-sense judgments about rationality lack the agent-sacrificing character of our common-sense moral judgments. In that case, perhaps we can supplement common-sense morality, not with any form of virtue ethics, but with (the entire body of) our intuitive beliefs about rationality to arrive at an acceptable foundation for our ethical thinking. For if common-sense thinking about rationality treats what the agent does on his own behalf as having positive (rational) value, then a foundational or central core of ethical thinking that combines common-sense (or Kantian) moral judgments with ordinary, intuitive rational judgments will be able to accord some sort of positive value to acts that help their agents, and our earlier criticism of common-sense morality will no longer be relevant.

Of course, by supplementing ordinary or Kantian moral thinking in this way, we treat such morality as less exclusively or preeminently important than we would if we regarded it as the single central and/or foundational component of our ethical thinking.[21] But that is precisely the price we may have to—and even be willing to—pay in order to undercut the sorts of criticisms we have been directing here against both common-sense and Kantian morality. Earlier in this century and possibly as a result of lingering Victorian, and more generally Christian, high-mindedness, the selflessness of common-sense morality went largely unnoticed and entirely uncriticized.[22] But in recent years many moral philosophers have advocated a healthy self-assertiveness on the part of moral agents.[23] And although much of this recent thinking has been directed against Kantianism and consequentialism, rather than common-sense morality, a climate of opinion has nonetheless been created in which it is easier to make and perhaps sympathize with our earlier criticism of the agent-downgrading and evaluationally selfless character of common-sense (as well as of Kantian) morality. But these charges, as we now see, do not entail the rejection of common-sense or Kantian morality. They entail, rather, that we *either* reject these forms of morality *or* supplement one or the other of them with some other form of evaluation that can allow for agent-favoring ethical judgments and function in conjunction with such morality within the foundational or central core of (a) substantive ethical theory. And properly to canvass the possibilities, we must now, therefore, consider the merits of a foundational theoretical approach that combines moral judgments with judgments about rationality in an attempt to evade the difficulties that beset both common-sense morality and Kantian morality when each is taken on its own.

## Notes

1. On these points see, e.g., S. Scheffler's *The Rejection of Consequentialism*, Oxford, 1982, *passim*.

2. I am not talking about masochism, where what seems like self-sacrifice may in some way or degree not be, but of cases where a person could, but won't actually, sacrifice her own dearest projects, etc. In such cases self-sacrifice is permitted, but would be irrational. (It would be a mistake to say of such a person: if she sacrificed the projects, she wouldn't have them as projects and so wouldn't be acting irrationally. This counterfactual claim cannot be defended. Cf. my "Time in Counterfactuals," *Philosophical Review* 87, 1978, pp. 3–27.)

3. It has been suggested to me that the reason why we are allowed to harm ourselves or avoid some benefit, where we would not be permitted to harm another person or prevent her from receiving similar benefit, lies in the consent implicit in actions we do to ourselves. If I harm myself or avoid a benefit, I presumably do this willingly, whereas the agent whom I refuse to benefit does not consent to this neglect (and when she does there is nothing wrong with what I do). It might then be thought that agent-sacrificing asymmetry is not a deep feature of common-sense morality, but rather derivative from and justifiable in terms of the moral importance of consent.

But such as explanation will not do. It makes a significant difference, common-sensically, whether I negligently cause another person unwanted harm or negligently do so to myself. Yet consent seems *equally absent* in these two cases. More persuasively, perhaps, if I can either avoid an enduring pain to myself or a short-lived one to you, you and I might both agree that it would be foolish of me to prevent the shorter one to you; so you might not consent to my taking the longer pain upon myself to save you from the shorter pain. Yet there would be nothing morally wrong, commonsensically, in such a sacrifice. But when positions are reversed and I can avoid a short-lived pain to myself or a longer one to you and it is morally right that I should do the latter, you will presumably not consent to my doing the former, and it will be wrong if I do so. Again, consent/lack-of-consent seems not to make the relevant common-sense moral difference. The agent-sacrificing moral asymmetry eludes the distinction between consent and non-consent, and is not thus easily accounted for.

4. On "agent-neutrality," see Derek Parfit, *Reasons and Persons*, Oxford, 1984, p. 27. Note that non-optimizing forms of utilitarianism and consequentialism are also strictly agent-neutral. If, for example, one accepts some form of "satisficing consequentialism," one's criterion of right action will be whether a given act has *good enough* consequences (relative, perhaps, to its alternatives);

but such a form of consequentialism will in no way distinguish among agents in its ultimate determinations of what counts as good enough consequences. On this point see my *Common-sense Morality and Consequentialism*, London, 1985, Chapter 3.

5. Even non-optimizing forms of consequentialism have the feature just mentioned. And because of this feature, such views allow for moral supererogation in a way that more standard utilitarianism and consequentialism do not.

6. See W. D. Ross, *The Right and the Good*, Oxford, 1955, p. 168; and also his *The Foundations of Ethics*, Oxford, 1939, pp. 72ff., 272ff.

7. See Foot's *Virtues and Vices*, California, 1978, pp. 125f.

8. See her "Morality as a System of Hypothetical Imperatives," in *Virtues and Vices*, pp. 159f., 168. In more recent and as yet unpublished work, Foot seems to be moving back toward her earlier ideas.

9. I am leaving it open whether we want to emphasize the distinction between character traits and personality traits and so argue, for example, that charming-ness, however desirable or admirable, is not a virtue.

It has been suggested to me that self-regarding virtues may count as such because they involve admirable self-control, rather than because they benefit their possessors. But one could press a similar argument with respect to other-regard-ing virtues; and if we intuitively feel that other-regarding virtue has to do with benefiting others and not just with the agent's demonstration of self-control, isn't there reason to say something similar about self-regarding virtue? I might also mention that some self-regarding virtues seem not at all, or at least predomi-nantly, to be a matter of self-control. Farsightedness, for example, is not readily viewed as a matter of self-control, and even self-assurance is a matter not so much of controlling self-doubt (so as to be able to act effectively despite it) as of not having doubts in the first place. Cf. Foot's remarks on honesty in the title essay of *Virtues and Vices*.

10. On this point, see Foot, *op. cit.*, p. 119 and Sidgwick, *Methods of Ethics*, seventh edition, London, 1907, pp. 327f., 332, 356.

11. See Hume, *An Enquiry Concerning the Principles of Morals*, Book IV, section 262. However, we return to this issue later in Chapter 8 when we discuss some of Hume's views on the virtues.

12. See Ross, *The Right and the Good*, p. 161.

13. See Ross, *The Foundations of Ethics*, p. 271.

14. For more on the conditional character of certain virtues both in general and in Kant's ethics, see Christine Korsgaard, "Two Distinctions in Goodness," *Philosophical Review* 91, 1983, pp. 169–95 and my *Goods and Virtues*, Oxford, 1990, Chapter 3.

15. See *Goods and Virtues*, Ch. 3.

16. In speaking here of the concerns and well-being of moral agents, I am leaving *simple desires* out of account. But common-sense morality arguably makes concessions to less-than-deep, less-than-serious desires (or intentions)—it

is not entirely clear how far common-sense agent-favoring permissions extend in this direction. See my *Common-sense Morality and Consequentialism*, pp. 141f.

17. See, e.g., Kant's *Fundamental Principles of the Metaphysics of Morals*, London: 1909, pp. 13f., 16n.

18. For what I take to be an example of such thinking, see the final two pages of Henry James's *The Ambassadors*.

19. Even if Kantianism can treat prudence and prudential action as (non-morally) valuable and admirable, such evaluations will presuppose the moral goodness of the agent or trait-possessor's will and will thus be conditional, e.g., on whether the individual in question is doing what he should in regard to other people's happiness. To that extent, prudential action will lack the *fundamental* value of moral action (although this doesn't mean that the agent is a mere means to other people's happiness). Clearly this view devalues the moral agent and makes him play second fiddle in relation to other people. Of course, for Kant even the value of seeking others' happiness is conditional on the simultaneous honoring of perfect duties, but then the value of prudence will be doubly conditional, whereas, for Kant, the virtue of promoting others' happiness is not conditional on whether one seeks one's own happiness. It may be conditional on proper self-respect, or non-servility, but in Kant's ethics the latter doesn't require the pursuit of one's own happiness. (On this point, see T. Hill, "Servility and Self-Respect," *The Monist* 57, 1973, pp. 87–104.) I am indebted here to discussion with Nancy Sherman.

20. However, as Louis Pojman has pointed out to me, Kant's employment in the *Critique of Practical Reason* of the notion of the complete good—of the postulate of proportionality between happiness and moral desert—may be said to undercut the claim that he depreciates the well-being of the moral agent, but to do so in religious/metaphysical terms that are philosophically unacceptable nowadays. Most precisely, then, the charge to be brought against Kant or ordinary moral thinking is that it either unacceptably devalues the moral agent or is forced to make unacceptable religious/metaphysical assumptions.

21. Recent attempts to criticize the "overridingness thesis" (according to which one can never be justified in doing what one takes to be morally wrong) also call the preeminent importance of morality into question. The argument of the main text above constitutes, however, a new way of questioning that importance.

22. Ross in the two works previously cited is clearly aware of the "selflessness" of common-sense morality, but in no way sees this as a limitation or defect.

23. See, e.g., important recent work by Philippa Foot, Samuel Scheffler, Michael Stocker, Bernard Williams, and Susan Wolf. The recent revival of virtue ethics as against moral theory narrowly construed may represent some sort of dim or implicit recognition of the attractions of its greater assertiveness in behalf of rational/moral agents.

# 2

# Morality and Rationality

Our present task is to consider how judgments about morality can be combined with judgments about rationality to create a total, or at least a larger, ethics that is immune to the forms of criticisms we investigated in Chapter 1. We must see whether we can supplement either common-sense morality or Kantian morality with a set of judgments concerning what it is rational to choose or do that enables the total thus composed to escape the charges of agent-devaluation and valuational selflessness that threaten each of these forms of morality when it is taken on its own. However, before we can proceed with this main task of the present chapter, we should consider an assumption made by Sidgwick which, if true, undercuts the whole idea of supplementing moral with rational judgments.

## The Right and the Rational

In *The Methods of Ethics*, Sidgwick speaks of the possibility that there is an "ultimate and fundamental contradiction in our apparent intuitions of what is Reasonable in conduct": if (utilitarian) duty and self-interest at any point conflict, practical reason must stand "divided against itself" and is subject to an unsatisfactory, but inescapable "dualism."[1] Sidgwick treats this possible contradiction as endemic to "one chief department of our thought,"[2] and lying behind this language and Sidgwick's reference to a potential or actual dualism of practical reason is an extremely important assumed premise about the nature of our ethical concepts. The assumption I am speaking of is absolutely crucial to Sidgwick's whole procedure in *Methods* as well as to the pessimistic conclusions about dualism and contradiction that he draws in the final moments of the book, yet the assumption has not received the critical attention it deserves, and I in fact believe it is false and can be shown to be false. The present chapter will discuss this underlying premise and consider some interesting problems and opportunities that arise from its rejection.

The fundamental assumption I am talking about concerns our ethical concepts or language. According to Sidgwick, practical reason operates with a single underlying concept that can be variously expressed by the terms "reasonable," "right," and "rational."[3] Certainly, if Sidgwick is right about this, then our ethical concepts—if not our ethical theories—possess an admirable, a desirable unity, but I in fact believe that Sidgwick, at least in this one area, misdescribes the phenomena. In common usage, "right" and "rational" express different concepts (I simplify the discussion by not focusing on "reasonable"); and this fact has some very significant implications both for Sidgwick's general project and for the pessimistic conclusions he moves toward at the end of *Methods*. Later, in Chapter 4, we will see that the dualism of theories, the conflict between Egoism and Utilitarianism that Sidgwick finds himself unable to resolve, is not exacerbated and may even be alleviated by a recognition of a dualism of our fundamental ethical concepts and, in particular, by recognizing that the concept of the right and the concept of the rational are not identical. But for the moment, our purpose in demonstrating such a dualism is to make conceptual room for attemps to defend Kantian and/ or common-sense morality by supplementing them with rational judgments, attempts that make sense only if the concepts involved in the latter judgments are not identical with those involved in making moral claims.

Differences between concepts or meanings are most typically demonstrated by discovering possible cases where it seems in no way self-contradictory to apply one term and withhold another. And there are a whole variety of possible cases where the terms "right" and "rational" seemingly fail to coincide. In common-sense terms, it may be irrational for me, having locked my front door, to return several times to check on whether it really is locked, but such behavior would not normally be considered wrong or immoral. (Compulsive it may be, but the behavior is also voluntary: In checking again and again, I *act* in a way that is rationally, though not morally, unacceptable.) Here is another example: Someone finding that she cannot have everything she wants in a given situation, decides in a fit of pique to *take nothing*. Once again it seems intuitively irrational for the person to refuse to take anything, but there also appears to be nothing *morally wrong* with her doing so.

To be sure, counterexamples in the other direction, cases where I act rationally but immorally, are harder to find. The well-known and widely accepted overridingness thesis, according to which one cannot be (rationally) justified in doing what is immoral rules out such counterexamples, and it is not easy to find cases that test or undercut that thesis.[4] But there is no need to discuss such possibilities here, since the just-mentioned examples of commonsensically irrational but morally acceptable action seem obvious enough, I think, to justify the claim that "right" and "rational" do not have the same meaning in English, are different concepts.

Further evidence for this conclusion can be found, moreover, in our own present-day reactions to Sidgwick's *Methods*. It is easier for most of us to regard egoism as a view of rationality that philosophers need to reckon with than to take it at all seriously as a theory of right and wrong.[5] And so a certain amount of discomfort should and, I think, does attend our recognition of Sidgwick's indifference to the distinction between egoism as a theory of right and wrong and egoism as a theory of what is rational and irrational. By contrast, utilitarianism nowadays is primarily viewed as a theory of right and wrong, rather than of rationality (or of reasons for action in general). And indeed apart from Sidgwick's own example, most traditional defenders of utilitarianism have put it forward as a view of what is right and morally obligatory and have not explicitly treated it as a theory of rationality.[6]

But if egoism is a non-starter as a theory or conception of morality, then the dualism and contradiction Sidgwick so greatly feared can perhaps to some extent be alleviated by noting the conceptual distinction between rightness and rationality. Assuming, as Sidgwick assumed, that common-sense morality is inferior to utilitarianism, the latter may take first place as a view of right and wrong, and morality, therefore, may not be subject to the dualism/contradiction Sidgwick describes at the end of *Methods*. Even if right action is occasionally not in our self-interest, that fact may have no tendency to undermine the *moral* value of acting optimifically, but against self-interest; and utilitarianism may therefore emerge as the sole victor on the battleground of moral theories.

What will then remain is the issue of rationality, the question whether it is rational to sacrifice self-interest or one's central life project when it conflicts with utilitarian duty. This question is, of course, a very interesting one, and has been more or less directly touched upon in recent years by a whole host of philosophers. But it is not specifically, or narrowly, a question of moral theory, and if we are mainly concerned with the latter, there may simply be no dualism of the sort Sidgwick felt himself forced to acknowledge. A Utilitarianism of reasons (or rationality) may be fundamentally irreconcilable with egoism—and more recent studies may have uncovered alternatives that are superior to either of these views about rationality. But at least our views of what is morally right are in better shape than Sidgwick imagined, and it is, in addition worth noting that in those passages toward the end of *Methods* where Sidgwick attempts to bring out the contradiction inherent in practical reason, he stresses the potential *irrationality* of acting against self-interest, rather than urging that such action may plausibly be seen as morally unacceptable or defective. Egoism as a theory of the right is not the egoism stressed by Sidgwick in his description of the dualism of practical reason, and it is only because he has earlier so clearly indicated and claimed the equivalence of the right and the rational, that we can see him as committed to viewing this final disturbing impasse as involving a contradiction about what is right, and not merely about what is rational.

However, as I have indicated, we have a serious problem about what is rational (supported by reasons), even after egoism drops out as a competitor in moral theory. After we admit that rightness and rationality—or morality and rationality—represent fundamentally different concepts, the particular dualism Sidgwick spoke of remains in a somewhat attenuated form as the problem whether it is ever rational to do the (utilitarianly) right act when doing so works against the agent's self-interest. However, the fundamental dualism of concepts we have been arguing for not only creates problems for ethical theory, but also, as we will see, reveals a new way to defend utilitarianism as a theory of rationality or reasons for action. Sidgwick's enterprise may actually be helped, rather than hindered by our disagreement with Sidgwick in regard to the conceptual distinctness of the fundamental concepts of rightness and rationality. But that, as I said earlier, is a matter to be left to Chapter 4. Our present task is to plumb the implications of the analytic or conceptual non-equivalence of rightness and rationality and to see, in particular, whether judgments involving rationality can helpfully supplement judgments made using rightness.

## Fearful Asymmetries

Given Sidgwick's preference for systematic unity in moral theorizing, one can see why it would be preferable to suppose that ethics contains only one fundamental concept. For if there are two concepts, and the two have differing criteria of application, it will be difficult to attain the kind of systematic unity in ethical theory that Sidgwick—and many others—have craved. However, even though there may be something at least slightly unfortunate about a dualism of fundamental concepts, I want in the present section to argue that the situation is in some respects even worse than the mere fact of conceptual duality would seem to entail.

If we supplement common-sense judgments of rightness and wrongness with common-sense judgments of rationality and irrationality, the total view we arrive at has some exceedingly odd and undesirable features, and we shall thus see that the attempt to combine common-sense moral and rational judgments leaves us in no better shape than we were in when we took common-sense morality by itself as the basis or center of our ethical thinking. (In the next section we will also see that Kantian morality cannot consistently be supplemented in this way.)

We have already seen that ordinary intuitive morality, the so-called morality of common sense, is subject to an agent-sacrificing asymmetry regarding what an agent may permissibly do to herself and what she may permissibly do to others. But our ordinary or common-sense understanding of rational choice and action is subject, in fact, to a precisely opposite, *agent-favoring* self-other asymmetry. For certain ways of failing to help oneself would naturally be taken to count against the prudence, the wisdom, the rationality of one's actions in a way that parallel failures to help others would not. In common-sense terms, it seems irrational for me not to take advantage of a business or personal opportunity in a way, or to a degree, that it does not seem irrational for me not to enable some perfect stranger to take advantage of a similar opportunity. And by the same token acting negligently with respect to one's own good or one's own self-regarding desires seems intuitively to be more irrational, less prudent, than negligence or carelessness concerning the desires and good of random others.[7]

It seems clear, therefore, that common-sense ethical thinking is structured by a pair of symmetrically or diametrically opposed self-other asymmetries. What we are assuming to be the two fundamental concepts of ethics are both subject to self-other asymmetries, but, in addition, the asymmetry attending our common-sense thinking about moral permissibility and rightness (or what counts as moral—as opposed to immoral) moves in an agent-sacrificing direction that runs counter to the agent-favoring asymmetry that attends our ordinary thought about what it is rational (or rationally acceptable) for an agent to choose or do.

I believe that the diametrical opposition that holds between the right and rational represents a more serious problem for common-sense ethics (or indeed for any ethics with similarly fundamental opposition between its concepts of right and rational) than the mere fact of non-identity between those notions. Sidgwick was worried that the single concept right/rational led to an irrecusable clash of ethical theories, but if there are two concepts here and they are lopsided, asymmetrical, in opposite ways, one is tempted to conclude that the two notions in some way cancel each other.

Our general theoretical preference for symmetry can make one uncomfortable, to begin with, with the common-sense asymmetries of rightness and rationality taken individually (e.g., it is a seeming advantage of utilitarianism that its judgments of right and wrong are symmetrical with regard to the good of the agent and of others). But now it has turned out that in their ordinary employment these two fundamental notions are partial or lopsided in mutually opposed ways, and when, therefore, one views them together, it naturally occurs to one to wonder whether ethics wouldn't get along much better, much more *economically*, without these opposing asymmetries. Common-sense rightness and common-sense rationality tug in opposite directions with equal force, and it seems that a lot less ethical energy would be wasted if the fundamental work of ethics could be accomplished in some way that avoided these two modes of asymmetry.

It is also worth noting that the oddness of the tug-of-war between common-sense rightness and common-sense rationality is not merely oddness from a utilitarian or consequentialist standpoint. Ordinary usage of these notions exhibits a failure of economy that one might very well be reluctant on sheer methodological grounds to admit as fundamental to our ethical thought, and although such theoretical considerations appeal to consequentialists and utilitarians, they appeal far more widely within the ethical sphere.[8]

Note, moreover, that the argument against combining common-sense morality and common-sense rationality is not based merely on an appeal to oddness and diseconomy. There is perhaps no reason to worry about redundancy or diseconomy in the use or application of fairly superficial or derivative ethical concepts, and it is only when we suppose that the mutually opposed—and, in some sense, mutually cancelling—asymmetries of ordinary morality and ordinary rationality occur on the ground floor, or at the very heart, of our ethical thinking that there seems to be something objectionable about them. To assume that ethics is fundamentally characterized by such an uneconomical or redundant opposition is to sin against obvious methodological imperatives, and on purely theoretical grounds there is, other things being equal, every reason to reject such a basis for ethics in favor of some more unified and unifying set of ideas. If, therefore, we accept both common-sense morality and common-sense rationality, we have reason to seek for something more economical and unified from which each can be derived (or of which each can be seen as a special case). And this precisely means treating, or attempting to treat, the combination of these two forms of common-sense thinking as less fundamental or central than some other aspect or part of our ethics. So even if the addition of intuitively plausible views about rationality enables one to escape the charge of downgrading the moral/rational agent, one nevertheless ends up with a total view that is prima facie unacceptable as the basis or most central part of our ethical thinking.

This opens up the possibility that we should replace common-sense moral and/or rational thinking with some more theoretically plausible candidate for foundational status, or else, and less radically, that we should retain both these parts of our ordinary thought but seek to ground them both in some different but equally substantial ethical view. And although, of course, these possibilities might well—later, in fact, we will see that they do—provide virtue ethics and utilitarianism with interesting foundational opportunities, we must first consider whether we shouldn't simply replace common-sense morality with Kantian morality. The latter are, as we have seen, closely related and equally open to the charge of downgrading moral agents, but perhaps there is some way of supplementing Kantian morality that can undercut such criticism without opening the resultant view to the objection of being too uneconomical or odd for us to be comfortable in treating it as foundational or central to ethics.

But such a move cannot, in fact, get off the ground, if we attempt to supplement Kantian morality with foundational views about rationality that are consistent with Kant's (other) general assumptions about ethics. For, according to Kant, there are no categorical imperatives of self-interest, no categorical rational or moral obligations to seek one's own well-being or happiness of the sort he believes he can demonstrate in connection with people other than the agent. This means that, for Kant, no agent-favoring judgments of rationality can properly be used to supplement agent-sacrificing morality and help it, and Kant, to elude the charge of downgrading the agent that we earlier brought against both Kantian and common-sense morality. Even if Kantianism allows or were to allow for the conditional value and virtue status of certain sorts of self-regarding prudence, such value exists, as we have seen, at a less fundamental level than the moral value of pursuing the happiness of others, and so is incapable of undercutting the charge in question. Or, approaching matters from a somewhat different direction, we can say that Kantian practical rationality gives rise to other-regarding or other-favoring categorical moral imperatives but to no categorical imperatives of rational self-interest, with the result that, unlike common-sense rationality, Kant's views about rationality cannot be used to counteract the criticisms lodged against Kantian morality in Chapter 1.

But why *doesn't* Kant accept any agent-favoring (i.e. agent-happiness-favoring) embodiment of (categorical) rationality? At least in part, it seems, because he held that the concept of one's own happiness is too indeterminate or individually variable to function as a basis for impera-

tives having the depth and force of those other-regarding moral imperatives that derive from (various versions of) the Categorical Imperative.[9]
And as a general thesis this doesn't seem entirely plausible. Individual
preferences and individual ideas of happiness may vary widely, but
indifference to certain sorts of personal goods seems categorically irrational, and someone whom we criticize for neglecting her health or failing
to avoid avoidable suffering or pain cannot make herself immune to such
rational criticism by claiming that she is indifferent to health and freedom from pain. Speaking at the very least intuitively, it is simply irrational to have such a structure of preferences; from a rational standpoint,
one just *shouldn't* be indifferent to health and freedom from future pain,
and these elements of happiness or well-being or individual good are
certainly determinate enough to give us imperatives of self-interest of a
kind Kant explicitly denies.

However, even if we were to grant Kant that our own happiness is too
indeterminate to give rise to categorical imperatives, Kant would have
great difficulty in reconciling that assumption with his own stated commitment to categorical imperatives concerning the happiness or well-
being of others. It is completely unclear how the argument from indeterminacy can fail to hold in the latter case and still, as Kant evidently
believes, serve to undercut rational/categorical imperatives relating to
the agent's own good or happiness,[10] so perhaps Kant *ought* to have held
that there are agent-favoring imperatives or principles of rationality
roughly corresponding to those to which common-sense thinking subscribes. But inasmuch as Kant actually denies the existence of strong
agent-favoring principles of rationality, he has no way out of the criticisms mounted in the last chapter, and so although he avoids the particular oddness and diseconomy that attach to common-sense morality-cum-
rationality, his total view seems no more capable than the latter of serving
satisfactorily as a foundation or central core of our ongoing ethical
theory. If neither common-sense morality nor Kantian morality taken on
its own can fulfill our foundational requirements, the addition of some
appropriate body of claims about rationality cannot help us to do any
better.

## Notes

1. See Sidgwick, *The Methods of Ethics*, seventh edition, pp. 404n., 507ff.
2. Sidgwick, p. 508.
3. Sidgwick, Book I, Ch. 3, esp. pp. 23, 32; also pp. 5ff., 77, 344. For further

discussion see J. B. Schneewind's invaluable *Sidgwick's Ethics and Victorian Moral Philosophy*, Oxford, 1977, Chapter 7.

4. For possible counterexamples to the overridingness thesis, see Philippa Foot's "Are Moral Considerations Overriding?" in her *Virtues and Vices*, California, 1978; and my own "Admirable Immorality", Chapter 4 of *Goods and Virtues*, Oxford, 1983. There have been numerous replies to these two critiques of overridingness.

5. See Derek Parfit, *Reasons and Persons*, Oxford, 1984, p. 129, and Schneewind, p. 353.

6. See, e.g., Bentham's *An Introduction to the Principles of Morals and Legislation*, London, 1982; G. E. Moore's *Principia Ethica*, Cambridge, 1959; and, more recently, S. Scheffler's *The Rejection of Consequentialism*, Oxford, 1982.

7. Cf. Sidgwick, p. 120 and Schneewind, p. 353. Also Shelly Kagan, *The Limits of Morality*, Oxford, 1989, p. 389.

8. For Sidgwick's commitment to the idea of (a scientific) ethical *theory*, see, e.g., the concluding chapter of *Methods*, but Sidgwick's favorable attitude is evident throughout. Cf. Schneewind, p. 214. For opposition to the ideas of ethical theorizing, see Bernard Williams's *Ethics and the Limits of Philosophy*, Harvard, 1985, pp. 149ff. For an argument in defense of ethical theory and its use of quasi-scientific methodology, see Chapter 3.

9. See (e.g.) Kant's *Fundamental Principles of the Metaphysics of Morals*, in T. K. Abott, ed., *Kant's Theory of Ethics*, London, 1909, pp. 35ff. Kant also says that because one inevitably wills one's own happiness or well-being there can be no (agent-favoring) duty or obligation to pursue one's own happiness or good (see the introduction to Kant's *Doctrine of Virtue*, ed., M. Gregor, New York, 1964, pp. 44ff.). But it is doubtful whether everyone always seeks or wills her happiness, and in any event (as we will be seeing in Chapter 3) Kant's argument for the non-existence of duties to pursue one's own good or happiness is inconsistent, or at the very least in tension, with others of his ethical views.

10. See Lewis White Beck, *A Commentary on Kant's Critique of Practical Reason*, Chicago, 1960, pp. 98f. Of course, Kant does allow for (basic) categorical imperatives regarding the development of one's own natural talents and moral self-perfection. (See Chapter 6.) Notice too that if the *hedonism* of Kant's conception of happiness makes the pursuit of one's own happiness seem less valuable than certain ancient conceptions of happiness, thereby supporting Kant's failure to place fundamental value on such pursuit, it must at the same time tend to *undermine* the valuation Kant places on promoting the hedonistically conceived happiness of others.

# 3

# Incoherence in Kantian
# and Common-Sense Moral Thinking

We have just seen some reasons for denying that either common-sense or Kantian views about what is right and what is rational can serve as a proper foundation for our ethical thinking. But this still leaves open the possibility that those views *taken together* with a (common-sense) ethics of virtue or the virtues might form an adequate basis for ethical thought in general. And the possibility also remains that the ethics of virtue plays a fundamental role, while Kantian or ordinary thinking about rightness and/or rationality plays a secondary or more superficial role, within some acceptable totality of ethics. In either case, virtue ethics would need to be accompanied by common-sense morality and the latter would remain part of our (developing) ethical thought and theory.

But it is time now to show my hand. In what follows I am going to argue that we in fact have no need either for common-sense or Kantian moral thinking and that virtue ethics, a critical commonsensism about the virtues, can best operate on its own. I hope to show you that the common-sense and Kantian conceptions of morality are both—though in somewhat different ways—internally incoherent. Our everyday sense of what is plausible or intuitive eventually leads us to contradictory conclusions, and Kant's general theory, taken together with what Kant himself regards as its implications for more specific moral questions, leads to contradictions that to a substantial extent overlap those we shall point out in our common-sense moral thinking. So we may not have to worry any longer about how or where common-sense or Kantian morality fits together with common-sense or other forms of virtue ethics. And I shall provide reasons for thinking that both of the former should be discarded altogether in our search for an acceptable ethics. Let us begin this process by considering some notable criticisms of the whole notion of ethical or moral *theory* that have recently been raised by defenders of an intuitive approach in these areas.

31

## Moral Theory and Anti-Theory

It is by no means self-evident that moral philosophers should be pursuing moral theory as that notion is commonly understood. Substantive ethics is standardly distinguished from metaethics, that is, from the semantics and epistemology of ethical concepts/terms, and many philosophers who think it appropriate to consider metaethical questions about the meaning, objectivity, and rationality of ethical "judgments" would question whether our more substantive ethical and, more particularly, moral ideas ought to be the starting point of a theoretical enterprise that seeks to replace the complexity and diversity of common-sense or intuitive moral judgments with some more systematic or unified moral view.

The clearest example of what I mean by the latter is provided by utilitarianism. Some utilitarians have distinctive or, at least, definite metaethical views; but utilitarianism as a substantive conception of what makes acts right and wrong commits itself to correcting common-sense morality (our substantive ordinary ideas, e.g., about what things are right and wrong), and it claims the superiority of its own substantive view over the moral beliefs of ordinary individuals, in part on the basis of the supposed virtues of utilitarianism as a *theory* of right and wrong: its superior unity, economy, explanatory power, simplicity, etc. But many philosophers who are willing to countenance moral theory in the sense of (non-substantive) metaethics think there is something unsatisfactory, even perverse, about replacing our commonplace substantive moral judgments of right and wrong with a theory of right and wrong that picks and chooses among those judgments in the light of and in the name of some scientific ideal or imperative of systematic theory construction. To take just one example of the direction from which such criticism of utilitarianism and other attempts at moral theory can be made, consider the following passage from Bernard Williams's *Ethics and the Limits of Philosophy*:

> Theory looks characteristically for considerations that are very general . . . because it is trying to systematize and because it wants to represent as many reasons as possible as applications of other reasons. . . . Theory typically uses the assumption that we probably have too many ethical ideas, some of which may well turn out to be mere prejudices. Our major problem now is actually that we have not too many but too few, and we need to cherish as many as we can.[1]

Why, then, do we *think* we need theory or system? Williams holds that the answer lies in the assumption that in the absence of any system our ordinary diverse moral ideas lack any foundation, are unjustified or to some degree uncertain. Though there are other reasons why one might urge theory and system and I mean to discuss some of them, Williams has come up with one important reason that motivates the drive toward systematic moral theory. But that reason also clearly begs an important question concerning moral knowledge, or the justification of moral judgments.

Some notable philosophers have held that morally sensitive, morally educated individuals have an ability to discern (e.g.) what is right and what is wrong in many or most of the situations they encounter during the course of their (adult) lives; and they have held, in addition, that such discernment, such moral perceptiveness, in no way requires us to have access to a (unified) set of general moral principles and indeed goes beyond anything we even *could* put into the form of general principles. Some defenders of such "intuitionist" metaethical views have asserted, with W. D. Ross, that our ordinary moral thinking can or should make use of "prima facie principles" of obligation or duty and thus regard our moral evaluations of particular actions in particular situations as to some extent guided by general considerations; but these intuitionists claim nonetheless that the relevant prima facie principles cannot be strictly prioritized, lexically ordered, or spelled out in such a way as to rule out all exceptions; and as a result they also hold that in cases where the principles yield opposing prima facie directives, their relative weight can only be determined by a delicate weighing that will vary in its results from situation to situation. Other intuitionists, like Aristotle, give an even smaller role to ethical principles or general claims in the process of moral discernment and defend the possibility of a perceptual or at least a modifiable sensitivity to situational moral requirements that amounts to knowledge of the moral or ethical properties of various actual and possible acts.

Both sorts of view can treat moral judgment as analogous, for example, to our ordinary considered judgments of grammaticality. And since, presumably, we can in many or most cases tell what is or is not grammatical without being able to cite a general theory or unexceptionable syntactic principles that dictate the particular judgment we make, it may be plausible to make a similar claim about our ordinary moral capacities, and in that case the defender of moral theory and system who bases his views on the doubtfulness or insufficient warrant of moral claims made without the benefit of systematic theory will have difficulty defending his own views about the need for moral theory.[2]

Another motive for ethical theory is mentioned, however, by Sidgwick, who claims that we can use the general principles arrived at through a scientific or systematic approach to resolve doubts or conflicts about particular cases.[3] The idea seems to be that, on analogy with what occurs in science, the desirable systematic unity embodied in a single moral principle, or a closely related set of moral principles, may give us reason to resolve interpersonal conflicts or individual doubts about particular moral issues in one direction rather than another and may even cause us to have doubts in cases where we had previously been confident about our moral judgments. But even granting that there are many cases where moral intuitions conflict or are almost non-existent, the moral anti-theorist may simply question the proposed analogy with proper scientific methodology and hold that it is better to accept limits to our (present) moral knowledge than to forge ahead in the illusory hope that we can remedy our ignorance by imitating science. Moral anti-theorists have quite frequently exaggerated the (present) capacities of moral intuition and sensitivity by ignoring the number and the variety of ways in which moral intuition speaks vaguely or conflictingly about particular cases; and Sidgwick does us a favor by pointing out a number of specific moral issues about which intuition, in one way or another, typically or currently fails us. But there still may be reason to doubt that theoretical considerations or scientific method can properly be used to resolve the unclear or "don't care" cases of the moral life; it may be better to admit the present incompleteness of our moral knowledge than attempt to remedy our ignorance through a factitious appeal to scientific methodology. And in that case our only real remedy may lie in a collective and potentially long-term process of concrete, critical moral reflection.[4]

The issues I have just raised are extremely complex, and it would probably take a book-length treatment to do them justice. But I do at this point want to mention a further reason for taking seriously the idea of ethical or moral theory. It is one thing to point out the incompleteness of our common-sense moral ideas and intuitions, to recognize that intelligent and sensitive individuals may differ over particular moral issues or lack any well-defined sense of what to say about other particular moral issues; it is quite another to claim that our intuitive moral thinking is internally incoherent or inconsistent. But it is just this sort of stronger and more troubling claim that I want to urge upon you in what follows.

In other areas of philosophy, we have long been familiar with the consequences of discovering intuitive inconsistency. When Frege's intuitive axiom five was found to lead to inconsistency or contradiction, that discovery motivated a move away from intuitive set theory to a set theory whose content was in large measure dictated by the goal of avoiding contradiction. And quite similarly, when it became apparent that our common-sense intuitions about what statements confirm which others lead to inconsistency, that very fact served as a prime motivation for the development of technical and systematic theories of confirmation. Once inconsistency is revealed in our ordinary use of a concept, it takes theoretical ingenuity to avoid such inconsistency while still achieving as many as possible of the original purposes that concept served, and any enterprise devoted to such a task has clearly gone beyond ordinary thinking into the realm of theory. And I want to argue now that our common-sense thinking about morality is internally inconsistent and that such inconsistency gives us reason to pursue systematic theory in ethics in the way it has been pursued in other areas of philosophy.

## Moral Luck

One of the unnerving accomplishments of recent discussions of the idea of moral luck is to point to a nest of inconsistencies in one major area of our intuitive moral thinking. Consider, for example, our everyday moral reactions to the unforeseen or accidental consequences of people's actions. Ordinary moral thinking distinguishes the moral status of attemped murder from that of murder, for example, and although this distinction is exemplified in legal distinctions between the status and punishability of murder and attempted murder, its moral significance is by no means exhausted by the role it plays in specifically legal contexts. Thus, quite apart from legal differences between murder and attempted murder, we think much worse of someone who has killed an innocent victim than of someone who accidentally fails to kill an intended innocent victim. We think much worse of him and of what he has done, and these differences can be seen in our inclination to heap greater blame upon an actual murderer (for what he has done) than we do upon an unsuccessful one and also, I imagine, in the greater revulsion we feel in confronting (knowingly sitting next to) a murderer than in confronting (knowingly sitting next to) someone who has merely attempted murder.

To the extent that common-sense morality accepts and encourages these differences of feeling and moral judgment, it allows actual unforeseeable consequences a role in determining moral judgment, thus making room for a certain kind of "moral luck." But as has been frequently pointed out, the very idea of moral luck affronts our common-sense moral intuitions. So our moral intuitions about cases taken singly are in conflict with a general common-sense moral conviction that judgments of morally better and worse, or greater or less culpability or blameworthiness, cannot properly be subject to luck or accident. And the cases where such inconsistency arises are quite numerous and varied.

To take one further, and perhaps more clear-cut example, imagine someone driving a car along a country road and pointing out noteworthy sights to his passengers. As a result of his preoccupation, the car suddenly swerves to the middle of the road; fortunately there are no cars coming in the opposite direction and no accident occurs. However, in another scenario the person is similarly preoccupied, and because a truck happens to be coming, has a major accident. He is then responsible for a great deal of harm to others and would normally be accounted blameworthy or culpable in a way that (to a degree that) he would not be thought blameworthy or culpable in the first-mentioned case. This example is borrowed from "Moral Luck," Thomas Nagel's groundbreaking paper. But as Nagel also points out, something in us revolts against the idea of moral luck, inclining us to the view that the driver must have the *same* degree of culpability in the two cases mentioned above.[5] There is something repelling in the idea that one can be more or less culpable depending on events outside one's ken or control. And in regard to the just-mentioned pair of examples, therefore, it may seem as if we should be able to insert some kind of probability estimate into the example, so that whether the driver who swerves is culpable and the degree, if any, of his culpability would depend solely on whether he was sufficiently aware of the likelihood of an accident and on how likely an accident was, given his preoccupation with the scenery—judgments that are constant between the two imagined cases and that might allow us to say the man was culpable (or not culpable) in both cases to the same extent for having paid attention to the scenery while driving.

But (following Nagel) I think that no such solution really squares with the moral judgments we make in the ordinary course of events, before we begin to worry about moral luck in a self-conscious way. I think no matter how constant one imagines the (awareness of) probability in the two situations, common-sense morality sees some difference in the culpability or reprehensibleness of the agent. (Actually, it doesn't matter whether the two situations are viewed as counterfactually possible relative to one another or are viewed as involving similar persons—or one person at different times—facing relevantly similar situations.) Common sense appears to subscribe to a mutually contradictory set of assumptions with regard to putative cases of inattention, carelessness, or negligence, and we therefore need to go beyond our ordinary thinking in this area of morality.[6]

We have just spoken of one particular form of moral luck: luck with respect to results or consequences of one's actions or inactions. But as

Nagel in his original article and many others as well have pointed out, moral luck can come about in other ways than through unexpected or unforeseeable results. Thus if some of us would have done nothing to stop the Nazis, had we been living in Germany before and during the Second World War, then arguably any lesser or negligible guilt we have through not having in fact been in Germany during that period is attributable to moral luck in our *circumstances*. And such assumptions of circumstantial luck lead to inconsistencies that resemble those uncovered in connection with luck in *results* or *consequences*. Finally, I should also mention constitutive luck with respect to inborn traits of intelligence, energy level, and the like. But I don't want to dwell on the difficulties such traits raise for our common moral judgments. The problems already unearthed are clearly sufficient for our purposes.

## Deontological Restrictions

One of the most notable features of act-utilitarianism and of act-consequentialism generally is its appeal from the standpoint of impersonal benevolence. When (and if) we abstract from our particular identities and our personal desires and concerns, and view what happens in the world benevolently but as it were from outside, we wish for optimific acts to be performed and are glad when they are performed. And such acts are the acts that act-utilitarianism and act-consequentialism designate as morally right or obligatory.[7]

On the other hand, common-sense morality differs from utilitarianism and from consequentialism generally in holding that certain kinds of acts are morally obligatory even when they produce less overall good than certain alternatives open to a given agent, and the prime illustration of such obligations has been those moral restrictions which dictate, for example, that one may not kill an innocent person even if doing so will save five innocent lives, indeed even if it will prevent the killing of five *other* innocent people by people other than oneself. Here it is assumed that acceptance of the restrictions involves accepting the idea that killing can be a wrong thing to *do* even when from an impersonal standpoint a better state of affairs (series of events) will *occur* if one does kill, and clearly such deontological restrictions on what a person may do even in the name of maximizing the good are involved in the morality most people accept.

Now with regard to situations where one has a choice between *killing* one innocent person and *failing to save* the lives of five other innocent people, it is clear what stands *in favor* of the former choice: if one makes it, then things overall will *turn out better* than if one doesn't make it. But common-sense morality nonetheless disallows that choice, and in that case it makes sense to ask what, from the standpoint of common sense, stands *against* that choice and does so with such sufficient weight as to make it clearly wrong to kill a single innocent to bring about an overall better (much better?) result. In *The Rejection of Consequentialism*, Samuel Scheffler points out that a certain kind of response is most typically and naturally made to such a question: those confronted with a request for a justification of some common-sense restriction on overall optimizing most frequently try to find some feature of violations of the restriction that is "very bad or has high disvalue" and that will allow them to say that it is because violations have this objectionable feature that they are commonsensically forbidden.[8] Thus it will be pointed out, for example, that when someone *s* deliberately kills an innocent person *p* to prevent others from dying of disease or accidental injuries, what is bad or objectionable about *s*'s act is the very fact that it is the deliberate taking—the deliberate *violation*—of an innocent life.

Such a justification may appear to work well enough when we merely consider cases where one has to choose between killing an innocent person and letting others die through some non-human or non-intentional instrumentality; for in such cases the highly disvaluable or objectionable feature that characterizes violations of the restriction that forbids killing will be entirely absent if one refuses to kill and lets a number of other people die through disease or as a result of some accident. But the restriction is also supposed to apply to cases where one has to choose between killing someone innocent oneself and letting others kill a number of (other) innocent people, cases, that is, where deliberate or intentional killing of the innocent will occur no matter what one does. And the kind of justification that most naturally, most commonsensically, most frequently occurs to one as a way of defending deontological restrictions forbidding killing and the like simply cannot work for the latter sort of case. For the objectionable, bad or highly disvaluable feature that characterizes the killing of an innocent person—be it the fact that someone is used as a mere means or that someone violates the innocence of another or whatever else of this sort one may choose to focus on—will also be present if one merely lets someone else deliberately kill innocent people. And indeed if it is such a bad thing that someone should use or be used by someone else as a means, one may well wonder whether that isn't a reason to *violate* the common-sense prohibition against killing the innocent in cases where one has to choose between using someone oneself and allowing a *greater number* of such usings by others. Whatever objectionable or disvaluable feature attaches to violations of the prohibition will be present on a larger scale if one doesn't violate the prohibition, and so if the use of another as a means or the violation of innocence is objectionable, the difficult question arises how it can be wrong or objectionable, by killing an innocent person, to act in such a way as to *minimize* such objectionable acts.

So, although it is natural to attempt to base common-sense deontological restrictions on some bad or disvaluable feature that attaches to violations of such restrictions, such justifications actually tend to undercut what they attempt to justify. If in order to justify deontological restrictions, we focus on some bad feature attributable to the violations of the restrictions, we may also be led to realize that *more occurrences* of that bad feature will occur if one does not violate the restriction and this seems to give one reason to prefer such violation or at least to treat it as no less permissible than compliance with the restriction; and all this, of course, precisely undercuts our inherent sense that it is wrong to kill in order to prevent other killings and worse to do so than not to do so. So our common-sense thinking in this area is at odds with itself, is incoherent, because the reasons it tends to offer in its own support actually tend to cast (further) doubt upon it.[9]

## Asymmetry and Incoherence

The third and final area of common-sense morality where I believe we run up against an incoherent set of individually plausible, intuitive assumptions is that, roughly, of self-other asymmetry. Obviously, such asymmetry seems irrational and unmotivated if we adopt the impersonal perspective of utilitarian ethics, but problems arise for such asymmetry even from within the perspective of common-sense ethical thinking. Common-sense morality itself has a difficult time coherently making sense of its commitment to a self-other asymmetry of right and wrong because of some of the *other* things it says about right and wrong.

In particular, ordinary non-utilitarian morality treats our obligations to others as dependent on how near they stand to us in relations of affection or special commitment: obligations to our immediate family (other things being equal) being stronger than to our relations generally, obligations to friends and relations being stronger than to compatriots generally, and obligations to the latter, in turn, being stronger than to the people of other countries.[10] To that extent, ordinary morality reflects the normal structure of an adult's concerns. We are naturally more concerned about and have more reason to be concerned about the well-being of friends and relations than of more distant others, and common-sense morality seems to build such differences into the varyingly strong duties it assigns us to concern ourselves with others' well-being. However, by means of its self-other asymmetry, common-sense morality also superimposes an absolute moral discontinuity on the structure of concern in which each agent is normally situated. On the one hand, it encourages the idea that strength of obligation weakens as one gets further from the agent, but, on the other, it assumes that there is no moral obligation whatever (except indirectly) for the agent to benefit *himself*. Once one leaves the agent behind, the agent's obligations vary in proportion to his reason for concern, but where he has greatest reason for concern in the natural course of things, he has no direct obligation whatever. And this appears odd and unmotivated, even apart from any utilitarian or consequentialist perspective (though the latter provides one way out of the oddness).

In fact there is one very obvious way to attempt to justify the self-other asymmetry (or some aspects of it), but in the light of what has just been said, the attempt actually makes the picture appear even bleaker for common-sense morality by making it appear impossible to make sense of the above-mentioned discontinuity in common-sense thinking. Let me explain.

One can very naturally attempt to justify the (apparent) lack of moral duties to provide for one's own good, in terms of normal human desires and instincts and plausible assumptions about their influence on our actions. We can be expected to take care of ourselves most of the time, and that, according to the justification, is why there is no need for morality to impose obligations or duties to do so. But this readily available rationale—and it is, roughly, the account Kant offers for our having no duty to seek our own happiness—actually leads to incoherence when combined with the facts about our relations to other people that we mentioned above.[11] We can normally be expected to take better care of our spouse and children than of distant others, yet our obligations to the former are stronger than to the latter, and this is just the opposite of what one should expect if the above rationale were correct about duties to seek one's own good. But it is commonsensically very natural to try to justify the self-other moral asymmetry, and more particularly the absence of duties to seek one's own well-being in terms of what is normal and expectable in people, and I think this shows that common-sense really is at odds with itself in this general area. What seems like the only possible and sensible rationale for the self-other asymmetry makes nonsense out of another aspect of common-sense morality, and this internal difficulty of ordinary thought about right and wrong offers some further reason, I think, to look for something better than common-sense moral thinking.[12] But it also might make one look for a better explanation than common-sense thinking offers of why there are no duties to promote one's own happiness, one that is not at odds with other features of common-sense morality in the way that what I have been describing as the common-sense rationale is.

Thus Joseph Butler agrees with Kant that we tend to neglect others' interests more than our own so there is less need to have obligations to further our own self-interest than to have obligations to further the interests of others—but he makes this a matter of degree, rather than claiming an absence altogether of duties to oneself, because he recognizes our human tendency to ruin or hurt ourselves through stupidity, carelessness, laziness, overweening passion, etc.[13] But even such a softened account of duties to oneself runs counter to the other aspects of common-sense thinking mentioned above, and it is therefore interesting to note that Butler offers another, supplementary explanation of self-other asymmetry that seems in no way incompatible with ordinary views about the strictness or strength of our obligations to "near" and "distant" others.

Butler points out that imprudence typically leads to its own punishment, whereas ill treatment of others may not rebound to the disadvantage of the agent; so there is less need to blame someone who hurts himself than someone who hurts others, since an injury incurred by imprudence does something by itself to dissuade the agent from similar action in the future. The prevention of self-damage can rely on the injury the agent himself feels and so requires less indignation on the part of others. And Butler adds that someone who hurts himself is naturally an object of our pity for the injury he sustains, whereas someone who hurts others and receives no injury is not a natural object of pity. Since pity tends to lessen, or is even incompatible with displeasure with the object of pity, we have a further explanation of why an imprudent person who hurts himself receives less opprobrium than someone who injures others.

However, this rationale, though it doesn't conflict with things commonsensically said in other areas, seems inadequate on its own ground. We blame someone for taking an unnecessary risk with another person if the risk was serious and even if nothing bad came of it, but we do not (as much) blame someone who opens himself to serious unnecessary risk. We think it is not wrong or not nearly as wrong for someone to expose himself to such risk, even if he in fact escaped injury, but on Butler's account, there is need to blame him in such cases since the usual punishment for imprudence is absent and so, unless the agent is blamed severely, there will be nothing to discourage him from similar risk-taking in the future. Since, moreover, the risk taker sustains no injury, there is nothing to pity, so pity cannot explain why we don't feel as much blame and indignation toward him as we feel in other-regarding cases.

Even, therefore, if we renounce the rationale that initially suggests itself as the best way to account for and justify self-other asymmetry, we remain saddled with considerable difficulties. We may avoid the out-and-out incoherence that arises from the common-sense rationale taken together with our ordinary views about the way strength of obligation varies with closeness of relationship; but since other known candidates for the explanation of self-other asymmetry fail to square with the actual phenomena of such asymmetry, we are left without any account of the asymmetry. And the absolute discontinuity that exists between the way we are permitted to treat ourselves and the way our obligations to others vary (other things being equal) with the closeness of our relationship to them seems as odd and unmotivated as ever. More generally, our common-sense moral views in this area and in the areas of moral luck and of deontology lead to paradox and outright incoherence in a variety of ways, and this fact—together with the foundational difficulties of common sense described earlier in Chapters 1 and 2—give us some reason to be dissatisfied with common-sense morality and search for a better overall approach to the problems of ethics.

But in addition to pointing out the need for something better than common sense, the above discussion demonstrates that in certain crucial respects, and contrary to Williams's claims, our intuitive moral thinking leaves us with too many rather than too few ideas. The inconsistency and incoherence we have discerned come from a clash of intuitive commitments and could be avoided if we lacked some of those commitments, and here, as I suggested earlier, the situation with regard to moral thought is very much like what in an earlier era was seen to occur with regard to our thinking about induction and confirmation. Hempel's classical studies of confirmation reveal that our common-sense ideas about confirmation, our earliest attempts to formulate intuitive criteria for determining when one statement confirms another, yield contradiction in a number of different ways. In the words of Israel Scheffler, "Hempel's critique of Nicod's criterion and of the prediction-criterion, his discovery and treatment of the paradoxes of confirmation, and his discussion of conflicts among certain criteria [make it seem] unlikely that *any* consistent . . . choice of criteria will wholly avoid violating *some* criterion which appears, in itself, to be perfectly plausible. [T]here is thus some degree of theoretical license legitimately claimed by anyone seeking a systematic account [of confirmation]."[14] In a similar vein, Nelson Goodman claims that "[s]ince our commonsense assumptions taken in combination quickly leads to absurd conclusions, some of these assumptions have to be dropped; and different theorists may make different decisions about which to drop and which to preserve."

For our purposes, Hempel's work on confirmation is important, not for its positive theoretical suggestions but for its illustration of the way an incoherence or conflict of ordinary intuitions in a given area justifies a recourse to theoretical considerations and systematic theorizing. We here have similar reason, I think, at this point to turn to considerations of systematic ethical theory in order to get beyond the conflicts we have found in ordinary intuitive morality. The mere incompleteness of ordinary moral thinking may be no reason to yield to the temptation—a temptation felt by some philosophical mentalities, but not others—to use theoretical methodology in an attempt to find and formulate an adequate substantive ethical view; such incompleteness by itself *may* simply illustrate Williams' point that we have too few ethical ideas and therefore shouldn't in ethics apply standards of simplicity and systematic unity that tend to *reduce the number* of our ethical ideas by treating some subset of those ideas as if it could cover the whole realm, all the phenomena, that ethics has to deal with. But the state of our ethical thinking is more complicated and more parlous than anti-theorists have (explicitly) recognized, and the fact that our combined intuitions yield incoherence and/or inconsistency points up a sense in which, as I say, we have too many, rather than too few, ethical ideas. And this conclusion in turn seems to justify the ascent (descent?) into theoretical ethics that anti-theorists deplore.[15]

There is some irony in our having reached this conclusion by way of a reply to the anti-theoretical position articulated and asserted by Bernard Williams in *Ethics and the Limits of Philosophy*. For in other, previous contexts Williams has shown himself well aware that our moral/ethical intuitions can lead us to contradiction and so require the rejection of at least one of those intuitions. His own earliest treatment of moral dilemmas provides a perfect example, in fact, of the way in which, at least in some areas, we may have too many, rather than too few ideas.

In "Ethics and Consistency," Williams defends the claim that through no fault of her own an agent may enter a situation in which she (morally) ought to do *a* and (morally) ought to do *b* and yet cannot do both *a* and *b*.[16] Such a situation represents a moral dilemma for a particular agent, and although there are many ways one can doubt or deny the possibility even in principle of such dilemma, Williams defends that possibility both in the above-mentioned article and subsequently in other essays. In the first article, however, Williams is quite clear that if we accept the possibility of moral dilemma, one or another intuitive principle of deontic logic will have to be given up; for if agent $p$ ought to do $a$ and ought to do $b$, it seems independently plausible, via what Williams calls the principle of agglomeration (but is elsewhere called the principle/rule of conjunction introduction), to infer that $p$ ought to do both $a$ and $b$. Since it is also plausible to assume that "ought" implies "can" and dilemma presupposes that $p$ cannot (ever) do both $a$ and $b$, we end up in a logical contradiction. So something clearly has to give, and Williams himself decides to hold on to "ought" implies "can" and the possibility of dilemma, but to reject the principle of agglomeration.

However, this particular choice among independently plausible assumptions is hardly self-evident. Confronted with similar contradiction, other ethical thinkers have opted to deny "ought" implies "can" and (at least implicitly) to retain the principle of agglomeration; and it is difficult to deny that this choice is appropriately influenced by theoretical considerations, even if it may also involve an appeal to the comparative strength or force of clashing intuitions.[17] So Williams himself has provided us with a prime example of a situation where a contradiction among intuitive ethical ideas makes it plausible to maintain that we have too many ideas, rather than too few. The appeal to theoretical considerations and our progress or groping toward substantive theories or conceptions of ethics can be justified in terms of what a more intuitive, but thoroughgoing common-sense approach reveals to be its own internal difficulties.[18] And since, in particular, uniformity, symmetry, (systematic) unity, and economy are both in and outside of science (e.g., in linguistics and mathematics) considered to be theoretical desiderata, we have reason to appeal to such factors in the way we have done up till now, and I will continue to do so in what follows.

## The Inconsistency of Kantian Ethics

One of the bases of the difficulties just uncovered in our common-sense moral intuitions is what I have called the common-sense rationale for agent-sacrificing self-other asymmetry. But I also indicated that Kant used a similar explanation or justification for that asymmetry, and at this point I think we ought to consider whether Kant's views have anything like the inharmonious character we have attributed to certain (juxta-positions of) common-sense views or entail the sort of inconsistency or incoherence that we find among common-sense intuitions or opinions. The difficulties we have uncovered in common sense to some extent propel us in the direction of systematic moral or ethical theory, and Kant's ethical philosophy represents a subtle, powerful, and complexly articulated example of such theory that we cannot afford to ignore as a potential alternative to common-sense or intuitionist views.

In Chapters 1 and 2 we saw that Kantian and common-sense morality are in similar ways unsuitable for a foundational role in ethical theory. The fact that neither treats enhancement of the agent's well-being as a basis for (comparative or positive) favorable evaluation of an agent's actions constitutes a reason for thinking that neither of these forms of moral theory can constitute *the* foundation or central part of our ethical thought in general. And there are problems of redundancy and disecon-omy with any attempt to treat common-sense rationality and morality as (roughly) coequal parts of our foundational thinking. Since Kant rejects the idea of categorical imperatives of self-interest, his view of rationality is clearly inconsistent with agent-favoring asymmetrical common-sense rationality, and so his overall view also rules out the possibility of foundationally combining agent-favoring rationality with his own form of agent-sacrificing morality. Kant appears, then, to have no way of avoiding the charge of deprecating or devaluing (the projects and con-cerns of) moral or rational agents.

But, in addition to all these difficulties, Kant's views about morality lead to paradoxes and inconsistencies that resemble, or perhaps I should say partially overlap, those we have mentioned in connection with com-mon-sense morality. For Kant there are no duties or obligations to pursue one's own happiness, and he seeks to account for this fact via the claims that every man "inevitably and spontaneously" seeks to promote his own happiness and that the concepts of duty and obligation apply only where an end is adopted reluctantly.[19] But this set of claims leads to incoherence and disharmony only if they are conjoined with the assump-tion that the strength or strictness of our obligations to benefit others (roughly) varies with the closeness of their personal relations to us. And in fact Kant seems to make this very assumption in the same work where he makes the above points about the absence of any obligation to adopt one's own happiness as an end.[20] So the same incoherence that we earlier attributed to common-sense morality in connection with self-other asymmetry and the variable strictness of duties to others also appears to characterize Kant's moral thinking and constitutes, I believe, an equally strong objection to the latter.

If one believes, on the other hand, that *one* set of contradictions, or *one* incoherence, is much less formidable than the three different nests of difficulty earlier ascribed to common-sense moral thinking, then one may at this point insist that Kant's views are in much better shape than common-sense morality, because, in addition to the just-mentioned difficulty, the latter faces both the problem of deontological restrictions and the problem of moral luck that we described earlier in the present chapter. And even if Kant probably has no clear answer to the problems raised by Scheffler and myself concerning the justification of deontology,[21] he clearly avoids the inconsistency of our intuitions about moral luck, by allowing luck or accident no role whatever in determining moral merit or culpability. However, Kant immunizes moral values from factors of luck by connecting them to non-empirical facts of noumenal willing, and though such a treatment may evade the *inconsistencies* in our common-sense ideas about moral luck, it makes itself hostage to metaphysical assumptions and methods most of us nowadays are likely to be wary of.

Moreover, the argument that Kant's ethics is in better shape than ordinary moral thinking depends on the assumption that the former is subject to no incoherence that fails to characterize common sense as well, and I believe that assumption can be shown to be mistaken. Kantian moral theory is subject to its own distinctive form of incoherence, an incoherence resulting partly from the well-trodden ways of self-other asymmetry and partly from an absence of such asymmetry in one of Kant's main formulations of the Categorical Imperative.

Kant's End-in-Itself formulation of the Categorical Imperative runs:

> Act in such a way that you always treat humanity, whether in your own person or in the person of any other, never simply as a means but always at the same time as an end.

And I believe that such a view sits badly with what we have seen Kant to be saying about the absence of duties to pursue one's own happiness. (This may be obvious, or almost obvious, to those who have been following the argument of the present chapter, but, as far as I am aware, the lack of fit, the inconsistency I am about to point to in Kant's thinking, has not been mentioned by other critics.)

Kant employs the End-in-Itself version of the Categorical Imperative to argue not only for the wrongness or impermissibility of killing others, but for the impermissibility of suicide as well. Although Kant's views about sacrificing one's own life for the lives or the happiness of others are complex and seem to have developed over time,[22] he very clearly holds that committing suicide when one despairs of one's future or is tired of life is morally unacceptable, and such a prohibition clearly fits in with the self-other *symmetry* of the Categorical Imperative as expressed above. Prohibitions against treating people in certain ways (even as a means to producing certain sorts of overall good results) are quintessentially deontological, and it is obvious that Kant's commitment to deontological restrictions is more self-other symmetric (at least in certain of its aspects) than common-sense morality seems to be. But questions about whether one may permissibly fail to benefit certain people in certain ways fall outside the area, so to speak, of deontology. Roughly speaking, deontology tells us we may not *actively treat* people in various more or less specific ways, and it differs from consequentialism through its claim, among other things, that such treatment cannot be morally justified in terms of overall desirable results. But obligations to confer well-being/benefits exist if we may not *fail to confer* such benefits and (again, very roughly) they represent a common element or aspect of common-sense, consequentialist, and Kantian moral views. And the relevance of this sketchily drawn distinction to our present purposes is the contrast it allows us to draw between Kant's deontological views and what he says about obligations to confer benefits.

We earlier saw that Kant espouses an agent-sacrificing self-other asymmetric view about the pursuit of mere benefits or happiness. One has an obligation to help others in their pursuit of happiness, but one has no obligation to pursue one's own happiness (except perhaps derivatively as a means, if one's happiness is one, to the happiness of others or to one's own personal or moral development). Yet Kant's deontology—under one of its aspects—requires self-other symmetry in the treatment of human beings: one may use neither oneself nor anyone else merely as a means. And this odd discrepancy, the tension, as I take it to be, between Kant's deontological and his extradeontological moral views is in itself perplexing and even troubling.

Now this discrepancy exists between Kant's views about perfect duty (the duty not to lie, not to kill, not to mutilate, etc.) and his views about the imperfect duty to confer benefits (which one doesn't have to fulfill at every moment); in an attempt to clarify and defend Kant, one might at this point attempt to justify Kant's alternation between self-other asymmetry and self-other symmetry by means of the distinction between perfect and imperfect duty. But that simply won't work. At a critical juncture Kant clearly refuses to put weight on the distinction between the two kinds of duty, and his failure to do so leads to what in all fairness can, I think, be called an incoherence in his total ethical view.

Kant's claim that we have no obligation or duty to pursue our own happiness is based partly on the assumption that what we inevitably and spontaneously do cannot be obligatory or a duty. Kant makes no distinction here between imperfect and perfect duty, and so he is committed to holding that what we inevitably, etc., do cannot constitute one of our *perfect* duties. Now as we have seen Butler point out earlier, many people seem to aim for something other than and even incompatible with their own happiness, so one might certainly question Kant's factual assumption that we all willingly and unavoidably pursue (what in fact constitutes) our own happiness or welfare. (However, see note 11.) But for the sake of argument let us grant Kant this point in fact, and see how well what he says to justify the absence of a duty to pursue benefits to oneself or one's own happiness (and a consequent extradeontological self-other asymmetry with respect to the pursuit of happiness) fits in with the End-in-Itself version of the Categorical Imperative.

Kant attempts to derive the wrongness of despondent suicide and killing others from the prohibition against using people merely as means, but he draws out a number of other implications as well: among them, the (notorious) prohibition on masturbation ("self-abuse") and, more relevantly to present purposes, a prohibition on mutilating either oneself or another person. But do we really need a prohibition against wilful *self*-mutilation? If Kant is allowed to have been justified in claiming that we inevitably and spontaneously aim for our own good or happiness, surely there is similar reason to hold that we inevitably and spontaneously (or typically and naturally) refrain from mutilating our own bodies, and so it would appear that the argument Kant uses to justify the absence of a duty to seek one's own happiness can also be used to argue against the existence of any obligation to refrain from wilful self-mutilation. And since the self-other symmetry of Kant's End-in-Itself formulation of the Categorical Imperative entails that there is such an obligation (Kant at least argues that it does), we really do end up with an incoherence or inconsistency in Kant's theory treated as a whole.

However, precisely because common-sense morality is relatively tolerant of self-mutilation, the problems here uncovered do not infect common-sense thinking about morality. Kant's End-in-Itself formulation of the Categorical Imperative is an important, a central, element in Kant's total moral conception, and so there seems to be at least one important form of incoherence that infects Kantian theory, but is not ascribable to common sense. I think we had better not try to decide, therefore, which of these two approaches to morality is in relatively worse, or better, shape as a result of our present criticisms. We have found internal conflicts both within ethical Kantianism and within common-sense morality and we cannot remain contented with either of these views.

## Can We Patch Up the Difficulties?

But how far do we need to move away from Kant and common sense? Perhaps, instead of opting for some totally different approach to ethics, we should try to amend one or the other of these views in such a way as to eliminate all disharmony and inconsistency. Certainly, if the problems we have uncovered concerned relatively superficial aspects or areas of Kantian or common-sense moral thinking, such a piecemeal or patchwork approach would naturally recommend itself. But I don't think the problems in question are superficial, and so I am somewhat skeptical about the possibilities of a patchwork solution to them. Nonetheless, it is far from *obvious* that such a less radical solution would inevitably be inadequate, so I would like to consider some of the possibilities of patchworking that might naturally occur to one as potential solutions to our various difficulties.

One possible move, for example, would be to abolish self-other asymmetry throughout Kantian and/or common-sense morality—and without moving all the way to consequentialism and its particular form or deployment of self-other symmetry. Now I am not taking this to mean we should allow people to (fail to) do to and for others what commonsensically they may permissibly (fail to) do to and for themselves, for this might approach some kind of amoralism or moral antinomianism, and it is hard to imagine common-sense morality, much less Kantianism, finding an emended version *of itself* in such a view. But consider the alternative emendation: treating it as wrong to (fail to) do to and for oneself what (on either Kantian or common-sense moral views) it is wrong to (fail to) do to and for others.

Presumably this would entail a larger change in common-sense morality, with its thoroughgoing commitment to agent-sacrificing asymmetry, than in Kantianism, with its symmetric, if inconsistently adopted, End-in-Itself formula of the Categorical Imperative. But Kantian moral theory would at least have to abandon its supposed justification for the absence of obligations or duties to seek one's own happiness; and its claim that beings with a holy will are not subject to categorical imperatives would also have to be either jettisoned or modified. Sidgwick and numerous others have criticized Kant's (arguments for the) claim that there are no categorical imperatives of self-interest, but if we abandon self-other asymmetry regarding the pursuit of happiness along the lines now being considered, we will have to accept the existence of such imperatives within the sphere of morality, and it seems to me—subject to correction by Kantians who may well know better—that the introduction of categorical imperatives of self-interest would entail radical revisions in Kantian moral theory. Perhaps such revisions can be made without the loss of what is distinctively Kantian, but I think they clearly extend well beyond my own expertise.[23] If the present arguments elicit such a set of revisions—if the problems of the present and previous chapters can be overcome in a Kantian manner—then we needn't abandon the Kantian approach to ethics for the more radical solution to those problems that will be suggested in what follows.

But we shouldn't neglect the implications for common-sense morality of a totally symmetric approach conceived as adding to the moral obligations the agent has to herself, rather than subtracting from those she has to others. As I mentioned, this would entail an even larger change, at least regarding symmetry, since common sense is more consistently and/ or extensively agent-sacrificing than Kantian moral theory. But even if such a radical alteration did away with all the incoherence that arises in connection with self-other asymmetry,[24] it is difficult to see how it would do away with the problems concerning moral luck and concerning the justification of deontological restrictions that common-sense moral thinking must face. If we allow that one can be morally defective or reprehensible not only for what one does to others but also, and to an equal extent, for what one does to oneself, moral luck and its difficulties remain in full force, and indeed the area of the difficulties actually widens out as self-regarding action becomes subject to the same puzzles and perplexities that were obviously confined, at least as far as common-sense morality is concerned, to other-regarding action. Luck and accident can affect the results of our self-regarding actions—for example, suicide attempts—as easily as they can affect those of our actions toward or involving others, so the acceptance of total self-other moral symmetry forces a revisionary common-sense approach to accept a more extensive set of difficulties in one area at the same time it solves problems in another area.

Something similar happens in connection with the problems for common sense that specifically arise from Scheffler's discussion of the intuitively felt obligation not to kill in order to prevent other killings. If we abandon self-other asymmetry in such a way that it becomes as morally objectionable to kill one's innocent self to prevent a greater number of deliberate killings of innocent people as we ordinarily take it to be objectionable to kill others for the sake of such an end, then the problems that develop from Scheffler's work remain in force and simply spread themselves to a new area. In addition to the difficulty of explaining how, if it is so objectionable to kill an innocent other, it can be objectionable to (seek to) minimize the number of such objectionable killings, we will have the further difficulty of explaining how, if it is so objectionable to kill oneself, it can be objectionable to (seek to) minimize the number of such objectionable killings (by killing oneself as a means, assuming it is one, to preventing others from committing immoral suicide). So even if the removal of self-other symmetry can help solve some of the deepest problems of common-sense morality, it exacerbates some of its other difficulties, and it is not clear that such a trade-off is really worth the effort.

Further, the Kantian who eliminates all self-other asymmetry faces these same difficulties. Kant has a number of arguments for the differing versions of the Categorical Imperative and their differing applications to specific moral issues like killing. But it is not clear to me how any of Kant's arguments serves to undercut the problems about justifying deontology that we have seen emerge from Scheffler's discussion of that topic. The difficulties raised in the last paragraph for a self-other symmetric common-sense-based view of deontology strike me as equally difficult for Kant's defense of deontology. And unless someone can specifically show how Kant's arguments for the wrongness of self- and other-killing enable us to explain why and how it can be objectionable to kill in order to minimize the overall number of killings, I think Kant's ethics will continue to have problems in this area, and one is given reason (additional to any one may already have) for suspecting the soundness of Kant's arguments for (specific forms of) deontology.

The other major problem faced by Kantian ethics—even a version cast in self-other symmetric form—revolves around the issue of moral luck. Kant denied the possibility of moral luck and had recourse to the metaphysics of noumenal will in his effort to establish conditions of moral evaluation entirely free from contamination by luck or accident. But I think many present-day ethical Kantians would tend to resist, and be right to resist, a noumenal metaphysics (even one in which the noumenal is regarded merely as an inevitable *postulate* of the moral point of view) as the price to be paid for luck-free moral judgment. In that case they owe us an account on how the determinants of moral evaluation—the factors of circumstance, constitution, and causation that give actuality and substance to moral thought—can reasonably be conceived independently of all luck or accident; and it is difficult to see how such a thing could possibly be accomplished.

Of course, it is possible that I have missed something in Kant's arguments that only a Kant scholar is in any position to see clearly, and in that case, as I indicated earlier, there may be more vitality in the Kantian approach to ethics than I have granted, and the move toward utilitarianism and virtue ethics that I shall now be recommending may be otiose or at least not clearly inevitable. But for the remainder of this work, I will not attempt to develop or correct Kantian and common-sense views of morality and will focus on the alternative possibilities of utilitarian and virtue-oriented ethics.

In so doing, we will certainly be pursuing ethical *theory* with a vengeance, but I think we have seen that our accumulating perplexities and inconsistencies justify a move toward the substantively theoretical, and in fact the preceding discussion of how best to amend Kantianism and/or common sense is already well and truly entangled with theoretical considerations and aims. What I am suggesting is that we now give serious and extended consideration to two forms of ethical theory that (as I will argue) have the resources to evade or eliminate the problems we have confronted in the past three chapters. But neither of these approaches to theory utterly lacks connection to our common-sense pretheoretical understanding of evaluative matters. Utilitarianism, after all, is based on the moral significance of sympathy or benevolence. It treats the attitude of benevolence or sympathy as helping to provide the basis for moral or other evaluations, and of course benevolence is commonly (if not in Kant's theory) recognized as relevant both to moral evaluation and to moral value.[25] But utilitarianism also systematizes our understanding by ruling out those aspects of commonplace morality that cannot be subsumed under sympathy or benevolence—that is, it systematizes by simplifying what moral and other forms of evaluative discourse ordinarily take into account in making their judgments. It is customary for defenders of common sense and others to say that utilitarianism oversimplifies, in its insistence on a single kind of intuitive moral factor or consideration, thereby impoverishing the richness of our common-sense intuitions and beliefs about the moral. But we have now seen where intuitions without system lead us, and what we have seen makes it reasonable at this point to see what system without certain intuitions can do for us. Since we now know that we are going in any event to have to drop some intuitions, the move to a consideration of utilitarianism perhaps makes especially good sense in the light of all that has been said in the past three chapters.

The move to a consideration of virtue ethics understood as I will be understanding it here may be more suspect at this point, because it involves the total elimination of the moral as a separate concept and category. I am not saying that fundamental other-regarding considerations won't importantly enter into the common-sense virtue ethics we will be developing and exploring later, but I am saying that those considerations will enter in only through commonplace evaluative concepts—like that of a virtue—which are not specifically tied to the moral (as opposed to the prudential, etc.). And this method of proceeding in ethics clearly seems problematic in a way that even utilitarianism does not. After all, utilitarianism offers or seems to offer *some sort* of view of the moral, but the form virtue ethics or virtue theory I am going to propose deliberately avoids the concept of the moral altogether, and this seemingly (or in this respect) more radical move must at this point (at least to most of you) appear suspect and even foolhardy. But it will later emerge that utilitarianism has large problems of its own that virtue ethics largely avoids. For the moment, indeed for a long span of pages to come, this claim must remain in the form of a promissory note, one that (unfortunately) I can at best pay off only after a discussion of utilitarianism, a discussion of virtue ethics, and a section devoted to a comparison of these two forms of ethics.

In any event, our most immediate concern is with utilitarianism, to which we shall be turning next. (I will be interested in consequentialism more generally, but utilitarianism is a particularly neat, simple, usable form of consequentialism, and we will therefore focus primarily on the utilitarian form of consequentialism.) I want to consider how utilitarianism escapes the difficulties that attach to both common-sense and Kantian morality, and since our focus will be on systematic or total ethical theories, we also need to consider the place of (some conception of) rationality in or alongside the utilitarian conception of morality or right action. But the alert reader may well be wondering at this point why we are going to bother with an elaboration of utilitarianism's advantages and defects and of its character as a systematic approach to ethics, when we have already argued, or at least assumed, in Chapter 1, that utilitarianism is too demanding and devaluing of the moral agent to count as an acceptable view of morality.

Of course, a charge of devaluating agents can also be brought against common-sense morality, but in what follows I hope to show you that utilitarianism has means of answering the charges of overdemandingness and agent-devaluation that are unavailable to common-sense against the accusation that *it* devalues agents. Standard forms of utilitarianism (and consequentialism) perhaps do downgrade the moral individual (though it is harder to prove this than one might think); but the foundations of utilitarianism actually can only justify something considerably weaker than familiar optimizing (act)-utilitarianism, and such weaker utilitarianism turns out to be immune to the criticism of overdemandingness or agent-devaluation. However, these distinctions and arguments will emerge only toward the end of the next chapter, after our unfolding discussion of utilitarianism allows us better to see what utilitarianism has to say about rationality claims and other forms of evaluation.

## Notes

1. *Ethics and the Limits of Philosophy*, Harvard University Press, 1985, pp. 116f. and Ch. 6, *passim*.

2. On the idea that sensitive perception, unaided by general principles or theory, can tell us how we should act in (all) the varying circumstances of our lives, see Martha Nussbaum, *The Fragility of Goodness*, Cambridge Press, 1985, Ch. 10 and John McDowell, "Virtue and Reason," *The Monist* 62, 1979, pp. 331–50.

3. *The Methods of Ethics*, 7th ed., pp. 99–103, 338, 353ff., 360f.

4. Cf. Williams, *op. cit.*, Ch. 6; and Annette Baier, "Theory and Reflective Practices," in *Postures of the Mind*, Minnesota, 1985, pp. 207–27.

5. Nagel, "Moral Luck," reprinted in *Mortal Questions*, Cambridge University Press, 1979.

6. One might reply at this point that common sense can deal with only one case at a time, so that the comparison of cases required for the inconsistency/paradoxes of moral luck already takes us beyond what common sense can tell us and into the realm of theory. But this would be a mistake. Transsituational comparisons are frequent in common-sense moral thinking: e.g., whenever one deliberately chooses one course of action over another because one thinks the results of the first course will be better than those of the other. Consider too the intuitive plausibility of Aristotle's (transsituational) claim that foolhardiness is nearer to courage than cowardice is.

7. The connection here assumed between act-consequentialism and optimality will be questioned in Chapter 4.

8. See Scheffler, *The Rejection of Consequentialism*, Oxford, 1982, p. 87, Ch. 4, *passim*, and p. 121.

9. The ordinary prohibition against killing concerns two kinds of cases: cases where one may not kill to prevent other killings and cases where one may not kill to prevent merely accidental deaths (i.e., deaths no one has deliberately brought about). The objections made above against common-sense deontology specifically relate only to the first kind of case, and this leaves open the possibility of

maintaining a more limited form of deontology that requires us not to kill in the second kind of case. However, once the slide has started it is difficult to stop it short of a total rejection of deontology—on this, see Scheffler, pp. 105ff.

Incidentally, some philosophers seem to believe that common-sense justification of the ordinary prohibition on killing to prevent more killings should rely not on considerations concerning the disvalue or objectionableness of killings (of the innocent), but on the idea (elaborated by Sen) of what is better or worse *from the standpoint of the agent.* It may not be *objectively* worse or more disvaluable if *I* kill one person rather than someone else killing more (and different) people, but from my standpoint as an agent it may be worse if I kill one than if *someone else* kills more people, and it might be held that this is all we need to (commonsensically) justify agent-centered restrictions of the sort Scheffler calls into question. But in fact it is very difficult to make this argument work. If betterness from the agent's standpoint produces an obligation not to kill as a means to preventing another from killing, then it presumably also produces an obligation to seek something good for oneself whenever it would be better from one's own standpoint to enjoy that good thing rather than give it to someone else. Yet ordinarily we think we are only permitted, not morally required or praiseworthy, to prefer ourselves in this way, and the upshot, I think, is that it is no easy matter to justify deontology by reference to goodness from the agent's standpoint.

10. Cf. Sidgwick, *op. cit.*, p. 246.

11. See Kant's *The Doctrine of Virtue*, Harper, 1964, p. 44. Contrast, however, Kant's *Fundamental Principles of the Metaphysic of Morals*, London, 1909, p. 15, where Kant seems to allow for empirical distractions from the pursuit of one's own happiness.

12. Even if common-sense moral thinking is incoherent or at odds with itself in the manner just indicated, there may be reason to advocate, or oneself hold onto, common-sense views for everyday practical purposes, e.g., as useful rules of thumb. This is a line utilitarians typically take with regard to common-sense morality, but the present point is that there may be non-utilitarian reasons, reasons generated by an incoherence or disharmony *within* common-sense morality, for treating the latter in the way utilitarians so often say it should be treated.

13. See Butler's "A Dissertation upon the Nature of Virtue" in his *Analogy of Religion*. This can be found in A. I. Melden, ed., *Ethical Theories*, Prentice-Hall, 1961, pp. 241–46.

14. See Scheffler, *The Anatomy of Inquiry*, New York, Knopf, 1963, p. 253; for the following quote from Nelson Goodman, see his *Fact, Fiction and Forecast*, Indianapolis, Bobbs-Merrill, 1965, p. 68n.

15. Perhaps one shouldn't give up on common-sense morality altogether until and unless one sees that systematic ethical theorizing has something better to offer, but theoretical considerations enter even when one is merely trying to patch up common sense in the best, or least offensive, way possible.

16. See his *Problems of the Self*, Cambridge Press, 1977, Ch .11.

17. See T. Nagel's "War and Massacre" in *Mortal Questions*.

18. Compare Bertrand Russell's claim, in various of his works, that common sense leads to science and that science, in turn, leads to the rejection of common sense.

19. See *The Doctrine of Virtue*, p. 44.

20. *Op. cit.*, p. 119. Also p. 49.

21. In "Agent-Centered Restrictions from the Inside Out" (*Philosophical Studies* 50, 1986, pp. 291–319), Stephen Darwall takes us *some of the way* toward an answer to Scheffler, but, in doing so, makes use of somewhat controversial contractarian ideas that take us considerably beyond anything explicitly in Kant.

22. See Kant's *Lectures on Ethics*, New York, Harper and Row, 1963, pp. 150–54, and compare with *Critique of Practical Reason*, Indianapolis, Bobbs-Merrill, 1956, p. 162; *The Doctrine of Virtue*, pp. 84ff.; and *Fundamental Principles of the Metaphysic of Morals*, London, 1909, p. 47. Also see M. Gregor, *Laws of Freedom*, Blackwell, 1963, pp. 135ff.

23. For Sidgwick's arguments against Kant on Categorical Imperatives, see *Methods*, 7f., 15, 35ff., 112ff. To some extent Sidgwick anticipates the recent disagreement between those who think practical rationality consists merely in certain sorts of relations (e.g., of consistency or of transitivity) among whatever desires/preferences one may have and those who think rationality also sets conditions on the content of our desires, so that, for example, it is irrational to neglect one's health however consistently, etc., one does so. (On this clash, see David Gauthier's *Morals by Agreement*, Oxford Press, 1986, Ch. 2, and my *Beyond Optimizing: A Study of Rational Choice*, Harvard Press, 1989, pp. 19f., 176; and Chs. 3 and 4 *passim*.) If there are "content" conditions on practical rationality, then the way to Categorical Imperatives of (non-moral, self-interested or self-regarding) rationality is considerably smoother than if one holds that there are only formal conditions on rational choice and action. Cf. Gregor, *op. cit.*, pp. 176ff.

24. We have said that the incoherence that common sense falls into here depends both on self-other asymmetry and on the way our obligations to others vary in strength with the (social or personal) nearness of those others. Lest someone should think that the first condition may actually entail the second and thus be a sufficient condition of the difficulties we have mentioned, let me briefly point to our common-sense thinking about gratitude. Such thinking is clearly subject to self-other asymmetry: we can have obligations of gratitude to other people for specific favors (at least we often think we can), but we wouldn't normally speak of obligations of gratitude to oneself resulting from things one has done on one's own behalf. (The point is made, e.g., in Thomas Aquinas's *Summa Theologiae*, 2a2ae, 107, 3.) But on the other hand, and apart from underlying differential obligations to those near or far from one, there is no greater obligation of gratitude for specific favors or benefits to those who are near and dear to us than to those who are socially or personally more distant. So there would appear to be a merely contingent connection between the exemplification of agent-sacrificing self-other asymmetry and some sort of proportionality (or

direct variation) between strength of obligation to another and nearness of relationship to that other. By itself any form of asymmetry may be somewhat undesirable, but the more deeply problematic incoherence or incongruity discussed earlier depends on something more than, and independent of, self-other asymmetry. (Thus I see no way to evoke a similar sense of incongruity in connection with obligations of gratitude.)

25. However, as should become clearer in Chapters 11 and 14, the fact that utilitarianism uses the notion of benevolence or sympathy, together with further notions like impersonality and rationality, as its fulcrum for moral evaluation doesn't mean that utilitarianism treats sympathy or benevolence as (always) good motives. Their goodness depends on their actual consequences (on particular occasions or in general). So actual benevolence may end up being condemned form the standpoint of (impersonal, etc.) benevolence; but that is probably no odder than the fact (which most utilitarians find entirely acceptable) that there may be good utilitarian reasons for not wanting people to be practicing utilitarians.

# 4

## Utilitarianism

In this chapter, I lay bare enough of the structure of utilitarianism to enable us eventually to compare its merits—and those of consequentialism generally—with those of (one form of) virtue ethics. And I want to begin by showing that a particular form of utilitarianism—direct utilitarianism—escapes the problems of incoherence and the methodological defects that we saw afflicting both Kantianism and intuitive morality.

### Rule-Utilitarianism

Direct forms of utilitarianism (or consequentialism) evaluate whatever they evaluate in terms of the effects or consequences of what is evaluated, whereas any indirect form of utilitarianism (or consequentialism) evaluates what it evaluates in terms of the effects of *something other* than, but significantly related to, the entities it seeks to evaluate. Act-utilitarianism thus counts as a form of direct utilitarianism because it evaluates acts exclusively in terms of *their own* consequences or results, and the best-known form of indirect utilitarianism is probably rule-utilitarianism, which ties the moral evaluation of acts to the consequences, not of the acts themselves, but of certain rules they fall or fail to fall under. Rule-utilitarianism and rule-consequentialism more generally treat an act as right if it accords with a set of rules whose adoption (or whose being followed—there are different versions of the view) would have consequences at least as good as would be obtained through the adoption (or efficacy) of any alternative set of rules. But rule-utilitarianism and indirect consequentialism in general are well known to be problematic,[1] and I think it is even possible to characterize what is problematic with such views in terms similar to those we have used to criticize ordinary moral thinking.

The explanations rule-utilitarianism and rule-consequentialism offer of some of their judgments regarding particular cases tend to undermine themselves in a fashion very similar to what we saw happen with respect to certain aspects of common-sense morality in Chapter 3. Thus rule-utilitarianism agrees with ordinary morality and opposes act-utilitarianism by denying that one may permissibly optimize on every occasion. But consider how rule-utilitarianism justifies and/or explains its divergence from act-utilitarianism. It says that on certain occasions optimizing would go against the best and most justified (or, allowing for ties, *a* best and most justified) set of moral rules. And according to rule-utilitarianism, such bestness and justification is a matter of the optimificness of (acceptance of) the favored set of rules relative to other possible sets, so optimizing action is wrong on those occasions when such action contravenes a set of rules whose acceptance would lead to better results than any alternative set of rules.

However, this form of argument tends to undermine itself by raising the following further question: If optimificness makes for a morally best or most justified set of rules, why shouldn't the optimificness of *an act* (always) render it a morally best or most justified act, with the result, as against rule-utilitarianism, that it is always morally permissible to make optimizing choices (act optimifically)? Rule-utilitarianism has never found, and seems incapable of offering, a satisfactory answer to this question; yet its own efforts to justify non-optimific action require a satisfactory answer to it. And in the absence of such an answer, rule-utilitarianism seems inconsistent in its treatment of acts and rules and, by raising problems it cannot cope with, undermines its own credibility. So for reasons similar to some of those cited earlier for rejecting ordinary and Kantian morality, we have good reason to prefer act-utilitarianism and other forms of direct utilitarianism to any form of indirect utilitarianism like rule-utilitarianism.

## What Utilitarians Have Said about Rationality

In Chapter 1, we saw that common-sense and Kantian morality both depreciate the moral agent by not counting the agent's welfare as relevant to the moral *value* or *disvalue* of her actions. We saw, however, that this criticism is not applicable to act-utilitarianism. Moreover, in addition to denying our common-sense deontological restrictions and special obligations to near and dear ones a direct utilitarianism of moral obligation or rightness—what is commonly called act-utilitarianism—lacks the agent-sacrificing character of our common-sense moral *obligations* and *permissions*. In what follows, I hope to be able to show, furthermore, that utilitarianism has the resources for defusing the problem of moral luck and the familiar accusation that it makes unreasonable demands on moral agents, but for the moment, I think we should turn our attention to some of the problems we mentioned in Chapter 2.

We saw there that common-sense rationality and common-sense morality uneconomically pull in opposite directions and argued that there was something repugnant in supposing that such a state of affairs existed at the foundational level of our ethical thought. The upshot appears to be that the concepts of rightness and rationality either are not the most fundamental ones for our understanding of ethical phenomena or else are misapplied by ordinary people thinking in ordinary ways. As I will be developing it later, virtue ethics takes the first of these alternatives and denies the fundamental character of rightness and rationality in favor of its own notion of what is admirable and/or exemplifies a virtue. Utilitarianism, by contrast, takes the second alternative mentioned just above and claims (in the version to be defended here) that common sense is mistaken in its application both of the concept of the right and of the concept of the rational. The particular view of rationality it urges then allows us to avoid the problems about common-sense rightness and rationality discussed in Chapter 2.

As I have already mentioned earlier, utilitarianism is at least nowadays not regarded as a theory or conception of rationality, but rather as a moral view or theory. The principle of utility states the act-utilitarian's substantive view of what is right and what is wrong, but has nothing explicitly to say about what is rational or irrational, and although defenders of utilitarianism and of the principle of utility may and frequently do have views, for example, about the rationality of doing what is wrong, those views are not typically treated as part of (act-)utilitarianism itself. But as we saw in Chapter 2, the matter stands somewhat differently with Sidgwick, because of his assumption that rightness and rationality are conceptually identical and his consequent assumption that the principle of utility can be conceived either as a substantive principle about what is right or as a substantive principle about what is rational. At least two other views about what rationality amounts to have been taken, however, by other utilitarians, and I think it might be useful to mention these before returning to Sidgwick's view of rationality and seeing what we may be able to say in defense of it.

In his "An Outline of A System of Utilitarian Ethics," J. J. C. Smart construes "rational" as essentially a moral term, but as having a somewhat different range of application from either the term "right" or the term "obligatory."[2] Utilitarianism is sometimes formulated as saying that an act is right if and only if its consequences (for human happiness) are as good as those of any alternative open to its agent; but sometimes it is held, rather, to be the view that an act is right if its consequences (for human happiness) are as *expectably* good as those of any alternative.

The difference between these formulations comes out most clearly in cases where an act has consequences that could not reasonably have been anticipated. If, against all odds and reasonable expectations, a benevolently motivated act I do turns out to have terrible consequences, then that act may count as wrong according to the first formulation of utilitarianism given above, but right according to the second, and this sort of example, and numerous others, make it clear that act-utilitarianism as tied to actual consequences is in no way equivalent to an act-utilitarianism that evaluates in terms of probable or expectable good consequences. In his "Outline," Smart, noting this distinction, proposes that we use "right" in accordance with an actualist version of the principle of utility and "rational" in accordance with the probabilist or expectabilist formulation of the principle: an act would then count as right if and only if it was actually for the best and rational if and only if it was expectably for the best, and so understood and applied, the terms "right" and "rational" have an equally good claim to being considered terms of morality.

Clearly, Smart wants to have a separate term to mark each of two possible versions of utilitarianism and of the principle of utility. But he himself admits that his particular assignment of terms is somewhat arbitrary, and indeed, as far as I can see, one could just as easily have stipulated that "right" be used in accordance with an expectabilist version and "rational" in accordance with an actualist version of the principle of utility. Also, in treating the question of how to apply the term "rational" as one of stipulation, Smart avoids a substantive moral issue that I believe it is important for us to consider here. We have seen how common-sense morality-cum-rationality possesses features that make it, on methodological grounds, seem inappropriate or unsatisfactory for a foundational role in our ethical thinking. And in considering now the merits of utilitarianism, and in particular its suitability to foundational status in ethics, we need to see whether there is any view of rationality that attaches as naturally and inevitably to utilitarianism as the latter's familiar views about right and wrong, as typically expressed in the principle of utility. Given that one or another familiar form of the principle of utility constitutes the correct utilitarian standard of moral rightness, the question before us is, first, whether there is any correct utilitarian view or standard of rationality and, second, assuming there is one, whether the *utilitarian* view of rationality combined with the *utilitarian* view of rightness is capable of eluding the criticisms lodged earlier against the combination of *common-sense* rationality and *common-sense* rightness.

Smart's resort to stipulation constitutes an implicit refusal to ask these questions. Smart assumes, in effect, that there is no distinctively utilitarian conception of rationality and that we are (therefore) free to use "rational" as a strictly moral term arbitrarily tied to an expectabilist, rather than an actualist, version of act-utilitarianism, and in addition to tying our hands in the ways mentioned just above, such a move also debars us from considering another important issue we will be discussing much later, in Part IV: that is, whether utilitarian moral theory is best put or expressed in actualist or in expectabilist form. Smart's decision to tie "right" to actualism and "rational" to expectabilism assumes that what might otherwise be thought to be incompatible conceptions of utilitarian morality are in some sense both to be accepted. Rather than deciding whether the principle of utility should make actual or should make expectable good consequences the criterion of right action, the utilitarian, according to Smart, can simply use the actualist criterion as the basis for applying "right" and the expectabilist criterion as the basis for applying "rational." But if it makes sense, from a utilitarian standpoint, to ask whether it is theoretically preferable to formulate the principle of utility in expectabilist rather than in actualist terms, then Smart's stipulation(s) are evasive and unhelpful with respect to this important issue. And since I can see no reason to doubt that this question makes utilitarian-theoretic sense, I believe we have been given a further reason for avoiding Smart's position about the terms "right" and "rational."

Quite recently, however, Peter Railton, in defending an act-utilitarian view of right action, has defended a conception of rational choice and action that differs both from Smart's stipulative approach and from Sidgwick's view of utilitarian rationality. According to Railton, individual rationality is understood as a form of instrumental rationality, as the agent's efficient pursuit (roughly) of his own ends or, perhaps more broadly, of his own interests or his own good. Moral value is then treated as a form of *social* rationality that can be understood on analogy with individual rationality. Railton holds that "moral norms reflect a certain kind of rationality, rationality not from the point of view of any particular individual, but from what might be called a social point of view," and so (again roughly) the moral rightness of an action depends, for Railton, on whether it "would be rationally approved of were the interests of all potentially affected individuals counted equally under circumstances of full and vivid information."[3]

Such an understanding of the relation between the moral and the rational leaves open the possibility of a more or less frequent gap between what is right or obligatory for a given individual and what it would be rational for that individual to do. That is because (yet again very roughly) Railton treats rationality in a relatively egoistic fashion, but has a basically utilitarian conception of moral right and wrong. Railton is well aware of the gap he has left between the right and the rational and his view runs counter to the widely accepted overridingness thesis that treats it as in every case irrational (rationally unjustified) to do what is morally wrong. But this may not constitute an objection, or at least a particularly strong objection, in the light of the numerous attacks that, as I mentioned earlier, have been mounted against the overridingness thesis in recent years.

Moreover, Railton's views seem very much in keeping with what was said earlier about the implications of Sidgwick's failure to distinguish the right from the rational. In Chapter 2, we noted that once one makes this distinction conceptually, egoism seems much more plausible as a theory of rationality or reasons for action than as a theory or view of moral right and wrong, and in great degree Railton's views reflect this differential plausibility, by understanding rationality along egoistic lines and at the same time rejecting egoism as a moral view in favor of utilitarianism. This leads, however, to what I believe to be problematic in Railton's approach.

Certainly, the idea of understanding the morally right and the rational in analogous ways has a deep-seated appeal, and a number of philosophers have noted the attractions of such an approach to these two important concepts/areas of evaluation.[4] But remember too that in accepting an (approximately) egoistic view of rationality alongside a utilitarian conception of morality, we treat these as parts of a larger ethical view, and it is well worth considering, at this point, both the possible merits and possible demerits of a conception of morality-cum-rationality that would include an egoism of rationality and a utilitarianism concerning morality as its individual parts. If we accept such a larger theory, we treat its moral part as attractively analogous with its rational part, but we also pay a price for this desirable feature. For the egoistic rational part involves an agent-favoring self-other asymmetry, whereas the utilitarian moral part is, as we know, free of (such) asymmetry, and this clearly, therefore, leads to an asymmetrical overall view of the right and the rational. By comparison, the mutually opposed asymmetries of common-sense morality and common-sense rationality lead to a relatively symmetrical combination of views, and the fault we found in the agglomeration or conjunction of these two aspects of common sense was more the diseconomy of such a larger-scale mutual opposition than the invidiousness of its smaller-scale asymmetries. But the combination Railton offers us is lopsided in the large, and I think that points to a serious internal defect. In what follows, I attempt to show that anyone who accepts a utilitarian view of morality should in all consistency also accept a utilitarian, rather than an egoistic, view of rationality. And given, therefore, that egoism is unacceptable as a moral theory, we may also be able to show it unacceptable, at least for any defender of utilitarian morality, as a theory of rationality as well. This would clearly enable us to do (at least some of) what Sidgwick in *Methods* sought to do, yet in the end despaired of doing, namely, defend a utilitarian view both of the right and of the rational against competing conceptions of rightness-cum-rationality. But Sidgwick based his arguments on the assumption that "right" and "rational" express a single meaning or concept, and we earlier found reason to deny that assumption. In what follows, however, we see that it is possible to defend a unified utilitarian theory of rightness and rationality by means of symmetry arguments and without assuming that there is only a single evaluative concept/meaning involved in such a larger utilitarian theory.

## Utilitarian Justice

Consider the gerrymandering that utilitarianism does as a theory of right and wrong, with respect to our ordinary thinking about these matters. In utilitarian terms, an act that damages the agent (more than is necessary) and hurts or affects no one else counts as wrong, and in reckoning whether a given act maximizes happiness overall, the agent's happiness counts as much as that of anyone else. So utilitarian morality is self-other symmetric in a way ordinary moral thinking is not. But we do not usually assume that the utilitarian, in ironing out the ordinary asymmetry, is working with some different concept of "right."[5] It is possible to distinguish concepts/meanings on the one hand from conceptions/views/theories, on the other; and although we clearly want to say that utilitarians disagree with our ordinary moral views as to what is right, we have no good reason, I think, to claim that they alter the meaning of the term "right." Indeed, unless we assume that "right" has the same meaning for them as it has for ordinary speakers, it is almost impossible to make any sense of the utilitarians' belief that they disagree with and are correcting ordinary views about right and wrong. Reasons of simplicity and symmetry may persuade the utilitarian to apply "right" differently from ordinary non-philosophers, but the disagreement here seems substantial, not terminological, and indeed utilitarianism and common-sense morality substantially disagree about matters other than rightness and wrongness.

Utilitarianism sometimes also addresses moral questions about justice, and we must now consider how and why its views about this topic differ from common-sense views about justice. One quite typical utilitarian view of justice treats that notion as applicable, fundamentally, in virtue of the very same criteria that govern the notion of moral rightness. On such a view an act is just if and only if it conforms to some appropriate version of the principle of utility.[6] By contrast, our ordinary concept of justice is subject to an asymmetry exactly parallel to that we find in the notion of right action. What it is unjust to deny to or load upon others, it may not be unjust to deny to or load upon oneself—the idea that one cannot do oneself an injustice goes back all the way to Aristotle. And it is clear that certain ways of failing to help or of hurting others count commonsensically against the justice of one's actions in a way, or to a degree, that relevantly similar failures to help or hurtings of oneself do not. Yet this agent-sacrificing self-other asymmetry of everyday moral thinking about justice is done away with in any distinctively utilitarian conception of justice.

However, a defender of utilitarian views of the right need not adopt a distinctively utilitarian view of justice. For example, in "An Outline of a System of Utilitarian Ethics," J. J. C. Smart treats the dictates of justice as *opposed* to those of the principle of utility.[7] That is, he takes our ordinary or common-sense views about what is just as constitutive of justice, but questions whether it is always right to perform the sorts of just actions that are morally acceptable according to common sense. Where the dictates of justice conflict with those of utility, it is the latter that determine, for Smart, what it is actually right to do. So at least one notable utilitarian has chosen to retain a self-other asymmetric notion of justice while urging a utilitarian view of the right which eliminates all such asymmetry, whereas others, as I indicated, develop distinctive views about both justice and rightness. And what I think we need to consider next is whether there is any reason for the utilitarian to prefer one of these strategies to the other.

Presumably the utilitarian believes herself to be justified in adopting a conception of the right that effectively smooths out the agent-sacrificing self-other asymmetries of common-sense morality—the utilitarian treats harms/goods to the agent and harms/goods to others as equally relevant to the rightness of actions. But if the self-other asymmetry attaching to ordinary conceptions of justice is parallel to that attaching to ordinary conceptions of the right, won't there be similar reason to adopt a utilitarian theory of justice that smoothes out such asymmetries? To be sure, the utilitarian morality of right also does away with our whole common-sense deontology of the right, but since ordinary views of justice are similarly deontological, there seems, again, to be no reason to adopt a utilitarian conception of rightness that is not likewise a reason to adopt such a conception of justice. Theoretical consistency in fact clearly dictates that the asymmetries and deontology of different common-sense moral notions be treated in parallel or symmetric fashion unless one can cite a reason for differentiating among them. And I can think of no reason why we should find the deontology and asymmetry of ordinary rightness unacceptable, but be willing to accept such deontology and asymmetry in connection with the notion of justice. So I believe utilitarians have every reason of consistency or symmetry to treat justice and rightness in parallel fashion, and Smart's adherence to ordinary justice therefore seems an unacceptable move for an act-utilitarian.

This fact seems all the more undeniable when one remembers Smart's argument against Rule-Utilitarianism in the same book where he adopts a common-sense view of justice. Smart takes it to be a devastating criticism of Rule-Utilitarianism that it refuses to justify certain acts in the same consequentialistic terms it uses to justify rules,[8] but such inconsistency, or as he puts it "irrationality," is just what is involved to accepting a utilitarianism of the right but refusing to accept a utilitarian criterion of justice. A utilitarian of rightness should be a utilitarian about justice too, and indeed most act-utilitarians have (implicitly) agreed with this assessment.

That is by no means, however, to say that such utilitarians think "just" and "right" mean the same in English, or that they necessarily come to mean the same after the adoption of utilitarian views. There are many things that it would be natural to call wrong, but very odd to call unjust, for example, the unintentional but negligent harming of another or the refusal to save a drowning stranger when one can do so easily and at no personal cost. And many people would wish to allow that it may sometimes be right to do what is unjust, if a sufficiently important end is served in doing so. These intuitive possibilities give us reason to believe that the two concepts are not the same; but the utilitarian can perfectly well accept this point. The coincidence he so typically argues for between justice and rightness need not be regarded as embodying some sort of analytic equivalence. And he can say that although we are working with two different concepts here, there are ethics-theoretic reasons for regarding both justice and rightness as governed by the principle of utility. And so, using the terminology mentioned earlier, we may say that the utilitarian *conception* or *theory* of justice treats that notion as coinciding with, or equivalent to (utilitarian) rightness, but that the utilitarian need not or may not regard "right" and "just" as expressing the same *meaning* or *concept* within his theory. Any reasons the utilitarian has for disagreeing with common-sense views about rightness are also reasons for rejecting common-sense views about justice; and anything that theoretically justifies the acceptance of a utilitarianism of rightness appears equally to support a utilitarianism of justice.

But these reasons, these justifications are not definitional; they stem in large part from an assumed methodology of ethical theorizing, a methodology at least partially analogous with scientific methodology and treating such features as symmetry, uniformity, economy, unity, and explanatory power as desiderata for the application of ethical concepts. The relevance of such methodology to the field of ethics is certainly not universally accepted by moral philosophers. But we defended that relevance in Chapter 3. And if this sort of methodology is valid in ethics, it would appear to be no more definitional or meaning-altering than methodological principles as used in science. Such principles may be fundamental to the process of scientific or theoretical inquiry, but if they are not analytic, then the results, the theories, we arrive at by using them should not be regarded as analytic or merely definitional. And the point clearly applies to the utilitarian theoretical conclusion that justice and rightness are both to be reckoned solely in terms of overall good consequences.

What we need to see now is whether the above conclusions and the methods we have used, and seen the utilitarian committed to using, in obtaining them can be applied to apparent differences between rightness and rationality. The utilitarian removes the common-sense agent-sacrificing asymmetry of justice and rightness in his own application of these notions; and we may at this point wonder whether there are similar reasons to smooth out the agent-favoring asymmetry that we find in common-sense views of rationality. We will then have to see whether such methods eventually lead to a utilitarian reconciliation of the right and the rational.

## Utilitarian Rationality

I begin, however, with the concept of prudence. In common-sense terms both prudence and rationality are subject to an agent-favoring asymmetry as described above, but the notion of prudence seems more specific than the idea of rationality: it involves or invokes a particular way of being practically rational and it bears to rationality in general a relation similar to that of justice to moral rightness. It is very difficult, though it is possible, to think of unjust acts that are morally right or acceptable, and similarly, it is very difficult, though not absolutely impossible, to imagine rational but imprudent choices;[9] so I would like to begin by noting the parallelism between the just and the prudent and from there move on to the more perplexing question of what relation utilitarians ought to assert between the right and the rational.

We have seen that the utilitarian, the act-utilitarian, has reasons of consistency to treat justice in a self-other symmetric way. Her conception or view of justice abandons the agent-sacrificing asymmetry of ordinary justice. But our ordinary view of prudence is also self-other asymmetrical and we should now ask whether there is any reason to eliminate the asymmetry of ordinary justice but refrain from doing so with ordinary prudence. Of course, the asymmetry involved in such prudence is an agent-favoring one, but there seems to be no good theoretical reason to treat agent-favoring and agent-sacrificing symmetries in different ways. If asymmetry itself is considered theoretically undesirable, then there would appear to be no reason to criticize and eliminate agent-sacrificing asymmetry that is not equally a reason to reject agent-favoring asymmetry.

So if the utilitarian has reason to smooth out the asymmetry of justice, she has similar reason to smooth out, in an opposite direction, the asymmetry we find in common-sense ideas of prudence, and this would 'ead her to treat prudence as governed by the principle of utility in the same way that justice is. If (the virtue of) justice can be freed of its usual, familiar agent-sacrificing asymmetry (and its deontological impediments) this can also, though in an opposite direction, be done to (the virtue of) prudence. A consistent utilitarianism, that is, a utilitarianism that gives a uniform consequentialistic treatment to concepts unless some reason can be shown for not doing so, has reason to treat both prudence and justice in symmetrical manner and, therefore, to regard an act or choice as prudent (or provident) if and only if it conforms to the (or an acceptable form of the) principle of utility.[10]

That means a utilitarian will have to count an act as imprudent if it serves the interests or desires of its agent but is overall harmful to what people want or to their good. And this seems decidedly odd. However, it is also odd to suppose—as a utilitarianism of justice forces us to—that it is unjust not to enjoy a good dessert, when there is no one else around to share it and no other act one can perform that affects anyone's interests. If we can, or should, get used to the latter oddness, why not treat the former oddness in similar fashion, allowing for the prudence of acts that don't serve the agent's interests and for the imprudence of some acts that do? I can see no possible basis for the utilitarian to balk at ironing out the asymmetry in common-sense prudence, when she is committed to ironing out similar, symmetrically opposed asymmetry in common thinking about justice and rightness.

At this point, however, one might argue that a utilitarian account of prudence goes against the very meaning of the term by tying its application to the good of other people—in English "prudent" just means "(expectably) in the agent's long-term interest." But this is simply not true about ordinary usage of the term. We don't commonly regard it as imprudent when someone acts against his own self-interest to do the just or honorable thing.[11] And someone charged with the well-being of others can be said to act prudently in their behalf (and without our having to suppose, in so saying, that such action also serves the self-interest of the person charged with others' well-being). Prudence is not tied by chains of meaning to the well-being or preferences of those who possess that trait, and, in the end, as I have already indicated, it seems no more untoward to say that prudence often involves a concern with the interests of others as to say that justice often involves the agent in concern for her own interests. A utilitarianism of justice and prudence must say both these things, but reasons of symmetry, of uniformity or consistency of treatment, would appear to dictate such a treatment of justice and prudence to anyone who accepts the principle of utility as a criterion of moral rightness or permissibility.

But now it is time to make the final move in this asymmetry-smoothing chain of symmetry arguments; we must ask whether considerations of the sort we have mentioned also tell in favor of a utilitarian account of rationality that treats the interests of all sentient beings as equally relevant to the rationality of a given agent's choices or actions. In the light of the steps we have already taken, it becomes much easier than one might initially expect to arrive at such a conclusion. We have seen that prudence, an agent-favoring, evaluative notion, can plausibly be smoothed of its asymmetry, if such notions as justice and rightness can be smoothed of their agent-sacrificing asymmetries. And, in addition, we have seen that in common-sense terms rightness and justice are subject to similar asymmetries and have argued that if the asymmetry of the former can be evened out, that of the latter can be as well.

As I mentioned earlier, common-sense justice is the (a) major part of common-sense rightness in the sense that it is very hard or rare for something to be (arguably) right if it is unjust. But the same relation holds between prudence and rationality. It is very hard or rare for an imprudent choice to count in ordinary terms as rational or rationally justified. Furthermore, as I also noted earlier, rationality is subject to the same agent-favoring asymmetries as prudence. In common-sense terms it counts more against rationality that one ignores or is negligent about one's own pain or happiness than that one ignores, or is negligent about, another's. So ordinary prudence bears to rationality a relation analogous to that which ordinary justice bears to rightness or morality, and the same considerations, therefore, that methodologically recommend the propagation of symmetry from rightness to justice and thence to prudence also dictate its further propagation to the notion of rationality, so that the principle of utility is applied not just to prudence but to rationality as well. Starting with a utilitarianism of right action framed in terms of (expectable) overall human (or sentient) happiness, we thus end up with the view that the rationality of any action is not tied exclusively to (expectable) effects upon its agent, but rather is solely dependent on how it affects the (expectable) happiness of mankind generally.

However, there are possible objections to such a utilitarianism of rationality that we ought now to consider. One may, for example, wish to argue at this point that the implications of applying the principle of utility to rationality are so far from our ordinary views about rationality as to make it unlikely that the meaning of "rational" has remained constant throughout. But one can with equal reason make a similar point about the utilitarian view of justice or rightness, and it is hardly obvious that the ordinary meaning of "just" and "right" renders it impossible to say the kinds of things utilitarians have wanted to say about justice and rightness. Moreover, even if utilitarianism changes the meaning of various terms, it is far from clear that that fact would undermine or count against the validity of utilitarian views. If theory is allowable within the sphere of ethics, then perhaps the kind of *explication* that occurs in science and mathematics can properly take place in ethics as well. Since explications can serve useful theoretical purposes without preserving all aspects of the meaning of the terms they are intended to explicate, a defender of a utilitarian criterion of justice or of rationality need not assume he has left the ordinary meaning of those terms totally intact.[12] And I think we can plausibly remain neutral as to whether utilitarianism *in fact* changes the meaning of any value terms. (However, this issue will recur in a somewhat different guise in Chapter 11.)

In any event, we have seen how it is possible to arrive at the idea that it is both right and rational to conform to the principle of utility, by assuming merely that egoism and common-sense morality are mistaken about what is right and that the only viable alternative is utilitarianism. But it is clear that egoism lacks force as a moral view only if one is clear, in a way that Sidgwick was not, about the conceptual or analytic distinctness of (the ordinary notions of) rightness and rationality. The considerations that seem to favor egoism and which Sidgwick found so difficult to refute are considerations that at best favor egoism as a theory of rationality, and once we distinguish between rightness and rationality as concepts, we are in a position to divide and conquer regarding the validity of egoism. Egoism can simply be ruled out of contention as a moral theory or view and, in that case, and given the limits of the choice Sidgwick presents us with, we can accept a utilitarian view of morality, if we can show, as Sidgwick thought he could, that utilitarianism is superior to common-sense morality. So we may be in a much better position to defend utilitarianism as a moral view than Sidgwick reluctantly concluded that we were, but this superior defensibility of utilitarian morality precisely depends on distinguishing the concepts of rightness and rationality in a way that Sidgwick fails to do.

In addition, we have seen that if utilitarianism is assumed to be correct as a moral view, there is no less reason to regard it as a correct view of rational choice and action, and it now would appear that our conceptual distinctions and arguments from symmetry allow us a strong defense of the full thesis that Sidgwick eventually despaired of adequately defending: the thesis that it is both right *and* rational to act according to the principle of utility. Once egoism is rejected and utilitarianism accepted as a theory of morality, we have reasons of consistency, of uniformity of treatment, also to accept a utilitarian conception of rationality; and that, in turn, *rules out egoism as a theory of rationality as well.*[13]

We have seen that the terms "right" and "rational" are ordinarily applied in symmetrically opposed asymmetrical ways, and this both indicates the non-synonymy of those terms and provides a basis for the criticisms made earlier of common-sense morality-cum-rationality. But if a utilitarian criterion of both rightness and rationality is employed, then neither term is applied in an asymmetrical fashion and the mutually opposed and mutually cancelling asymmetries of common-sense usage are totally eliminated. A utilitarianism of rightness and rationality thus escapes all our earlier criticisms of common sense, and we have, therefore, been given reason to prefer a utilitarian criterion of application for both these fundamental ethical concepts.

However, it might be thought that in applying two (ordinarily) different concepts according to a single criterion the utilitarian conception of rightness and rationality takes us from the frying pan of common sense to a frying pan of its own. Common sense can certainly be criticized for its failure of economy, but what else but a failure of economy is the use of two different terms and concepts in accordance with a single criterion? If, as we have assumed, "right" and "rational" express different meanings or concepts but are applied in exactly the same manner, wouldn't economy dictate the elimination of one or the other of these terms/concepts, and wouldn't it be better for the utilitarian not to offer such a redundant theory of rightness and rationality?

Notice, however, that exactly the same criticism applies to the far more familiar combination of a utilitarian view of rightness with a utilitarian view of justice. And I think I can imagine the sort of response a Bentham or a Sidgwick might make in response to such a criticism. A utilitarianism of rightness and justice explicates both these concepts in terms of the maximization or production of (expectable) utility or happiness, and couldn't we therefore say that, far from containing a redundancy of concepts, utilitarianism shows us how to reduce both justice and rightness to the causal-evaluative notion of producing/maximizing overall (human) happiness or welfare? So both justice and rightness, even if they involve different concepts, can be reduced to or explicated by a single underlying property or concept, and as a result utilitarianism at its foundations is properly regarded as unified rather than redundant.

Exactly the same can be said about the utilitarian treatment of rightness and rationality (and justice and prudence). The fact that utilitarianism applies all these terms according to a single criterion may indicate the redundancy of certain *terms*, but the theory based on such a single criterion in effect reduces all its terms/concepts to the single concept embodied by that criterion and is therefore an excellent example of systematic unity, rather than of undesirable redundancy. (In Part III we will have more to say about the reductionist tendencies of utilitarianism.) So quite apart from the paradox and incoherence endemic to common-sense moral thinking, the combination of such thinking with our ordinary ideas about rationality entails a form of diseconomy one is loath to accept at the foundational level of ethics, whereas utilitarianism's view of rationality and morality provides for systematic unity at that level and is thus arguably superior to the common-sense approach as we have been describing it. But having been given reason to move in the direction of a utilitarian criterion of both rightness and rationality, it is time to see whether (direct) utilitarianism can deal with the other problem we discussed in Chapters 1 to 3. We have just seen that it can avoid the difficulties that arise out of self-other asymmetry, and of course it is obviously not open to Scheffler's criticisms of ordinary deontology. We now have to see whether utilitarianism can evade the intuitive paradoxes of moral luck and whether, finally, it can answer the criticism that it is overdemanding and devaluates moral agents.

## Utilitarianism and Moral Luck

To the extent it bases its assessments of acts on their actual consequences, rather than on expectable consequences, utilitarianism is up to its ears in moral luck. For an act done from benevolent motivation may have unforeseeable bad effects and count as wrong on this actualist basis, through a kind of moral bad luck. To be sure, we can insist on a probabilist or expectabilist version of utilitarianism and later, in Part IV, we will consider whether we should be actualists or expectabilists, but as far as moral luck is concerned, there is no particular advantage for utilitarianism in taking the expectabilist form and ruling out moral luck through unforeseeable circumstances. Utilitarianism and consequential- ism more generally have a way of defanging the problem of moral luck quite independently of whether they take an actualist or an expectabilist form in judging the rightness of actions, so there is no reason for utilitarians to adopt an expectabilist guise as means to avoiding moral luck and for simplicity I will use an actualist version of utilitarianism in what follows.

We noted in the last chapter that the utilitarian who allows an act to be wrong for unforeseeable reasons can cut the connection we ordinarily assume to exist between acting wrongly and acting blameworthily. It may be useful and right from a utilitarian standpoint to praise an act that in fact counts as wrong by the act-utilitarian criterion, and with respect to such a case the utilitarian typically says that the wrong act in question is not blameworthy, but rather praiseworthy. In other words, she treats blameworthiness as understandable simply as what it is right to blame.[14] The idea goes counter to common-sense opinion, because we ordinarily imagine there to be a difference between what it is right to blame and what is blame*worthy*. If, to avoid a human catastrophe, we must blame someone for an (innocent or non-existent) action, it is arguably right for us to do so, but no one ordinarily thinks that makes the person to be blamed blameworthy or reprehensible for the act in question.

But with respect to such cases, the utilitarian can say something analogous to what she says about justice. Bentham claims that if we are to make any sense of justice, we must use the term in accordance with utilitarian standards, even if that isn't the way we normally apply the term.[15] And the utilitarian can say the same thing about blameworthiness: if the term is to be used in a sensible way, we must tie it, she thinks, to the rightness of certain acts of blaming, not to some imaginary acquired (inner?) moral taint that cannot be cashed out in consequentialistic terms.[16]

By arguing thus, I believe the utilitarian takes—or hopes to take—the sting out of moral luck; for if the above is an acceptable view of moral blameworthiness/reprehensibility and moral praiseworthiness, then the dilemma faced by common-sense morality, the inconsistency we have seen generated from its assumptions regarding moral luck, can easily be avoided by denying the crucial premise that moral luck is morally problematic or intolerable. The unacceptability of the idea of moral luck for ordinary ways of thinking depends largely on the connection between moral evaluations of acts and agents and the attribution, in particular, of praiseworthiness and blameworthiness understood as these notions are ordinarily understood, rather than in purely consequentialistic terms. What we most deeply balk at in the idea of moral luck is the notion that the culpability, the reprehensibility, the blameworthiness of an individual for some act, omission, or sentiment can in any way be due to factors of mere luck or accident. But when we do thus balk at moral luck, we are thinking of culpability, blameworthiness, and the like in a way that is no more purely consequentialistic than ordinary attributions of rightness or obligation are purely consequentialistic. And the consistent utilitarian can and should tell us—and over the years many of them *have* told us— that if utilitarianism is superior to common sense as a conception of right and wrong, its consequentialistic conception of moral blame- and praiseworthiness is also superior to the way common sense understands and applies these latter notions.

Once, however, we treat blameworthiness, etc., in a consequentialistic manner, the problem of moral luck loses its sting. Whether one act or another will maximize utility often (or usually) depends on unforeseeable factors of luck; there is nothing odd or problematic in supposing this to be so. But if rightness is just a matter of maximizing utility, rightness can quite straightforwardly be a matter of luck. And parallel points are easily seen to hold for the utilitarian attribution of blameworthiness and the like. If blameworthiness really is just a matter of the utility of acts of blaming, then in relation to that assumption at least, luck regarding blameworthiness is no more problematic than luck regarding the long-term usefulness of blaming one act or another.

As I have suggested, the consequentialistic approach to blameworthiness, culpability, etc., has long been a familiar feature of utilitarian conceptions of morality; but since the problem of moral luck has only recently come to engage the attention of moral philosophers in a major way and since, in addition, that problem is especially easy to ignore when one is accustomed to a utilitarian criterion for the application of moral terms, I don't think utilitarians have in any substantial or explicit way based their advocacy of consequentialism about blameworthiness on the fact that such consequentialism allows us to avoid common sense's deep problems with moral luck. But if we view utilitarianism not from within, but rather from some standpoint that seeks to compare its merits with those of competing moral theories/conceptions, then utilitarianism's ability to draw the sting, the paradox, from the idea of moral luck gives it at least one distinct advantage over the morality of common sense.

Common-sense thinking about morality generates a contradictory set of conclusions from the judgments it makes about particular acts differing, as a result of luck or accident, with respect to their consequences, taken together with its general assertion of the impossibility of moral luck. But the utilitarian moral conception of things is readily squared with the possibility of moral luck, and so utilitarianism escapes the nest of contradictions common sense seems committed to. One may, of course, object to the means by which utilitarianism escapes these problems, that is, to the utilitarian conception of morality in general or in some of its parts or aspects; but if utilitarianism is acceptable as a general view of morality, then its ability to evade common sense's contradictions in the area of moral luck constitutes a definite and specific advantage over the latter, an advantage additional to those other advantages we uncovered in earlier chapters.

Let it be noted, however, that to reap this advantage, utilitarianism has to affront our common-sense intuitions by claiming that an act's blameworthiness, for example, amounts to nothing more than the rightness, the utility, of blaming (someone for doing) it. But this seems a no more serious divergence from common-sense views, once we have accepted a utilitarian view of the right, than the fundamental utilitarian decision to apply the notion of rightness in a strictly consequentialistic way. The latter decision, though it is out of keeping with our ordinary intuitions, can be justified in part by its ability to help us avoid the incoherence and/ or contradiction that arise from our common-sense intuitions, most particularly, from our intuitions about self-other asymmetry and our differential obligations to those nearer and further from us. But the utilitarian view of rightness is also in part justified by the systematic unity it allows us to bring to substantive morality and by a number of other methodological and substantive advantages we have discussed in prior chapters. And similar things can be said in favor of the utilitarian account of blameworthiness, except that the common-sense contradictions and paradoxes it allows us to avoid include not only those just mentioned but also, and most notably, those that attend the idea of moral luck.[17]

However, it is one thing to show, as we have attempted, that utilitarianism has certain advantages over common-sense morality, quite another to clear it of the earlier-mentioned charge that it is unreasonably demanding in what it requires of moral agents. As we have seen, both common-sense and direct utilitarian morality can be accused of devaluing (the interests of) the moral agent, though this common accusation is based on different foundations in the two cases. The basis of the accusation as it applies to utilitarianism lies precisely in the claim that it demands too much of moral agents. For remember that if, as familiar or standard utilitarianism tells us, it is wrong to act in ways that are not overall optimific, then most of us, at least many of us, in pursuing (innocent) projects and personal concerns, in seeking or retaining jobs that give us pleasure and in preferring the welfare of ourselves and our families to that of strangers, are failing to comply with the demands of morality. Whenever we perform actions or series of actions that do less than the most we could have done to advance the general welfare of mankind, we act wrongly (though perhaps not blameworthily) according to the principle of utility as commonly understood. And various critics of direct or "act"-utilitarianism have claimed that such a standard of right or morally acceptable conduct is overly demanding, asks too much of human beings. Unless utilitarianism can somehow free itself from this accusation, it will be problematic as a moral view—even if overall it may be in better shape (but that would hardly be self-evident)[18] than common sense. So it is important that we should now discuss how and whether utilitarianism can in fact deal with this familiar charge.

## Is Utilitarianism Too Demanding?

In recent years there have been a variety of attempts to undercut or mitigate the charge that act-utilitarianism is overdemanding.[19] But I don't propose to review these by now familiar defenses of act-utilitarianism because I think there are other, less familiar ways in which the charge of overdemandingness can be met that deserve a separate discussion of their own. I have elsewhere argued at considerable length that utilitarianism's most familiar foundational motivations are insufficient to support currently accepted forms of act-utilitarianism, and thus that utilitarianism has reason to *consider itself* too demanding. However, far from leading to the rejection of the utilitarian approach to moral theory, the arguments I have offered for this conclusion actually point toward ways of understanding or formulating act-utilitarianism that can avoid not only self-accusation but the arguments for overdemandingness that have been launched by external critics.

If we think of act-consequentialism, at its most general, as claiming that the evaluation of actions is a function of the evaluation of their consequences and those of their alternatives and conceive act-utilitarianism as a form of act-consequentialism that focuses on total (or average) happiness, then there can be forms of utilitarian act-consequentialism that do not require the optimization/maximization of good consequences as a condition of an act's being right. Bentham's earliest version of the principle of utility claimed that acts are right if and only if their consequences for human happiness are *on the whole good*, and not only does that version of act-utilitarianism not morally require the maximization of human or sentient good, but it is possible to formulate other versions of act-utilitarian and act-consequentialism more generally that treat acts as morally right when they have *good enough* consequences that are less than the best achievable in the circumstances in which those acts occur. All such non-optimizing (non-maximizing) versions of act-utilitarianism and act-consequentialism we can speak of as *satisficing* forms of these views, and, reviewing briefly what I have said on this subject elsewhere,[20] I want to claim that the considerations standardly adduced by act-utilitarians in favor of optimizing formulations of their doctrines are insufficient to support those views in the manner they assume.

One of the foundational ideas of (act-)utilitarianism has been the notion that moral judgment is most validly made from a standpoint of rational impersonal benevolence (or sympathy).[21] And it has long been taken for granted that the recently prevalent optimizing forms of act-utilitarianism (and of the principle of utility) follow quite naturally from such a foundational picture. But in fact various kinds of satisficing act-utilitarianism are just as much in keeping with the above picture as the familiar form of act-utilitarianism that considers an act to be right if and only if its consequences on balance for human happiness are, or are expectably, as good as those of any available alternative.

For a utilitarian, impersonal benevolence is to be understood as impersonal or impartial concern for the happiness/pleasure of all sentient—alternatively, all human—beings. But why, to begin with, should a being with such a benevolent concern for happiness generally approve only acts with (actually or expectably) optimal consequences? Granting that such a being will favor or prefer acts with (expectably) optimal consequences over alternatives with (expectably) less good consequences, does it follow that such a being will find those alternatives—even those with *very good* consequences—unacceptable, unworthy of her approbation? Perhaps the benevolent onlooker will be pleased by some acts producing less-than-optimal good consequences, even though some optimific alternative would have pleased her *more*. (Indeed, it is not even clear that someone with the *highest degree* of benevolence would have to *disapprove* of what she found less than ideal in the production of human happiness or well-being.)

Part of the intuitive force of act-utilitarianism lies in its use of the notion of benevolence, together with rational constraints like impersonality and in some versions, omniscience, to deliver its consequentialist view of morality. And it has certainly been assumed by Sidgwick and many others that these conditions uniquely determine an optimizing standard of right and wrong.[22] But the foundational moral psychology of act-utilitarianism (and, it could be shown, of act-consequentialism more generally) in fact seems to have no way to rule out satisficing forms of utilitarian act-consequentialism. Optimizing act-utilitarianism seems, therefore, to be underdetermined by the foundational considerations that have been brought forward in its behalf.

If we have no basis for choosing between satisficing and more familiar optimizing versions of act-utilitarianism, then at least at this point utilitarians have no reason to favor the kind of utilitarianism that is most naturally or frequently regarded as overly demanding. In that case, there are strong utilitarian reasons for considering present-day optimizing utilitarianism to be overly or unreasonably demanding. It demands more than it can itself justify, but that is no reason to opt at this point for some version of satisficing act-utilitarianism or act-consequentialism. For even if the charge of overdemandingness doesn't apply to (some) such views, each of them specifies some level of good consequences as necessary and sufficient for the moral rightness (or obligatoriness) of any action, and any such particular specification is (at best) likely to be underdetermined relative to utilitarianism's own foundational motivations and methodology.

Is that, then, a reason to give up on utilitarianism until such time as we find some way to defend some particular version over all its satisficing and/or optimizing competitors? Not necessarily. Rather, we may conclude that we have no reason, at this point, to assert anything more than *what is common* to all the versions of act-utilitarianism we have considered or referred to. But this weaker common doctrine may still represent a substantial enough form of act-utilitarianism to be defensible as the best version of act-utilitarianism now available to us. And as we will also, briefly, see, this new, weaker version of utilitarianism allows the utilitarian to obviate the present charge of underdetermination and the charge of overdemandingness at one and the same time.

The act-utilitarian views we have spoken of may differ as to how much resultant good to require for right action, but all agree in treating any act as *morally better* than a given alternative if and only if it has better overall consequences for human happiness than that alternative. All satisficing and optimizing forms of utilitarian act-consequentialism treat the goodness of consequences as the only thing relevant to moral evaluation, and in fact agree in their comparative moral judgments even while differing in positive assessments. They differ only as to where on the scale of goodness one should draw the line between right and wrong, but this then leaves a vast area of *agreement on comparative judgments* that may be used to form the basis of a utilitarian moral view that *restricts itself* to comparative moral judgments.

Thus the difficulty of supporting optimizing views over their various competitors may indicate that (presumptive) facts about good and bad, better and worse total consequences carry with them no (currently discernible) natural or non-arbitrary resting place for a distinction—even one that allows for vagueness—between morally right and morally wrong acts, and this implies that any attempt on our part to draw such a distinction will at this point reflect some sort of (possibly useful) convention or guess, rather than a defensible theoretical claim. The only recourse would then be a *scalar* form of act-utilitarianism that provided for all the comparative moral assessments common to differing forms of act-utilitarian consequentialism while deliberately excluding the positive judgments of right and wrong that give rise to their differences.

Thus, if disagreements among various forms of optimizing and satisficing utilitarian act-consequentialism are not presently resolvable in objective rational terms, a utilitarian ethics that seeks an objective account of morality will do best explicitly to exclude the making of judgments of right and wrong and confine itself to comparative judgments of morally better and worse. It could then make use of the traditional foundational psychology of all-knowing impersonal benevolence by focusing on the rather uncontroversial *comparative attitudes* of an impersonally benevolent being. Whether or not such a being would feel unfavorably toward an optimal act with bad consequences, she would clearly prefer or favor such an act over an alternative with even worse consequences; and whether or not an act with very good but non-optimal consequences would be approved by such a being, presumably an alternative with even better consequences would please her more. So one can preserve a version of utilitarianism and its underlying psychology on a purely scalar basis. However, any such theory clearly leaves out questions and answers that previous utilitarians have felt the need to insist upon. Without making judgments of right and wrong, a moral view may be deemed insufficiently action-guiding or practical and may appear incapable of giving us a complete account of morality.

But utilitarianism is in a particularly poor position to insist that correct moral theories be capable of a useful action-guiding role. The history of utilitarianism is strewn with disclaimers, in behalf of the principle of utility, of any reason to expect the latter to function as a practical moral guide.[23] And so, it would be difficult for utilitarians and for consequentialists generally to point to limitations in the action-guiding capacities of scalar utilitarianism as any argument against the fundamental correctness or present preferability of such a restricted view.

Of course, if one is a (utilitarian) act-consequentialist, one will presumably believe that there is a need for some sort of moral principles to govern conduct, but to the extent one holds that the non-practical principle of utility or any other non-practical consequentialist principle constitutes the sole objective standard of right action, one will have to view these other principles merely as useful practical expedients or rules of thumb. And this way of distinguishing between (e.g.) the principle of utility as a valid moral standard and merely useful practical moral principles opens the way to a similar defense of scalar act-consequentialism or act-utilitarianism.

For if the objective moral standard needn't share the practical character of the moral rules or principles that are needed to guide everyday action, there will, presumably, also be no need for that standard to draw the sort of distinction between right and wrong action that (we are assuming) enables the ordinary rules to be so practically effective.[24] And in that case some form of scalar act-consequentialism might represent the sole objective truth about the morality of actions while some other set of non-scalar and presumably non-consequentialist rules or principles provides people with the sort of useful practical guidance any utilitarian would herself wish, on utilitarian grounds, to see people provided with. If the practical need for non-consequentialist principles is fully compatible with the sole validity of (utilitarian) act-consequentialism as a moral standard, so too may the practical need for non-scalar principles offer no threat to our earlier claim that a scalar form of act-utilitarianism gives us our best present hope of providing a non-arbitrary and objectively valid utilitarian standard (theory) of morality.

We thus arrive at a form of utilitarianism, scalar act-utilitarianism, which, because it makes no judgments of right and wrong, cannot be said to set any requirements of right action, to make any demands of us. It is perhaps unfortunate that this is the only or best way at present for utilitarianism to evade or undercut the charge of overdemandingness; perhaps we ought to seek different arguments or evidence for some positive form that makes lesser demands. But on the other hand perhaps we should be happy when we consider that utilitarianism and its methodology can be used to show the inadequacies of certain forms of utilitarianism that are accused of overdemandingness and actually lead us to a form of direct utilitarianism that cannot be accused of that fault. When we come to discuss virtue theory, it will not have any advantage over utilitarianism in terms of being less demanding. Those who wish to support it will have to find some new reason for preferring it to utilitarianism. For we have now seen that utilitarianism is subject neither to the myriad difficulties of common-sense or Kantian ethics nor to those difficulties it itself often is accused of. However, in what follows I attempt to offer an ethics of virtue that likewise avoids the difficulties we have pointed out in common-sense and Kantian ethics. We will then see how this specific version of virtue ethics fares in critical comparison with utilitarianism.

## Notes

1. In *Utilitarianism: for and against* (Cambridge University Press, 1973), both J. J. C. Smart and Bernard Williams argue against the viability of rule-utilitarianism as a consistent form of utilitarian theory.

2. In Smart and Williams, *op. cit.*, pp. 47f.

3. See Peter Railton, "Moral Realism," *Philosophical Review* 95, 1968, pp. 163–207. The quotations are from page 190.

4. In *A Theory of Justice* (Harvard, 1971, pp. 22ff.), John Rawls says that the "most natural way . . . of arriving at utilitarianism . . . is to adopt for society as a whole the principle of rational choice for one man." But he makes it clear earlier that what he is regarding as rational for the individual—namely, to achieve one's own greatest good as far as possible—is to be thought of as relating only to situations in which no one else is affected by one's actions. In other words, Rawls leaves open the possibility that it may not be rational to maximize one's own satisfactions or welfare in situations where the interests of others are at stake, and so he clearly differs from Railton, who appears to want to define rationality

*ueberhaupt* and who thus seems committed to the irrationality of going against one's own interests or preferences, or one's own welfare, to serve the interests, etc., of other people. Railton argues for an analogy between the rational and the utilitarianly moral, whereas Rawls urges only the more limited analogy between what is rational in the absence of others and what the utilitarian regards as moral. For an attempt to demonstrate such a more limited analogy between self-regarding rationality and *common-sense* morality, see my *Beyond Optimizing* (Harvard, 1989), which also spends a great deal of time considering the differences between welfare-based and preference-based conceptions of rationality and morality.

5. Sidgwick and Bentham are both advocates of consistent, uniform, or symmetric approaches to moral issues. See, e.g., *Methods*, pp. 418f., and *Introduction*, pp. 19ff. For further criticisms of self-other asymmetry see my "Utilitarian Virtue," *Midwest Studies in Philosophy* XIII, 1988, pp. 384–97.

6. See Rawls, *op. cit.*, pp. 26, 187, and S. Scheffler, *The Rejection of Consequentialism*, Oxford, 1982, p. 33.

7. Smart, "Outline," in Smart and Williams, *op. cit.*, section 10.

8. See "Outline," p. 10.

9. Gauguin as described by Bernard Williams is a possible example of rationally justified imprudence. See the title essay of Williams's *Moral Luck*, Cambridge, 1981.

10. For applications of such a methodology of consistency, symmetry, or uniformity of treatment, compare Smart's attack on the rule-utilitarian in "Outline," p. 10; and Parfit's attack on egoism as a theory of reasons in *Reasons and Persons*, pp. 142–48, 448.

11. See Foot, *Virtues and Vices*, p. 187.

12. On explication and reduction, see W. V. Quine's *Word and Object*, M.I.T. Press, 1960, pp. 257–66. Bentham demonstrates his tolerance for changes in the ordinary meaning of ethical terms in the *Introduction*, pp. 13, 102, 120n. However, for some reasons to hold that utilitarianism doesn't alter the ordinary meaning of terms, see my "The Theory of Important Criteria," *Journal of Philosophy*, 1966.

13. For independent reasons to reject egoism as a theory of reasons or rationality, see Parfit, *op. cit.*, Part II.

14. Notice that a utilitarian conception of blameworthiness leaves open the possibility that a given act should be both blameworthy and praiseworthy, unless it explicitly rules this out by further qualifications.

15. Bentham, *Introduction to the Principles of Morals and Legislation*, p. 120n.

16. But why shouldn't the utilitarian treat blameworthiness and the like on analogy with justice and rightness, so that an act counts as blameworthy just in case *it* is wrong and is less than optimific, rather than in virtue of the rightness of the *different* act of *blaming* it? Utilitarians, as far as I know, always adopt the latter approach, and perhaps they do so because it allows one to say that certain acts that through sheer bad luck turn out to be wrong are nonetheless not blameworthy and may even be praiseworthy. But the ability to make such a

concession to common-sense moral thinking works only for some (or many) cases of the above kind, not for all. For there will certainly be times when a benevolent act, say, unforseeably leads to bad consequences and when, through additional bad luck, blaming it—and not praising it—would have optimal consequences. And in any event why should the typical utilitarian worry here about conflict with what we ordinarily would say or think, if with regard to so many other cases, she claims the right to be indifferent to the existence of such conflict(s)?

17. In addition to the conflicts we have been emphasizing, the utilitarian view of blameworthiness clashes with ordinary intuition by treating the rightness of blaming a certain act as a matter solely of the consequences of such blaming. But this is of a piece with the general incompatibility of common-sense and utilitarian criteria of right action, and represents, I think, no further problem beyond those familiar from our earlier discussion.

18. Unless the presence of mutually contradictory or incongruent assumptions automatically renders a set of views less acceptable than any consistent set of views, and unless—which hardly seems likely—this assumption is itself self-evident.

19. On these possible defenses of utilitarianism, see, e.g., S. Scheffler, *The Rejection of Consequentialism*, Oxford, 1982, *passim*; Peter Railton, "Alienation, Consequentialism, and the Demands of Morality," *Philosophy and Public Affairs*, 1984, 134–71.

20. See *Beyond Optimizing*, Harvard University Press, 1989, esp. Chapters 1 and 7. The first person in recent times to discuss non-maximizing forms of utilitarianism was Judith Lichtenberg in "The Right, the All Right, and the Good," *Yale Law Journal* 92, 1983, pp. 544–63.

21. Sometimes the characterization of the ideal utilitarian perspective contains, in addition, a condition of total knowledge or a stipulation that the benevolent rational observer observes *sub specie aeternitatis*. But at this stage of our argument, this addition need not concern us; it will concern us closely enough in Chapter 15.

22. See Sidgwick, *op. cit.*, pp. 241, 431f., for one example of this tendency.

23. See Sidgwick's *The Methods of Ethics*, London, Macmillan, 1962, 7th ed., pp. 413, 469, 480–92; and Scheffler, *op. cit.*, Ch. 3.

24. Scalar (act-)consequentialism is in numerous cases inconsistent with the *comparative* judgments common-sense morality seems committed to. Thus in some cases a scalar view must hold that it is morally better to kill one person to prevent two others from being killed, but common sense would subscribe to an opposite comparative judgment.

However, in another area where common-sense morality has been held to conflict with utilitarian consequentialism, namely, the morality of agent-relative permissions, a scalar view does away with some of the conflict. That is because the view that we are morally permitted to pursue our own innocent projects and commitments at some cost to overall impersonal optimality is usually maintained alongside the concession that such individual pursuit of projects and commitments is (typically) not as morally good or praiseworthy as actions serving a greater overall human good. (Cf. Scheffler, *op. cit.*, pp. 21ff.) So ordinary morality allows for agent-relative permissions—which are in greater or lesser conflict with utilitarianism depending on what level of good consequences the latter demands—while at the same time largely agreeing with utilitarianism about what is morally better or worse in this area. And I think the fact that scalar (act-)-utilitarianism agrees with ordinary morality's comparative judgments concerning agent-relative permissions, while disagreeing with its comparative judgments in the area of agent-relative deontological restrictions shows something significant about the disagreement between common-sense morality and utilitarianism. We have been given reason here to think that its comparative or scalar judgments are the bedrock of utilitarian consequentialism; in the light of what has just been said, this seems to indicate that the conflict between common-sense morality and utilitarianism is more fundamentally located in matters concerning deontology than in matters relating to agent-relative permissions.

# II

# VIRTUE ETHICS

# 5

# Rudiments of Virtue Ethics

Philosophical interest in virtue and the (particular) virtues has had a long and—though the term is inadequate—distinguished history. Although, in modern times, the interests of ethicists have largely shifted toward questions of right and wrong and toward the formulation of principles of duty and/or obligation, the predominant virtue ethics of the ancient world has exerted a significant influence across the centuries. In recent years, and for reasons it is difficult to be entirely sure of, there has in fact been a considerable revival of interest in virtue ethics. There have been a number of notable efforts to characterize both particular virtues and some interrelations among particular virtues, and attempts have also been made to offer more or less general accounts of what virtue, or a virtue, is. In addition, several philosophers have urged us to start approaching ethics as a whole through a primary or initial focus on virtue-related concepts, and these calls for change have often been defended by attributing major flaws to currently more prominent forms of ethical theory or by reference to a more pervasive sense of the futility or sterility of recent ethical debate. Yet despite—or because of—all the calls for a new approach, I believe no one has actually set about constructing ethical theory, from the ground upward, on a virtue-theoretic basis—no attempts, as far as I know, have been made to bring the foundational issues and conceptual distinctions that have animated recent discussions, say, among utilitarians, Kantians, and common-sensists into specific relation to the structures and content that characterize, or are likely to characterize, a fundamentally virtue-theoretic approach to the problems and phenomena of ethics.

The problems we have found in both Kantian and common-sense approaches to ethics give us an opportunity and a motive to pursue such a more foundational approach to the ethics of virtue, and the reasons are not difficult to state. The faults uncovered in Part I depended on our use of ethics-theoretic structural concepts like agent-neutrality and self-other asymmetry that have been of noteworthy use in attempts over the past few years to sort out the relative merits of (utilitarian) consequentialism, common-sense morality, and Kantianism; making use of such notions, we have learned, moreover, that utilitarianism avoids a number of difficulties that attach to the latter two approaches. But I hope now to show you that—for substantially different reasons—a certain kind of common-sensical approach to virtue ethics can also escape these problems, and this will involve us in facing the sorts of ground-floor conceptual and ethical issues that have dominated recent ethical debate[1] and that occupied us so thoroughly in Part I.

In order to show the superiority of virtue ethics to both common-sense and Kantian morality, we in effect must consider virtue ethics in an unaccustomed foundational light, and in the present part of this book, therefore, I will attempt a foundational approach to virtue ethics that will enable us to see how it evades the difficulties of the approaches we in effect discarded at the end of Chapter 3 and that will eventually enable us, in Part III, to compare its merits with those of utilitarianism. It is time we tried to make good on some of the larger promises that have been made on behalf or in the name of virtue ethics, and even if fundamental flaws sooner or later turn up in the particular development of such ethics to be undertaken here, the flaws themselves may point us toward a better understanding of how—or whether—virtue ethics can take its place among the major overall approaches to the problems of ethics.

## Distinctive Features of Virtue Ethics

In Part I we saw how an agent-sacrificing (self-other asymmetric) approach to morality gives rise, in Kant's ethics, to an agent-sacrificing notion of (what counts as a) virtue; but it was also pointed out that common-sense thinking about (what counts as a) virtue lacks the agent-sacrificing asymmetric character of our ordinary views about morality. Given the argument of Chapter 1, it is an advantage of our ordinary thinking about the virtues that it allows both facts about the well-being of others and facts about the well-being of the agent to support claims about the goodness of some trait possessed by the agent, claims, that is, about the trait's status as a virtue. And in the present chapter and those to follow, I make use of an appropriately self-other symmetric common-sense notion of what it is to be or to exemplify a virtue, as the foundational notion of a larger approach to the problems of ethics that can be shown to be free of the difficulties that undermined common-sense morality and Kantianism in Part I.

The idea of a virtue ethics is commonly regarded as involving two distinctive or essential elements. A virtue ethics in the fullest sense must treat aretaic notions (like "good" or "excellent") rather than deontic notions (like "morally wrong," "ought," "right," and "obligation") as primary, and it must put a greater emphasis on the ethical assessment of agents and their (inner) motives and character traits than it puts on the evaluation of acts and choices.[2] And if we understand the notion in this somewhat rough manner, then I think that not only much of ancient ethics—Aristotle, the Epicureans, and the Stoics, for example—but also the ethical view to be presented here and in the next few chapters constitute forms of virtue ethics. However, it is also worth noting at this point that these instances of virtue ethics are in a way less radically different from familiar deontology and utilitarianism than some advocates of a virtues approach may have hoped for or imagined.

Thus although Aristotle and I both make consideration of the virtues and of virtuous or admirable individuals central to our ethical views, neither of us altogether eschews the ethical evaluation of acts/actions and neither, in a sense I am about to explain, makes the ethical assessment of acts strictly derivative from the evaluation of persons or traits. For Aristotle, to be sure, an action will be noble if it is one that a noble or virtuous individual would perform, and Aristotle doesn't think we can *say* much about what acts or feelings are best without (perhaps not very helpfully) bringing in the notion of a good, or virtuous individual. But he also allows that properly instructed (or momentarily inspired) people can perform good or virtuous acts even if they are not themselves virtuous or good and, in addition, he characterizes the virtuous individual as one who *sees* or *perceives* what it is good or right or proper to do in any given situation. Such language clearly implies that the virtuous individual does what is noble or virtuous because it is the noble—e.g., courageous—thing to do, rather than its being the case that what is noble—or courageous— to do has this status simply because the virtuous individual will choose or has chosen it.

So for Aristotle, as well as for the view to be sketched and defended here, the ethical status of acts is not *entirely derivative* from that of traits, motives, or individuals, even though traits and individuals are the *major focus* of the ethical views being offered. Some philosophers recently advocating an ethics of virtue have advocated the more radical form of theory that would treat the evaluation of acts as an entirely derivative matter, and on some occasions this has been done because of a conflation of the notions just mentioned and consequent misidentification of (or confusion about) the ethical position of virtue theorists like Aristotle.

The fact, in other words, that Aristotle makes virtues and the virtuous individual the center of his discussion of ethics (assuming this to be an accurate characterization of the *Nicomachean Ethics* on the whole) in no way entails that he treats act-evaluation as derivative from agent-, motive-, or trait-evaluation, and one must in fact look elsewhere to find views that can be characterized in the latter terms.[3] Plato arguably makes the assessment of particular actions depend on how well they accord with a certain independently specifiable valuable ordering of the parts of the soul,[4] and in *Types of Ethical Theory*, James Martineau makes the evaluation of actions depend entirely on a prior evaluation of the motives whose conflict is assumed to precede those actions.[5] But clearly, if we wish to treat Aristotle as a bona fide virtue ethicist, we must not insist that any virtue ethics treat the evaluation of actions as an entirely derivative matter, and indeed the characterization of virtue ethics given earlier avoids such an insistence. Moreover, the virtue ethics I will be offering will be the less radical kind of virtue ethics offered by Aristotle; because it will allow for the independent aretaic evaluation of acts or actions, it will not (at least in this respect) depart as radically from familiar act-oriented deontology and utilitarianism as a view like Martineau's or Plato's seems to do.

However, I have added the just-used parenthetic phrase precisely because in another respect the virtue ethics to be developed here departs more radically from current-day moral theories than does Martineau's or even perhaps Plato's account of ethical phenomena. It is often assumed[6] that the predominant or fundamental aretaic notion of any proper virtue ethics will be the notion of moral goodness (as instantiated, e.g., in the notion of morally good character). But, unlike the views of Martineau and, perhaps, Plato, the virtue ethics I espouse will avoid making use of specifically moral notions. Its fundamental aretaic concepts will be those of a virtue or of an admirable trait, action, or individual and, as we noted as early on as Chapter 1, the latter notions in their common usage and application are not specifically moral. In common-sense terms self-other asymmetry of an agent-sacrificing kind is as much built into the notion of moral goodness or betterness as it is built into the notion of moral rightness or obligation, and this remains true whether moral goodness is being attributed to traits, to motives, or to actions. And since the problems we have seen attach themselves to common-sense morality give us reason to avoid such morality altogether, our common-sense ethics of virtue is going to avoid specifically moral notions and make use—not of the notions of moral excellence and moral goodness—but of the broader aretaic notions of a good or admirable character trait, an excellence of character, or, more briefly, a virtue. Our common-sense application of these concepts involves none of the self-other asymmetry that applies, with such devastating consequences, to our ordinary employment of specifically moral notions, and so in its attempt to avoid the problems of Part I, the virtue ethics we defend here will avoid specifically moral notions altogether. If the utilitarian approach of Chapter 4 gerrymanders the ordinary or common-sense application of moral terms, then, and in regard to the same problems, our virtue-ethical approach will take the different tack of remaining within common-sense modes of thinking, but making use only of widely ethical concepts which, in their common-sense application, possess none of that self-other asymmetry that gave rise to so many (but not all) of our problems in Part I.

We have already seen, in Chapter 1, that traits of character can qualify as virtues through what they enable their possessors to do for themselves as well as through what they enable their possessors to do for others, and so we saw there that our ordinary employment of the aretaic notion of a virtue gives fundamental evaluative significance to the well-being of the self (i.e., the agent of an act or possessor of a trait) and to the well-being of others. So it should be clear that our refusal to use specifically moral concepts doesn't force our virtue ethics in the direction of egoism. In the absence of deontic and/or moral concepts, egoism is roughly the virtue-ethical view that traits are virtues and acts instantiate virtues to the extent they favor their possessors/agents. And such a view, while it allows virtue traits to benefit other people, makes the virtuous character of such traits ultimately dependent on what they more or less directly do for their possessors. As such, it is not our ordinary or, for most of us, our considered view of what counts as admirable or a virtue, for most of us are disposed—and happy to be disposed—to feel a ground-floor admiration for acts and traits that help others (people other than the agent or trait-possessor). Few of us would maintain an egoistic view of what counts as a virtue, and in our present situation we have more than one reason for avoiding egoism in favor of a more even-handed common-sense view.

Given that we are thinking critically and theoretically about ethics, we may well wish to avoid asymmetry whenever other things are equal, and clearly egoism is asymmetric in a way common-sense views about admirability and virtue-status are not. But, more important, we have every reason, in formulating an ethics of virtue, to make only those large-scale or radical shifts from ordinary ways of thinking that we need to avoid the problems and inconsistencies of Part I. And it will turn out that we can accomplish this goal simply by abandoning all specifically moral notions and without taking the further, radical step of rejecting our everyday recognition of (or belief in) the fundamental evaluative significance of the well-being or preferences of others. A properly conservative approach seems to dictate, therefore, that we prefer a common-sense account of the virtues to the sort of egoistic view which, despite its predominance or prevalence in the ancient world, e.g., among the Stoics and Epicureans, is out of keeping with what we (post-)Judeo-Christians typically think about the conditions of admirable action and status as a virtue (or admirable trait of character). And I will therefore from this point on largely ignore egoism and attempt, instead, to articulate a common-sense form of virtue ethics that can solve the various problems we need to be able to handle in order to arrive at an adequate conception of ethics and of ethical theory.

But (arguably) neither Plato nor Aristotle is an egoist in the manner of the Epicureans and Stoics, so perhaps I should in what follows develop virtue ethics within a Platonic or Aristotelian framework. However, for reasons mentioned just above, I think it would be very risky to follow Plato (as I interpret him) in saying that there are no external conditions on right or admirable action except for the form of the Good. If we leave aside Plato's mystical appeal to the latter as a moral standard, then Plato (like Martineau) is saying (roughly) that whatever the virtuous or healthy person may do, her action will be right because of the kind of person it is done by; so without an appeal to metaphysical/epistemological assumptions most of us wouldn't want to make, the Platonist has to say that there are no objective or situational standards or requirements for the moral agent to perceive or learn about, and, very much like egoism, this assumption is so very far from present-day conceptions of ethics that I think we needn't consider it here. If we are trying to formulate an ethics of virtue that eliminates the problems of common-sense and Kantian morality but is otherwise conservative, we do well, in the absence of other compelling reasons, to avoid the extreme "agent-basing" that a Platonic approach would force us to.

Does that then mean that our (common-sense) virtue ethics ought to have a fundamentally Aristotelian structure? Not necessarily. Although Aristotle does advocate both self-regarding and other-regarding virtues (as well as mixed virtues), his fundamental doctrine of the mean (as has often been noted) seems ill adapted to helping us understand or justify duties of promise-keeping and truth-telling, so I think we have reasons of common-sense plausibility (perhaps this is just our common sense, not Aristotle's) to avoid the doctrine of the mean. Freed of that doctrine, our intuitive virtue ethics will readily allow us to criticize—though not to blame people for—promise-breaking and lying, but there will, nonetheless, be much that is reminiscent of Aristotle in what follows (though I might mention that the account we shall give of friendship avoids Aristotle's extreme rationalism at the same time that it argues against the moralism of much recent work on that topic). Furthermore, our approach all along has been much more explicit about issues of self-other symmetry than anything to be found in Aristotle. But nothing like the Kantian or Christian/Victorian view of morality was known to Aristotle, and here we have had to be, and will continue to be, explicit about issues of symmetry in an attempt to explain how a common-sense virtue-ethical approach may be superior to common-sense, Kantian, and even utilitarian forms of ethics.

## Some Issues of Terminology

I said above that I want, like Aristotle, to allow for the independent aretaic evaluation of actions, but the observant reader may have noted my tendency, especially in Part I, to focus on the (favorable) evaluation of traits (of character) as virtues and to treat the evaluation of actions as a matter of subsuming them under virtues. In other words, my references to virtue-theoretic praise of actions have typically invoked the idea that one or another action may or may not exemplify or instantiate a virtue (good character trait), but in fact I have been doing this simply as a matter of convenience, as a means to streamlining our discussion, and I certainly want to leave room for the direct evaluation of actions. To say of an act that it exemplifies or demonstrates a certain virtue, is typically to evaluate it indirectly, through its relation to a certain trait regarded as valuable or admirable,[7] but there is no reason I can think of why one can't also assess an act itself in virtue-ethical terms, and although the term "virtue" cannot be used for such direct act-evaluation, we have other aretaic terms available for this purpose. If we admire or think highly of an act (which may or may not obviously exemplify some familiar virtue), we can simply say that the act is admirable or that we think well of it, and in so doing, it is not at all obvious—and I certainly want to avoid being committed to saying—that we must base such an act-evaluation on some prior or implicit evaluation of certain general traits.

Moreover, the notion of the admirable (unlike specifically moral terms such as "morally praiseworthy" and "morally good") applies in the same self-other symmetric way that holds for "is a virtue." And it is perhaps easiest to recognize this, if one notices that calling a trait of character a virtue is essentially the same, in ordinary English, as calling it admirable. The aretaic term "admirable" can be as readily applied to traits of character (and people) as to particular actions, and what is done for the agent/possessor and what is done for others are both commonsensically relevant to the admirability of a trait of character in the way we have seen them both relevant to status as a virtue. By the same token, what is done for others and what is done for the agent are both ordinarily taken to be at least relevant to the admirability of a particular act, so the term "admirable" is not only more broadly usable than the expression "is a virtue" but also possesses in its ordinary application the highly desirable self-other symmetry that so clearly characterizes the latter expression.

In what follows I shall be making more frequent use of the notion of admirability than of any of the other aretaic, but non-moral notions that are available to virtue ethics. Of course, other aretaic terms apply equally to acts, traits, desires, and persons, so I think I should at this point mention why I think some of them are less appropriate for our purposes than the term "admirable." The virtue ethics I will be describing is largely based on our common-sense ideas and intuitions about what counts as a virtue and, more generally, as admirable. And in order to evoke, or at least not discourage, such intuitions,[8] I think we should try to avoid stretching the usage of terms and, whenever possible, use idiomatic or natural-sounding language in our discussion of foundational issues. I believe that using the term "admirable" as our most general term of aretaic commendation allows us to meet these conditions in a way that other terms that may initially recommend themselves ultimately turn out not to do.

Thus virtues are sometimes characterized as good traits or excellences of character, but when we try to use the terms "good" or "excellent" of particular actions and people, we end up, I think, with something less idiomatic than we could hope for—and in the case of "good" we run the additional risk of confusion with moral categories. Because we can speak in the broadest sense of actions or people we admire or lack admiration for, we can speak, in general, of acts or people that (we find) are admirable or not admirable. But the idea of excellent acts or actions—however much Greek usage pushes us in the direction of such neologism—is much less natural as English than similar talk using the concept of admirability—consider the difference between "I found what he did admirable" and "I found what he did excellent." And I think something similar can be said in connection with the concept of good(ness), even though one may be initially inclined to hold that it is—indeed must be—the most generally useful of our virtue-ethical aretaic notions. But to say

"I found his actions (or what he did) good" is to invite a request for further clarification in a way that use of "admirable" seems not to do. And part of the problem here may be that "good" also suggests moral goodness more strongly than we wish to do in the version of virtue ethics to be developed here. "Good person" more clearly implies specifically moral goodness than "admirable person" or "excellent person" suggests specifically moral admirability or excellence.[9] (Interestingly, and somewhat paradoxically, thinking *well of a person* is not tied to specifically moral evaluation in the way the notion of a *good person* ordinarily is; we commonly think well of whatever and whomever we find admirable.) And so for purposes of our present foundational discussion, I will for the most part avoid "good" and "excellent" and use "admirable" as the canonical general term of virtue-ethical commendation. However, terms like "laudable" and "commendable" seem as generally applicable as "admirable" and just as free of specifically moral import. So I will feel free to employ them as stylistic variants on "admirable," even if the term "praiseworthy" is probably too dangerous to use in this fashion because of the superficially moral connotations of its putative opposite, "blameworthy."

The last point raises, however, the additional problem of how to express the opposite of admirability. If we wish to express an attitude that is as fully negative as "admirable" is positive, it is not enough to speak of a less-than-admiring attitude or of behavior as less-than-admirable; and in fact English seems rather less rich in general terms of negative (non-moral) aretaic evaluation than it apparently is in general terms of positive or favorable aretaic evaluation. "Blameworthy," "reprehensible," and "culpable" are all specifically moral—Winston Churchill may have been careless or foolish, when on an early trip to the United States he stepped off a curb looking the wrong way and was injured by an oncoming car, but we wouldn't ordinarily regard him as even the least bit blameworthy, culpable, or reprehensible for such self-neglect. So what term or terms can be used for expressing the opposite of admirability?

I think our best bet is "deplorable." Although it can be predicated of accidents, events, or states of affairs—and in such usage it means something like "unfortunate"—the term "deplorable" can be used in other contexts to imply the kind of non-moral criticism we make when we accuse someone of careless or foolish behavior. If Churchill was sufficiently warned of the dangers for Britons of the American rule of the road, then we may regard his failure to look left as open to criticism, as deplorable; we may deplore his inattention, even if "blame" seems the wrong word for our critical attitude. But someone can also be considered deplorable for the harm he negligently or intentionally does to others, and so I think we can treat "deplorable" as the opposite of "admirable."[10]

## Modes of Symmetry

In Part I we saw that common-sense morality is subject to certain asymmetries. What it is permissible to do to, or fail to do for, oneself it can be wrong to do to, or fail to do for, people other than oneself, and although how much one does for others makes a difference, other things being equal, to how morally good we ordinarily take an act or trait or disposition to be, what one is enabled to do for oneself doesn't in this way count toward a (comparative or non-comparative) favorable moral evaluation of one's behavior, etc. Such self-other asymmetry when conjoined with other aspects of ordinary morality leads the latter into difficulties that give one good reason, I argued, to look for something better than common-sense morality, and we have been and will be arguing that both utilitarianism and common-sense virtue ethics enable us to avoid the asymmetry of common-sense morality as just (roughly) characterized and thus to avoid the problems and paradoxes of such morality. However, there is another natural sense for the expression "self-other symmetry" according to which utilitarianism is symmetrical, but (non-moral) virtue ethics is not. It is time we took note of this distinction.

Under utilitarianism, the welfare or preferences of every individual are given equal weight in the reckoning of the goodness of results that constitutes the basis for its claims about moral rightness or betterness. So utilitarianism in that sense expresses or embodies an ideal of equal concern for all persons (or sentient beings): though it doesn't insist that moral agents themselves be equally concerned with every person's good, the calculations that determine the obligations of each agent (or what it is better or worse for the agent to do) are based on a reckoning of good consequences that treats the welfare of each and every person other than the agent as no more or less important than that of the agent. In thus making the standpoint of impersonal or impartial benevolence the fulcrum of all its evaluations, utilitarianism embodies an ideal of uniform or symmetrical concern toward *every* individual that is clearly as a result, also *self-other* symmetric. (From such an ideal standpoint, however, concern for the agent of a given action may be a small fraction of the total concern that is, as it were, expressed in the utilitarian evaluation of that action. The more people affected by a given action, the less important are the welfare or interests of the agent in determining how that action is to be evaluated.)

There is no reason in advance to suppose that common-sense virtue ethics embodies the particular form of symmetry just described, and one may therefore wonder whether, through a lack of such symmetry, our proposed virtue ethics is at a relative disadvantage vis-à-vis utilitarianism. In fact, common-sense virtue-ethics is not self-other symmetrical in the sense just introduced. But I don't believe this will cause problems for virtue ethics, because the latter can be shown to embody its own distinctive ideal of self-other symmetry, one that utilitarianism fails to embody; and so as far as the issue of desirable symmetry is concerned, there will turn out to be little to choose between utilitarianism and common-sense virtue ethics. Nonetheless, the distinction between the two kinds of symmetry we are now discussing may be the key to understanding the main differences between utilitarianism and virtue ethics as ethical norms or ideals, and although the literature of utilitarianism has already made us somewhat familiar with symmetry understood as uniform concern for self and any other person, the form of symmetry that characterizes our ordinary thinking about the virtues has been pretty well ignored. Yet it is well worth discussing both in its own right and for the understanding it can give us of the virtue-theoretical approach to ethics.

The form of symmetry we have just attributed to (direct) utilitarianism is clearly absent from common-sense morality. The judgments made by the latter are not predicated on any ideal of equal concern for everyone; on the contrary, the agent counts for *less* than others and *greater* concern for those near and dear as opposed to distant others is morally incumbent upon her. And, as it turns out, the virtue ethics of common sense also fails to embody the symmetry we have just attributed to utilitarianism. To be sure—and this is a point I will return to shortly—our ordinary thinking about the virtues treats benefit to the possessor of a trait as relevant to its status as a good trait of character. But nothing in our ordinary understanding of the virtues precludes the admirability of traits or acts that involve one in giving preference to certain people over others, and in fact it seems contrary to our usual understanding of the virtues, seems out and out deplorable, for one's actions and character not to give expression to greater concern, for example, for one's spouse and children than for random others. So there is some reason to believe that common-sense virtue ethics is incompatible with the sort of self-other symmetry exemplified by utilitarianism's equal concern for every individual.

Yet that ethics embodies another sort of self-other symmetry we have not yet considered. In Part I, I mentioned that traits admired for other-regarding reasons are not normally considered to have any sort of general precedence over predominantly self-regarding virtues. Kindness, justice, and generosity are not usually viewed as greater or more important virtues than self-regarding virtues such as prudence, fortitude, sagacity, and equanimity or "mixed" virtues like courage, self-control, and practical wisdom; indeed the language of common-sense ethics includes as many terms for self-regarding or "mixed" virtues as for other-regarding virtues. To that degree, our ordinary thinking about the virtues gives equal emphasis to, is equally concerned with, virtues helping others and virtues helping their possessors, and this latter fact, assuming it is a fact, expresses or embodies a kind of equality or symmetry of concern for self and others.

But note the important difference from the symmetry we have just discussed in connection with utilitarianism. (The symmetries that utilitarianism and common-sense virtue ethics share and which we discussed in Part I are not at issue here.) In describing a virtue as (basically) other-regarding, I am treating others as a class or category specified relative to some given choice of possessor, and in saying, therefore, that our ordinary thinking about the virtues seems to place equal weight or importance on virtues helping their possessors and virtues helping people other than their possessors, I am not saying that virtue ethics allows or requires us to have or act on dispositions that embody an equal concern for every single individual. Rather, I am saying that our ordinary thinking about the virtues treats the category of trait-possessor and the category of "other people" (i.e., people other than the trait-possessor) as of roughly equal importance, and this latter suggests (perhaps it does more than suggest, but I don't at this point want to claim any more than it suggests) an ideal of character and action that, for any given choice of agent/possessor, exemplifies roughly equal concern for the agent/possessor and for others treated as a class or category to which everyone other than the agent/possessor belongs. In that case, we can say that our ordinary understanding of what is admirable and what counts as a virtue embodies equal concern for self and others, where "others" is to be understood *in sensu composito*, that is, applying to other people as a class; whereas, by contrast, utilitarianism's ethical ideal expresses equality or symmetry of concern for self and others in a sense that understands "others" *in sensu diviso*, as applying to each and every other individual as compared to the concern shown for the self (the agent/possessor herself). And this means that utilitarianism and common-sense virtue ethics differ as regards the importance and evaluation of purely self-regarding traits and actions.

Utilitarian evaluation reflects an equality of concern for the self and for every single other individual, and where enough other people can be affected by a trait or activity, concern for the given self/agent/trait-possessor may be practically insignificant by comparison with the sum of concern for other people that is mandated by the situation. Since over a (good chunk of a) lifetime, most of us can affect thousands, even millions, of other people, the self is likely to be submerged in the sea of concern for others that gives rise to utilitarian ethical judgments. But our ordinary thinking about the virtues—though it may not rule out the possibility of self-sacrifice, even enormous self-sacrifice, as a condition of human admirability or non-deplorability—seems less committed to evaluations that take such little account of the agent/possessor's self-regarding concerns. If its ideal of character and of action involves an equality as between the self as a category, on the one hand, and other people taken as a category, rather than individually, on the other, then an evaluative balance is established between self-concern and concern for all others put together, and it is such a (two-way) balance that on my view constitutes the backbone of our ordinary thinking about what is and is not admirable in character, action, desire, etc. Utilitarianism, by contrast, sets up and commends separate balances, as it were, between the self and every single other person (sentient being), and although this in one sense represents an ideal of symmetrical treatment, it should by now be clear that the idea of a merely two-way balance between any given self and the totality or class of others also expresses an ethical ideal of symmetry, one that utilitarianism clearly and necessarily fails to embody.

In effect, I am saying that "equality of concern for self and other people" has two natural readings embodying two incompatible but attractive notions/ideals of self-other symmetry. But it may at first seem odd to have to suppose that forms of *symmetry* can stand in this sort of opposition to one another. In biology, for example, radial and bilateral symmetry are different but mutually compatible, and it seems natural to think that it is only forms of asymmetry, not forms of symmetry, that can be mutually incompatible. We may feel less attached to these initial thoughts, however, if we recognize the similarity between the notion of symmetry and notions such as sameness and similarity itself and if we also remember some of the ways in which projected or continued similarities may conflict. Goodman's New Riddle of Induction suggests that some rational creatures might see grueness as a more natural form of similarity than greenness, and Wittgenstein's example of the person who thinks, after having counted the first five hundred numbers of the series 2, 4, 6, 8 . . . , that saying "1004, 1008, 1012" is going on in the same way, should remind us of the possibility of conflicts between perceived similarities or samenesses and, therefore, between perceived symmetries.[11]

But the Goodmanian and Wittgensteinian examples concern conflicts between (the interpretations or perceptions of) two separate individuals, whereas the clash of symmetries I have just been talking about is supposed to be recognizable as such outside a distinctively utilitarian or virtue-ethical perspective. What we have described is not a situation where what seems to one person to be a symmetry or similarity turns out to be incompatible with what seems symmetrical or similar to someone else, but rather a situation where we can from one and the same perspective recognize two different and natural-seeming forms of symmetry and yet see their mutual incompatibility. And Goodman and Wittgenstein's examples don't in fact give us anything fully analogous with what we have been saying about the two forms of self-other symmetry we have focused on in this chapter.[12]

However, one doesn't have to move very far from the kinds of examples Goodman and Wittgenstein explicitly discuss to find a case of the right sort. For it is possible to describe situations where whatever a given individual does (at least as between two choices available to him) will seem in one natural respect to be going on in the same way—or doing the same thing—but in another natural respect not to be going on in the same way, etc. And I can perhaps best illustrate this possibility by describing a little experiment that I have sometimes done in classes on inductive methodology.

Standing in front of the class, I turn my back to the class and ask the students to notice what I am going to do. I then raise my right arm from a position against my body to one in which it is extended upward, in front of me, and to my right. Turning around to face the class, I ask them, finally, to do with their left arms what I have just done with my right arm.

The response is usually bimodal. Some move their left arms up and to the right, others lift their left arms up and to the left. And it isn't hard to understand why these two sorts of responses should occur. Obviously, some members of the class see my own original action as one of lifting my arm to the right, and when asked to do the same with their left arms, they move their left arms up and to the *right*. Others think of my action as one of moving my arm upward and away from my body, and given this description, this way of seeing what I have done, they naturally move their left arms up and to the *left*. So what seems natural in the light of one way of seeing my action conflicts with what seems natural in the light of another way of viewing that action, but since both views of my action seem natural even after (or especially after) one has described the bimodal results of the experiment, the situation is recognizably one in which clearly natural understandings of "doing the same" cannot both be followed or exemplified. And that is exactly what I am saying occurs with respect to our understanding of the two kinds of symmetry discussed in this chapter. Both are understandable, natural ways of ascribing symmetry, but neither utilitarianism nor common-sense virtue ethics allows both of them to be exemplified or adhered to. Rather, if we accept utilitarianism we give realization to an *in sensu diviso* form of self-other symmetry that virtue ethics rules out, and, by the same token, if we accept common-sense virtue ethics, we provide a place for *in sensu composito* symmetry of a kind that utilitarianism makes it impossible to realize.

As a result, the choice between utilitarianism and a virtue ethics that remains as close as possible to our ordinary sense of what is admirable entails a choice between two kinds of self-other symmetry, and as far as I can tell neither form has an overriding claim on our ethics-methodological sensibilities. I don't think any argument from symmetry alone is going to be able to distinguish in a decisive or important way between the merits of utilitarianism and those of the virtue-ethical approach I am in the process of describing. But in the light of the class experiment just mentioned, this conclusion is perhaps neither surprising nor particularly unpalatable. Utilitarianism and common-sense virtue ethics have been seen to embody natural but incompatible forms of self-other symmetry, but I also said earlier that our ordinary thought about the virtues is committed to some sort of (ideal of) balance as between what one does for oneself and what one does for other people (sentient beings). It is time to say some more about what such a balance entails and how it can be encapsulated in ethical principles.

## Notes

1. I here have in mind the sort of ground-floor discussion of the relative merits of utilitarianism and intuitive morality that one finds in recent work by Williams, Nagel, Parfit, Kagan, and Scheffler.

2. On these two distinctive elements of virtue ethics, see, e.g., Robert Louden's "On Some Vices of Virtue Ethics," reprinted in R. Kruschwitz and R. Roberts, eds., *The Virtues: Contemporary Essays on Moral Character*, Wadsworth, 1987, pp. 67–79; and Marcia Baron's "Varieties of Ethics of Virtue," *American Philosophical Quarterly* 22, 1985, p. 52n.

3. In her excellent book, *An Introduction to Plato's Republic* (Oxford, 1982), Julia Annas introduces the notion of an "agent-centered" ethical theory and cites

both Plato and Aristotle's ethical views as exemplifying it. But her characterization fluctuates between the two notions mentioned in the text above, and as we have seen only one of the two actually applies to Aristotle.

4. However, Plato's valued ordering of the soul's parts essentially depends on the rational part's being properly oriented to the source of all value, the Form of the Good. So although, for Plato, the value of actions may be a function of the value of certain states of the soul, the latter value is itself understood and/or defined by reference to what has the highest value of all, namely, the Form of the Good. Evaluation of states of the soul is thus, for Plato, not the most fundamental level or kind of evaluation.

5. See his *Types of Ethical Theory*, 2 volumes, 1885, 1891. In "Motive Utilitarianism" (*Journal of Philosophy* 73, 1976, pp. 467–81), Robert M. Adams introduces a view called "conscience utilitarianism" that evaluates acts in terms of whether they conform to a utility-maximizing conscience. On such an indirect utilitarian view, conscience is evaluated prior to the evaluation of actions, just as, for Martineau, motive-evaluation is prior to the evaluation of actions. But for Adams's view (as for Plato's) the evaluation of the "inner" is not the most fundamental level of evaluation. For conscience utilitarianism, the evaluation of conscience(s) requires a prior evaluation of the effects of one or another form of conscience, whereas Martineau seems to treat the (comparative) evaluation of inner motives as resting on no prior or independent form of evaluation and, therefore, as truly foundational.

6. See Louden, *op. cit., passim.*

7. This claim needs to be qualified to handle cases where a given virtue is exemplified but doesn't operate as a virtue, but I will ignore this complication in what follows. On this point, see Philippa Foot's title essay in *Virtues and Vices*, California, 1978.

8. We need a term for the opposite of an "intuition pump."

9. In *The Foundations of Ethics* (Oxford, 1939, pp. 270f.), W. D. Ross points out that "good man" has a moral content "admirable man" lacks and says that the latter is the broader notion.

10. The notion of an opposite is somewhat ambiguous. The opposite of admirability might be thought to be paltriness or negligibility (an admirable vs. a paltry effort, e.g.)—rather than the "negative" notion of deplorability. So we may need some new terminology here. We can say that "paltry" and "admirable" differ *in size*, but not *in sign*, whereas "deplorable" and "admirable" differ *in sign* but not *in size*. ("Criticizable" differs both in size and in sign from "admirable.") The notion of oppositeness is colloquially usable to refer either to opposition of size or to opposition of sign, but we have been looking mainly for a term that has the latter sort of relation to admirability—or, as we have also put it, we have been looking for the negative analogue of the positive term "admirable." It is also useful, however, to have terms available to mark differences in evaluative size, and some of these we have just mentioned.

11. See Goodman's *Fact, Fiction, and Forecast*, Bobbs-Merrill, 1965, Ch. 3; and Wittgenstein's *Philosophical Investigations*, New York, 1959, pp. 74e–85e. Paragraph 208 focuses on the specific notion of uniformity (of pattern).

12. The closest analogue of what I am describing here may be found, not in Wittgenstein or Goodman's work, but in C. I. Lewis's idea that we can discern a natural regularity or pattern in whatever course of events nature or the world may present us with. See *Mind and the World Order*, Dover, 1956, Ch. 11.

# 6

# Virtue Rules

In the last chapter I mentioned some reasons for the hypothesis that our common-sense thinking about the virtues places, if not (exactly) equal, then at least comparable weight on the self-regarding and other-regarding aspects of the traits it treats as virtues. In the present chapter, I would like to expand just a bit on this idea and give you some other reasons for thinking that an equality or balance of concern as between self and others taken as a class is characteristic of our implicit views about admirability and virtue-status. I don't expect to be able to present a knock-down argument, and, as far as I know, the idea of such a balance has not previously been explored by philosophers, but it can at any rate be shown to fit nicely with certain neglected aspects of our evaluative thinking that I will attempt to describe in what follows.

I mentioned in the last chapter that there seems to be no tendency, in philosophers who adopt a more or less intuitive approach to the virtues, automatically to assume the primacy of other-regarding over self-regarding or mixed virtues. But at this point it is also worth our while to notice that with respect to a particular mixed virtue like courage, the importance or stress we tend to place on its other-regarding aspects is not obviously greater than that placed on its self-regarding aspects. It seems just as important a fact about courage that people need it for their own well-being as that it enables its possessors to serve the needs of others. And for a much more minor virtue like patience, I believe the same rough proportionality also holds: we practically and evaluatively focus on patience as much for its usefulness to those who have it as for its beneficial effects on other people, and presumably there would be no reason to expect such a rough equality here and with respect to courage (and other mixed virtues) if our ordinary thinking about what is admirable and deplorable didn't in some sense recommend a rough equality as between self-benefit and other-benefit.

Obviously, we need to be able to say more, a great deal more, about what this sense is, about what this purported recommendation of balance amounts to. And we may perhaps begin doing this by considering a possible objection to the direction the argument has just been taking. Even if, the objection goes, the self-regarding and other-regarding aspects of the virtues are equally significant and valuable, a recommendation or commendation of attaining and acting on both sorts of virtues doesn't necessarily follow, since it is entirely compatible with such equal significance and value that it should be best to *specialize in virtue*, that is, cultivate and exhibit (for the most part) either self-regarding or other-regarding virtues, but not both sorts of virtue together. After all, even if we feel that being an architect and being a professor are (ceteris paribus) equally significant and valuable roles and careers, we will probably not want to recommend the pursuit of a dual career in architecture and, say, philosophy; there may be superior advantages and merit in specializing, and clearly most of us are willing to acknowledge this possibility.

Moreover, the idea of a similar form of overall *ethical* specialization is not so absurd that we can simply dismiss it out of hand. There is a distinction, after all, between saints and heroes, and perhaps that distinction can be taken as embodying some notion of equally meritorious forms of (supererogatory) ethical/moral specialization. So why can't our commonplace ideas about the admirable and the deplorable also make room for a form of specialization that allows not only for the equal value or importance of self-regarding and other-regarding virtues, but also for a thoroughgoing specialization in one or the other of these two classes of virtues. Why can't such specialization be no less admirable and no more deplorable than a "generalist" mixture of self- and other-regarding virtues in particular lives?

The answer to this question comes in part from a consideration of what we (nowadays) are willing to count as a virtue, or as admirable and in part from a general theoretical principle that I believe will recommend itself to us at this point. A virtue like kindness intuitively belongs to the category of the other-regarding, and fortitude (mainly) falls into the category of the self-regarding, yet neither of these putatively admirable traits seems in any obvious way to be incompatible with the cultivation and exemplification of virtues in the category it doesn't belong to. And it seems plausible to claim that any trait falling into one of these two categories that is (largely) incompatible with admirable traits of the other category should not be regarded and not count as a virtue.[1] And this supposition, if true, is evidence that common-sense ethics (re)commends balance, rather than specialization, with regard to self- and other-regarding virtues.

Why don't we think of selfishness as an admirable trait of character, a virtue? It enables one, after all, to do good things for oneself and seems compatible with the development of its possessor's artistic, intellectual, or even political talents so long as he is concerned only with how they affect himself: his own power, knowledge, achievements. (I am describing things somewhat roughly here.) So given that fortitude (or equanimity or prudence) is primarily self-beneficial, why do we consider fortitude a virtue, but selfishness not?

I think at least in part because selfishness precludes other-regarding, other-benefiting virtues as fortitude (or equanimity or prudence) does not. A selfish person may, of course, do things for others inadvertently or as a means to her own advancement, but fortitude and other basically self-regarding virtues are quite compatible with a fundamental concern and respect for the concerns and self-respect of others, and attributions of general selfishness are precisely meant to exclude such concern and respect. But in that case the fact that selfishness is not considered a virtue (hence the title of Ayn Rand's *The Virtue of Selfishness*) and is often criticized in a way that fortitude, etc., are not is some evidence that thoroughgoing specialization in a self-regarding, self-favoring direction is by our common lights deplorable, to be recommended against.

However, lest one think that we may here have uncovered some new form of self-other asymmetry, it should be pointed out that we needn't consider selflessness a virtue either. Selflessness is largely incompatible with what we intuitively take to be self-regarding, self-benefiting virtues, and even if it was highly admired in Victorian times, nowadays—perhaps because we are less priggish and highminded, perhaps because we think we know more about human psychology and are less willing to take things at face value—selflessness is a practically automatic object of suspicion. The person who not only shows a great concern for others but who, in addition, seems to deprecate or ignore his own needs whenever there is the slightest good he can do for others would typically be thought to have something wrong with him—consider, for example, how we tend to regard a character in literature like Pere Goriot, who pauperizes and then destroys himself in order to allow his daughters to go on leading their frivolous, luxurious existences. In the light of what seems to be a genuinely deeper understanding of human psychological phenomena, a totally self-sacrificing, selfless individual would automatically be suspected of masochism, of being burdened by inordinate and misdirected guilt, and one really doesn't therefore, have to be a Nietzsche or an Ayn Rand nowadays to take such a view of (Victorian, highminded) selflessness. (Interestingly, the idea that selflessness is based on inordinate or unusual guilt can be found in the work of that quintessential highminded Victorian, T. H. Green. In the *Prolegomena to Ethics*, Green claims that the great benefactors of mankind are usually motivated by a stronger, more stringent sense of duty than most of us have. What we consider supererogatory in their actions they tend to regard as absolutely incumbent on them, and so guilt would seem to threaten them from more directions than most of us seem threatened by it. But Green is still enough of a Victorian not to doubt the admirability of what is done from such a stringent conscience, and in any event he doesn't focus on cases where the agent, possibly in addition to showing concern for others, treats himself as unworthy of concern, as not worth considering—sacrifices himself to the minor needs or velleities of others.)[2]

We might say that the selfless individual who slights his own major self-regarding concerns to cater to the comparatively insignificant desires of others acts as if he had a positive duty *not* to do well by himself. However, since such a person may be unable or unwilling to put the matter in such stark terms, he may always look for possible excuses to do things, however insignificant, on behalf of others, so as to be able to bring his self-denying actions under the safer or higher moral category of altruism. But whatever we may wish to say about these possibilities, we in any event seem quite prepared to deny virtue-status to selflessness as we deny it to selfishness, and so our fundamental attitudes seem to tell both against exclusively self-regarding and against exclusively other-regarding forms of disposition and activity. Neither selfishness nor selflessness is admirable by our lights, indeed both are commonly deplored, criticized, thought badly of. And this is the evidence we need to show that our common attitudes and evaluations in this area favor some kind of balance as between an individual's treatment of her own self-regarding needs and concerns and her treatment of the needs and concerns of people other than herself.

But how much balance, what kind of balance? After all, even if we have so far seen nothing contrary to the idea of equal treatment of self and other, our argument from the status of selflessness and selfishness at most establishes that the extremes of (near-)total concern for oneself and (near-)total concern for others are evaluationally discredited by our common lights. And nothing follows about the evaluative preferability, the greater admirability, of an exactly or approximately even or equal balance as between self- and other-concern. (We will have to say more about the notion of concern in what follows.) I will not, therefore, attempt to argue that rough equality of self- and other-concern is mandated by our common ideas about what is admirable in human action and motivation, but nonetheless I hope to show that those ideals commend or recommend *some degree of balance* as between these two forms of concern. What is so far clear is that our common-sense thinking about the virtues treats both other-regarding and self-regarding virtues as important. What we do for others and what we do that doesn't directly concern others are both sources for significant common-sense claims to admirability, and we can represent these two sources of evaluation in a way that posits (some sort of) balance between them, without having to argue for a specific degree or kind of balance in the way that our earlier questions seem to presuppose that we must.

We can do so by spelling out principles of admirability and its opposite in such a way that we at least implicitly recommend and/or commend balance between the self-regarding and the other-regarding sides of (the) virtue(s). But it will also be useful to model such principles on a more familiar kind of principle that can be found in ethical views that make use of specifically deontic concepts like duty and obligation, permissibility and rightness. In particular, we need to employ, for purposes of example, Kant's notion of an imperfect duty. For there are analogues of such duties in the non-deontic realm of the virtues (or the admirable and the deplorable), and the notion of an implicit recommendation of balance is readily illustrated by citing Kant's actual views about our imperfect duties.

Kant distinguishes between *perfect duties* (like the duty not to lie and the duty not to mutilate oneself), which we must obey in any and all circumstances, and *imperfect duties*, which bind us in a less stringent or less all-or-nothing manner. According to Kant (roughly), a single lie is sufficient for the duty not to lie to have been violated; whereas a single failure to help others in circumstances where one is in a position to do so does not automatically constitute a violation of what Kant conceives to be our imperfect duty to promote the happiness of others. Rather, the latter is always in force and always exerts a certain moral pressure on the agent, without absolutely forbidding occasional or even frequent failure to do what one can to promote the good of others.

According to Kant we have two basic (sets of) imperfect duties: to promote our own moral (or other) perfection and to advance the happiness of other people. But he holds that there is no corresponding imperfect duty to bring about either one's own happiness or the (moral) perfection of others and gives as reasons arguments that are either problematic or lacking in persuasive power. We have already discussed the ways in which Kant's denial of any duty to pursue one's own happiness and the supporting claim that one cannot have any duty or obligation to do what one always automatically wishes to do get him into difficulties. But the argument for the denial of duties to promote the (moral) perfection of other people is perhaps even more obviously problematic. Kant says that "the *perfection* of another man, as a person, consists precisely in *his own* power to adopt his end in accordance with his own concept of duty; and it is self-contradictory to demand that I do (make it my duty to do) what only the other person himself can do."[3] And such an argument seems to make some questionable modal assumptions or else to rely on aspects of the Kantian metaphysics of freedom that we have every reason to question. The argument may also cause us to wonder whether an appropriately analogous argument might not be mounted against the possibility of doing something (now) to enhance one's (later) moral powers and so likewise call into question Kant's assumed imperfect duty to promote one's *own* moral perfection.[4]

But for the moment let us put aside the question whether Kant's views about our imperfect duties are entirely consistent or well grounded and consider *how* Kant expresses those views. He asks: "What ends are also duties?" and then immediately gives the answer: "They are *one's own perfection* and the *happiness of others*." In so doing, I think Kant is naturally taken to be recommending or commending a balance in people's lives between helping others and developing their own moral and other powers, but this (re)commendation is effected not through any explicit statement that asserts the importance or value of such balance, but through the making of *two separate claims* of imperfect duty and, perhaps additionally, through *their juxtaposition* in Kant's text. To be sure, the balance here implicitly recommended is not the specific balance I have said is implicit in our ordinary judgments about admirability, etc., but it is a balance, nonetheless, and Kant's way of developing his own particular views gives us a good example, therefore, of how balance, or some sort of equality of concern, can be recommended or commended without being explicitly discussed.

Notice that one could not be said to have followed Kant's recommendations if one devoted all one's time to self-development/self-perfection or, alternatively, if one devoted all one's time to advancing the happiness of other people. Someone who has had ample opportunity both to develop her own powers and also help others, but who has "specialized" by putting all her efforts into only one of these recommended forms of activity has not (fully) complied with the injunctions entailed by Kant's specification of our imperfect duties. In effect, Kant's specification of our duties here amounts to a *bipartite injunction* against neglecting the good of others and neglecting one's own development, and such an injunction can no more be obeyed simply, for example, by giving to others than the bipartite command, "Plant corn and plant cotton!" can be obeyed simply by planting an unusually large amount of corn. Since, moreover, the

latter bipartite injunction/command seems implicitly to involve a requirement to plant *both corn and cotton* in non-negligible amounts, it
should be clear in what sense a bipartite recommendation asks for or
requires a balance between the activities or actions so recommended, and
therefore we can now easily see how Kant's specification of imperfect
duties and the bipartite claims I have been and shall be making about the
general conditions of living admirably (as they can be summed and
summarized from our common-sense views on particular acts, motives,
and traits of character) both require or at least recommend a certain sort
of balance within the ethical life of individuals.

Now, of course, what Kant is recommending and what common-sense
virtue ethics recommends are both formally and materially different. Our
virtue ethics makes no use of specifically moral or deontic concepts of the
sort at issue in Kant's claims about perfect and/or imperfect duty. But I
shall for the duration of the present chapter ignore this difference,
because I believe one can show that virtue ethics is capable of grounding
forms of derivative deontic concepts, and I will attempt to do so after we
have revealed or supplied, more of the content, the substance, of the (a)
virtue-ethical view of things. I shall, in other words, assume that we can
put virtue-ethical views about what is admirable or deplorable into the
imperative mood or into the form of claims about what one ought to do.
And expressed or understood in this fashion, we can easily see that the
recommendations of virtue ethics differ substantively from Kant's particular views about our imperfect duties.

For Kant, there is no imperfect duty to benefit oneself (except indirectly as a means to self-development or to helping others); but if our
account of virtue ethics above is on the right track, then one can be
admirable for one's ability to help (or success in helping) oneself, and
certain ways of ignoring or thwarting one's own welfare or happiness can
be deplored or criticized. Presupposing, then, what needs to be shown
and will be defended later, we can say that the common-sense view of
what is a virtue or counts as admirable tells us, among other things, to
seek and/or develop our capacities for achieving our own happiness,
whereas Kant wants precisely to avoid issuing any such injunction or
recommendation. And as I now also want to make clear, the recommendations or expressed values of Kantianism and virtue ethics also differ in
another important respect.

Kant argues (ineffectually) that we have no duty to seek the (moral)
perfection of others; and unless we wish somehow to insist at this point
on a distinction between esoteric but valid virtue ethics, on the one hand,
and its exoteric, "noble lie" recommendations, on the other, it seems

obvious that virtue ethics will likewise not wish to command specifically moral development or self-perfection. But in speaking earlier about the way in which our thinking about the virtues seems to commend both concern for others and concern for oneself, I didn't explicitly limit such concern to concern for the well-being or happiness of the persons in question. And I want now explicitly to point out that in common-sense terms we admire both what a person is able to do to advance his own or other people's happiness and what a person is able to do to advance the admirability either of himself or others. We commonly admire people for their possession of both self-regarding and other-regarding virtues (I am deliberately using these terms vaguely—as placeholders, if you will), and we also admire people who help others to develop admirable or virtuous traits of character, so although it might be mistaken or misleading to claim that virtue ethics, in telling us to be concerned with others and with ourselves, is recommending moral self- and other-development, still there is a sense in which our implicit view of ethical phenomena recommends something other than the advancement of one's own or other people's (capacity for attaining) happiness or well-being. Even if the possession of self- and other-regarding virtues turns out to be partly constitutive of human happiness or well-being (and we will consider this issue in some detail later on, in Part III), I don't think we have to assume either the presence or the absence of such a connection to believe that the advancement of people's virtues is laudable. And so I think it is part of common-sense virtue ethics to assume that people should be concerned with the happiness and virtue (in our non-moral sense) *both of others and of themselves*, just as, less symmetrically, Kant advocates a practical concern with *one's own* virtue (in his sense of moral self-development) and with *other people's* well-being or happiness.

The difference in symmetry is worth dwelling upon at this point. Kant's arguments for asymmetry are weak and from the standpoint of the present work the absence of symmetry is itself at least a reason for questioning the ethical validity of what is thus asymmetric. By that standard, therefore, the even-handed (or at least *more* even-handed)[5] approach taken here has a certain advantage over the Kantian ethical view. Moreover, unlike Kant, common-sense morality seems to treat it as fundamentally obligatory that one should concern oneself with the development of various virtues in certain other people. Our duties, for example, to our children are normally taken to include a duty to advance their well-being as well as a duty to educate them morally and, more generally, to instill good values. We are supposed to help our children with the life-skills needed to advance their well-being, but we commonly also want them, and think we should help them, to be good or admirable people, and to a certain extent this injunction/desire is felt independently of the desire/injunction to make them happy. We would hesitate and probably more than hesitate to insure the happiness or contentment of our children at the cost of making them despicable or deplorable people willing to do great damage to those around them as a means to their own well-being.

But our concern for the morality of non-deplorability of our children is not the only instance one can cite of practical interest in more than the happiness of other people. We feel more responsible for the moral reform of an errant spouse or parent than we feel for the moral reform of more distant others, but even toward the latter we sometimes feel some measure of obligation to be concerned with whether morality or virtue is exemplified.[6] During and after the Vietnam War, Americans who had opposed the war felt a greater moral impulsion toward (re)educating their fellow Americans than they felt or would have felt toward equally benighted people in some other country who tolerated some equally intolerable war, and so I think it is in fact safe to say that the degree of our ordinary moral concern for people's virtue(s) varies with the closeness of people to ourselves (in some sense of "closeness" that no doubt needs further specification) and that, unlike the morality of our concern for happiness, this relation of variation includes one's concern for oneself as well as one's concern for more or less distant others. In the common-sense morality of concern for happiness, we saw that (strength of) obligation varied with closeness to the self or agent *except in the case of the agent's relation to himself*, where in common-sense terms there seems to be no substantial basic obligation to advance happiness or well-being. But what I am now saying is that with regard to the advancement of (the) virtue(s), common-sense morality does not allow an exception in the person's relation to himself. One's greatest or strongest obligation is to be concerned with one's *own* virtue. And this counts, I believe, as an additional strike against common-sense morality.

For in addition to the asymmetries and paradoxes discussed earlier, in Part I, it turns out that there is another form of asymmetry in common-sense morality that has emerged only here, in the present chapter. What common-sense morality recommends in regard to the advancement of virtue is asymmetrically related to its recommendations in regard to the advancement of people's happiness or well-being. And this asymmetry makes common-sense morality's lack of any obligation to advance one's own happiness seem even stranger than it previously has, because, in addition to everything we said earlier in this connection, it now turns out that common-sense prescribes a practical concern with both the well-being and the virtue of everyone other than the agent and also with the virtue of the agent, thus leaving concern for the agent's well-being as the sole exception to a large-scale and otherwise symmetrically contoured set of injunctions about human beings (or persons generally). This is an oddness additional to any we exposed earlier, and it gives us further reason—if we still need any—for discarding common-sense morality.

But since we have already given up on common-sense morality, we should at this point return to our exposition and development of a common-sense ethics of (the) virtue(s). And we are basing our understanding of what virtue ethics generally (re)commends for our behavior toward others and toward ourselves on an analogy with the imperfect duties that Kant asserted (asymmetrically) in relation to others and ourselves. The difference in content between Kant's views and our own—and the latter's advantages, at least on the face of them—have now been described, and we also noted the need to explain how aretaic characterizations can or may give rise to injunctions or recommendations. But leaving this issue, again, until later, I would like now to point out another aspect of parallelism between Kant's imperfect duties and what virtue ethics commends and deplores.

Just as imperfect duties can be complied with without one's having to follow their recommendations/requirements at every moment, common-sense virtue ethics is not to be thought of as requiring/recommending that we concern ourselves with others and ourselves, and in regard both to virtue and to happiness, at every possible moment. If common-sense virtue ethics considers it deplorable if one doesn't do enough for others or for oneself, it has no tendency to regard it as deplorable if one doesn't at every moment actively concern oneself with people's happiness and/or possession of (the) virtue(s), and since, to anticipate, we will later tie the notion of aretaic recommendation or injunction to the idea of conditions of non-deplorability, it should be clear that the common-sense-based, but (by philosophers) largely unrecognized bipartite injunction to concern oneself with (the well-being and virtue of) others and to be practically concerned with (the well-being and virtue of) oneself can be complied with by people who aren't always engaged in these recommended activities, but who show a sufficient amount of such engagement a sufficient part of the time.

In previous chapters, we spoke of individual virtues and pointed out a certain balance in our ordinary thinking as between self-regarding and other-regarding virtues. In the present chapter, I have presented two principles or a bipartite principle or rule that can, in the ways we have argued, be said to summarize or encapsulate the total impact of what common-sense wishes to say about admirable character traits taken individually. Just as to a large extent our common-sense views about what traits count as virtues or anti-virtues summarize and encapsulate our attributions of admirability or deplorability to particular actions and motives, so too, but at a level of even greater generality, does the bipartite principle formulated and defended here summarize and encapsulate our views about given virtues and anti-virtues, about the deplorability or admirability of various character traits. Our possession of such a more general or comprehensive virtue-ethical principle is desirable not only for its own sake, that is, for the unity it makes constitutive of virtue ethics, but also for the comparison it allows us to draw between common-sense virtue ethics and Kant's ideas about imperfect duty and for the (later-to-be fulfilled) promise it offers us of being able to make sense of recommendations and injunctions of a sort that can be grounded in a fundamentally aretaic approach to ethics.

But having said so much already about virtue-ethical analogues of imperfect duty in Kant's sense, we shouldn't ignore the virtue-ethical analogues of Kantian perfect duties. For Kant, we have a perfect duty not to lie because it is wrong *ever* to lie. Acceptable compliance with an imperfect injunction or duty doesn't require one always to be acting in accordance with it, but, for Kant, such constant or continuous obedience is necessary to morally acceptable compliance with a perfect injunction or duty like the duty not to lie (or the duty not to kill). By analogy, in the context of our common-sense thinking about virtue, we can say that lying and killing are never admirable, always deplorable—although, unlike Kant, we may wish to include a number of qualifications in our description of what we here take to be universally deplorable or lacking in admirability. And we may also wish universally to deplore certain (mainly) self-regarding acts or dispositions—like taking hard drugs or, more generally, impairing one's body. Clearly, there is no reason in principle why a virtue ethics may not criticize as deplorable every instance of a certain kind of act or trait in the very same way the Kantian or common-sense morality of perfect duty is capable of treating every instance of a certain kind of act or trait as wrong or reprehensible. So it seems plausible to conclude that the moral distinction between perfect and imperfect duty has analogues within the sphere of common-sense virtue ethics as we are understanding it here.

Even without the use of specifically moral concepts, the common-sense virtue ethics being developed here makes room for ground-floor ethical concern for the well-being and virtue of other people and, as we have just seen, it not only allows us to do this on the less general levels of our talk about the admirability or deplorability of particular acts or traits, but in addition permits the formulation of more general principles that play a role in the virtue ethics of common sense that seems entirely analogous to that played by (injunctions expressing) perfect and imperfect duties within morality. We have also, however, seen that virtue ethics—in crucial contradistinction to common-sense and Kantian morality—permits (potential) effects on the good of the agent/possessor/self to count in favor of favorable virtue-ethical evaluation of a given action or trait, and this feature precisely allows the common-sense ethics of virtue, as we have characterized it, to avoid some of the puzzles and pitfalls that led us to reject common-sense and Kantian ethics at the end of Part I. The puzzles and pitfalls I have in mind were largely (thought not entirely) the result of the self-other asymmetry of common-sense and Kantian morality, and we have now amply seen that common-sense virtue ethics is not self-other asymmetrical in this way. But neither, on the other hand, is utilitarianism, and we have already also seen how utilitarianism seeks to undercut the problems of moral luck. So if we wish to give as full a defense of common-sense virtue ethics as we attempted, in Part II, to provide for utilitarianism—if, that is, we wish to show that virtue ethics is as free of the problems raised in Part I as it has been argued that utilitarianism is—we must now see what such virtue ethics can say to blunt the force of the objections that arise, for common-sense morality at least, from our inconsistent intuitions in the area of moral luck. That will be the task of the next chapter.

## Notes

1. Clearly, this allows for traits *not* incompatible with either self-regarding or other-regarding virtue to lack virtue status for other (intuitive) reasons.
2. Green, *Prolegomena to Ethics*, Oxford, Clarendon, 1907, Book III, Ch. 5, Book IV, Ch. 1.
3. See Kant's *The Doctrine of Virtue*, ed. M. Gregor, New York: Harper, 1964, pp. 44f.
4. Sidgwick makes just this point in *Methods of Ethics*, seventh ed., p. 240.
5. Even given the (rough) self-other balance that common-sense virtue ethics assumes, it is not clear that it also assumes that individuals should be *equally* concerned with their own happiness and their own virtue, or that they should be *equally* concerned with the virtue and with the happiness of others. The topic calls for further elaboration, but I don't think we need to treat it any further here. I have also simplified by focusing on the development of (the) virtues in stating the content of our common-sense virtue ethics. But some admirable traits may

not count strictly as virtues, and our concern, in regard both to others and to ourselves, may also be with certain admirable *achievements*. In that case, our bipartite injunction is most generally and perhaps most plausibly stated as enjoining concern for one's own well-being and for what would in fact make one admirable and concern for the well-being and admirability of others.

6. On the subject of concern for the (moral) virtue or admirability of others, see Sidgwick, *op. cit.*, pp. 239ff.

# 7

## Virtue-Ethical Luck

We have now offered a highly general formulation of the fundamental ideas behind our common-sense virtue ethics, and we have also had several more specific things to say about the traits, acts, and motives that count as admirable or as deplorable by our common lights. However, we need to say more about how primarily self-regarding concepts like rationality, prudence, and sagacity fit into an overall virtue-ethical scheme and also about how such a scheme can deal in a general way with our relations to other people without making use of specifically moral concepts. But we will delay these further developments until the next chapter, because we seem to have a more pressing need to see how an ethics of virtue can escape the problems and contradictions that common-sense morality gives rise to in connection with the idea of moral luck. We should make sure that a common-sense ethics of virtue really can escape the perplexities and difficulties of Part I, before we proceed with the further elaboration of its positive content. And so we must focus once again on the problems of moral luck.

Even granting that our ethics of virtue makes use only of morally neutral concepts—that is, of concepts not specifically tied to the moral—we have seen that such concepts can have important, substantive implications for the evaluation of our treatment of other people; and of course virtue ethics also has important things to say about how we treat ourselves. So we may well feel the need to ask ourselves whether such concerns of virtue ethics may not give rise to problems, as it were, of virtue-ethical luck that are analogous, and just as deep and troublesome, as those encountered under the rubric of moral luck.

### Admirability and Luck

The issue of blameworthiness (or culpability or reprehensibility) is at the very heart of the issue of moral luck, because it is the idea that luck or accident can make a difference to blameworthiness, etc., that most grates against our antecedent moral intuitions. (Nagel uses the notion of culpability to make most of his points in "Moral Luck.") If we concentrate on praiseworthiness, the clash of intuitions is less evident or palpable because there is such a thing as non-moral praiseworthiness—we can praise an artistic performance or work that it would make no sense to regard as culpable or blameworthy—and because it is therefore not odd at all to suppose that non-moral praiseworthiness can sometimes depend on accident. Of course, we could distinguish moral praiseworthiness from praiseworthiness in general and claim that it grates on our intuitions to suppose that moral praiseworthiness can be subject to luck; but it is just easier to focus on blameworthiness, where ambiguity seems less capable of misleading us because all blameworthiness seems to be moral blameworthiness.

Clearly, the issue our virtue ethics must face is whether, by avoiding moral notions like blameworthiness, it can avoid difficulties and contradictions of the sort besetting our common-sense moral thinking. And since just about everything we do and feel is tinctured by some degree of luck or accident, we need to consider whether the ethical judgments we want to make in virtue ethics can non-controversially and even plausibly allow for luck and accident. Let us begin with a self-regarding case.

Consider a person who negligently hurts himself, damaging, say, some part of his body through carelessness or inattention while he is doing repairs to his home. In the normal course, we would not call such a person reprehensible, but we could certainly criticize—express a negative opinion of—his self-negligence and carelessness: we might, for example, say that it was foolish of him not to have paid more attention to what he was doing. And we therefore have here a fairly clear-cut example of how one may deplore or criticize behavior without making any attribution of blameworthiness.

However, the just-mentioned case is self-regarding, and since moral judgments of blameworthiness, etc., standardly or mainly apply in cases of other-regarding behavior, tendencies, or attitudes, it would be useful at this point if we could find an other-regarding example where our less than favorable evaluation of someone's actions, attitudes, or whatever commits us to no judgment of reprehensibility or blameworthiness. It would also be helpful if the negative or critical judgment in some degree depended on factors of luck and thereby enabled us to see the innocuousness of treating such a non-moral ethical judgment as subject to factors of luck. There are, in fact, a variety of such examples, and let me begin by citing one from the area of "role ethics."

To say that someone is or is not a good father or a good wife is to evaluate that person in a way that may not be clearly moral, but that clearly is, and is generally taken to be, ethical. One component of being a good father and, as we may now assume, a good mother as well is to be a good provider for one's family. Imagine, therefore, a father who is laid off work after many years on the job, but who, after several weeks of vain searching for another, comparable position, finds such a position through the sheerest luck (imagine, if you will, that thousands of people with his skills have been laid off and that they are in competition for the small number of positions requiring those skills that are available or opening up). In that case, if he takes the position and is again able to provide for his family in the manner to which they had been accustomed, he will eventually be considered to have been a good provider. But if, on the other hand, he had failed to find any good job and were never again able to provide his family with any sort of comfort, then the overall claim that he is or has been a good provider would be irremediably undercut. Circumstances of the sort just described are familiar from the historical example of the Great Depression of the 1930s, and in regard to such a period it seems in no way odd or problematic to claim that factors of luck played a (considerable) role in determining who was and who was not (able to be) a good provider for his family.

This conclusion fits in nicely with our earlier explanations of the problematic character of certain cases of moral or ethical luck. If luck with respect to being a good provider is less problematic than specifically moral luck, we have every reason at this point to attribute this difference to the unacceptable way in which moral judgments allow reprehensibility and the like to turn on accidental or fortuitous factors. Judgments about how good a provider someone has been can be (seen as) detached from any commitment to moral condemnation and allowed to function (merely) as forms of *ethical appraisal*, and it is certainly easy enough to see how a failure to be a good provider might in no way be either blameworthy or reprehensible. The people who were unable to find jobs in the Depression through no fault of their own cannot be considered to have been good providers, but in making such an appraisal we need not condemn or blame them; in fact it is difficult to see how anyone *could* blame them for failing, in such circumstances, to provide well for their families. (It is tragic that a whole generation of men and women should so largely have lacked access to this kind of normal human attainment, but that is another matter.)

So the just-mentioned example represents a clearly other-regarding case where evaluation hinges on factors of luck, but where, because moral blame and condemnation are entirely out of the picture, there seems to be nothing outré or offensive in supposing evaluation to depend, in part, on accidental circumstances. But other examples can be mentioned.

Consider someone who frequently turns on people unexpectedly—someone who acts angrily and/or aggressively toward people, without having been given the slightest provocation. We naturally think of such a person as vicious (as having, for example, a vicious streak in her), but the notion of viciousness at issue here is not the obsolete dictionary-notion of having many vices, but something much more specific of the angry, aggressive sort described just above. Obviously, viciousness in this sense has something important to do with a person's character and temperament, but I don't believe we automatically assume that every such vicious person can help being so or is morally responsible for having become or "turned" vicious. After all, the above characterization of viciousness is in no way incompatible with regarding certain *animals* as vicious. But in speaking thus of a vicious dog, we don't assume that the dog could have helped becoming vicious or is blameworthy for being so. It may have been made vicious by the cruel treatment of its master, and it is, and of course we know that it is, a matter of luck to some extent whether a given puppy is treated kindly or cruelly by those who raise it. Clearly, in the case of dogs, the judgment of viciousness in no way commits anyone to a judgment of reprehensibility or blameworthiness, and there is absolutely no reason to think human viciousness as described above should be conceived any differently.

We may know of a psychopathic killer that he was beaten and tortured as a child by his parents and so believe that through accident of birth and as a result of treatment he had no control over, he developed a vicious streak or, worse, became a vicious killer. But again this needn't commit us to seeing him as blameworthy for being what he is or for acting accordingly—we may merely want to stop him and, assuming he is unreformable, put him out of social circulation for a very long time. When we call a dog vicious or claim someone is a vicious killer or psychopath we are clearly evaluating in a non-superficial and important way, but such a negative assessment of what someone or something is deeply like does not commit us to the moral evaluations that land us in such difficulties in connection with luck. The vicious killer may not be able to help being as he is or acting as he does, but in characterizing him as we do, we are expressing a highly negative opinion about him. We are saying that one way he (centrally or deeply) is is a terrible way to be, and the example is a good one, therefore, of the possibility of ethical criticism without moral blame.

Finally, and briefly, one further illustrative example. A given person may relate poorly to other people, and the explanation of this fact may be that the person, through the bad luck of heredity, is psychotic. But the explanation doesn't undercut what it is supposed to explain; it leaves the criticism of how the person relates to others entirely intact, but simply gives us reason not to blame her, or find her blameworthy, for the way she deals with others. Of course, given a commitment to common-sense moral ideas, we may indeed wish to blame certain non-psychotic people for the way they relate to others. But the important point to be made here is that the mere or pure judgment/claim that someone relates poorly to other people (or has a vicious streak, etc.) commits us to nothing in the line of blame or blameworthiness—since it can be made both in cases where we find blame appropriate and cases where we do not and it is linguistically implausible to suppose the term is ambiguous across such differing cases (on this last point, more will be said below).

## Criticism Without Blame

We can thus adopt a perspective that sees certain things a person does as better or worse, that allows us to judge him more or less admirable or criticizable, without finding ourselves committed to specifically moral judgments, and that is the perspective from which a non-egoistic virtue ethics that avoids moral concepts insists on judging performance, motive, and character. Common-sense virtue ethics can avoid all common-sense or other *moral* judgments and restrict itself to intuitively plausible judgments of admirability and deplorability *that have no essential connection to blameworthiness*,[1] and what results from our move in this direction is a form of ethics that is already perhaps familiar from the example of Spinoza and that is also interestingly analogous to ordinary *aesthetic* evaluation.

In the *Ethics*, Spinoza argues against free will and rules out the possibility of valid blaming, or of blameworthiness, even though he also wishes to make claims about what human traits count as virtues and what traits count as vices or weaknesses.[2] According to Spinoza, reason can operate in man even in the absence of libertarian conditions of freedom, and true virtue means acting or living according to reason. But Spinoza's view of virtue is fundamentally egoistic: he allows a distinction between other-regarding virtues of nobility and self-regarding virtues of courage, but seems to regard concern for others as virtuous solely as a means to the individual's well-being.

Here, of course, we are not adopting an egoistic view of (the) virtue(s), but despite that difference from Spinoza's conception of virtue, Spinoza's system of thought allows us (better) to see how evaluation of action and character can take place in the absence of attributions of moral praise- and blameworthiness. Spinoza commends and recommends some forms of activity and disposition, while criticizing and attempting to dissuade us from certain others, but all this occurs in the absence of various familiar kinds of fault-finding moral judgment, and I believe there is no inconsistency in our own pursuit, therefore, of a form of moral-no-fault ethical evaluation that in addition places a fundamental emphasis on concern for others in a way that Spinoza does not.

In urging such a course of development for virtue ethics, we are making ethics in certain ways seem more like aesthetics, because like the latter we are committed to criticizing and praising without blaming. To be sure, we can moralize our relations to artists and art and speak of an immoral painting, as so many people have done over the centuries. And we can also criticize an artist as immoral for painting in a certain way or with certain subjects. But I hope we can all see the point of eliminating such judgments from aesthetics or treating them as irrelevant to aesthetic judgment, and as such aesthetic forms of evaluation do seem to offer an interesting model for—or some interesting analogies with—Spinoza's ethics and the virtue conception of ethics that is underway in this book.

We think better of some works of art than of others, and we may criticize the latter in very strong terms, but none of this need lead us to finding works of art or their artists, blameworthy, reprehensible, or culpable. And if, as I am proposing, we allow ourselves to think better or worse of certain acts and traits without committing ourselves to blaming those we think worse, or worst, of, then at least to that extent we are treating virtue on analogy with aesthetic merit. Such an analogy is nothing new: surely there is *some* significance in the fact that Greek and Greek philosophers use a term for honorableness or nobility that can also just mean "beautiful" and function as a term of purely aesthetic evaluation.[3] But we are not here simply limited to analogies with aesthetic evaluation. Baseball is not yet a fine art and praise and criticism for the performances of teams in the World Series, even if they aren't either aesthetic or ethical, needn't bring in issues of blameworthiness or culpability. ("Bonehead" Merkle may have lost his team the World Series through foolish inattention, but anyone who—as opposed to merely, in a more, neutral causal sense, blaming the Series loss on him—actually regards him as blame*worthy* for what he did has gone beyond evaluation in baseball terms to specifically moral criticism. However, sometimes such criticism is in order, as, for example, when the "Blacksox" were bribed to throw games in the 1919 World Series.) We can also deplore or admire a person's intelligence or lack of it, without having to suppose that someone can rightly be blamed for doing things a natively more intelligent person would not have done. And, of course, our examples of not providing well, of viciousness, and of relating poorly to other people have nothing to do with aesthetic evaluation. So the conception of evaluation being offered here is not exclusively or distinctively aesthetic, even if the analogy with aesthetics, among others, may clear the way for a better understanding of the ethical view I am elaborating.

What I am proposing for ethics in the end comes down to the assumption that "admirable" and "deplorable" (and "laudable" and "criticizable") are univocal across the broad range of cases where we apply them. We may call an other-regarding trait of character or a philosophy book or a painting or a self-regarding action admirable without the meaning of the term varying across the wide spectrum of such ascriptions. The justifying reasons for the ascriptions may widely differ, but that, of course, is another matter. When we ascribe existence to different kinds of entities or describe different sorts of arguments as bad arguments, our reasons may vary, but, in the light of the work of Quine and others, it is less and less plausible to suppose that "exists" or "bad argument" is being used ambiguously. And I think we have every reason to adopt the same attitude toward the different uses we can make of "admirable" and "deplorable."[4] And I can see no reason, therefore, to suppose that moral concepts must be involved in our assessments of character any more than they are involved in aesthetics or in the evaluation of the playing of games (or in the evaluation of basic intelligence to the extent this is *not* an aspect of someone's *character*). If the refusal to give expression to some of (what Strawson has called) our "reactive emotions" is a sign of detachment or objectivity or impersonality, then these last epithets may apply to the Spinozan-like perspective that our proposed virtue ethics adopts. But it adopts that perspective only for theoretical purposes, and an ethics of virtue might well be as contented to remain esoteric as utilitarian conceptions of ethics seem happy to do.[5] And so nothing in the common-sense virtue-ethical approach to ethics (and it is "common-sense" only in regard to the judgments it makes, not in regard to the moral judgments, common-sense or otherwise, that it excludes) requires us to suppose that people ought to become more detached and/or less willing to find things blameworthy. It holds that any judgments of blameworthiness people make are doubtfully true and subject to enormous theoretical difficulties; but it can or could allow that people are better off not knowing or at least not dwelling on those problems, and it may, therefore, have no basis for objection if those who accept it refuse to promulgate it and themselves go back to old habits of praising and blaming once they are outside the philosopher's study.

Thus virtue ethics may differ from the utilitarian approach by making no use of specifically moral judgments or concepts, but still take a page from the utilitarian book by distinguishing between the theoretically valid and the practically useful. For Spinoza, of course, the person who takes to heart the theoretical lessons of the *Ethics* will be more virtuous and better off. But an ethics of virtue need not, though it may, make the assumption that greater virtue means greater well-being or happiness (a topic we return to in Part III) and, in any case, it need not assume that knowledge of its own theoretical truth is a primary virtue or plays an important role in making people virtuous. I want to remain neutral on these issues—the common-sense virtue-ethical approach has enough problems to occupy it without having to leave further hostages to intellectual fortune—but the issues are nonetheless worth mentioning at this point if only because of the interesting stands that have been taken on them by others, for example, Spinoza and the utilitarians.

However, our main objective has been to show how a non-moral virtue ethics can avoid the paradox and contradiction that arises in common-sense morality with respect to moral luck, and we have attempted to do this by showing how a virtue ethics that avoids both specifically moral concepts and common-sense or other moral judgments can safely accommodate itself to luck and accident, that is, to their partial role in determining what virtue-ethical attributions apply or fail to apply.[6] But since our virtue ethics will not make moral judgments or claims of blameworthiness, in particular, it seems important to give further, more detailed attention to what our approach can or cannot say about interpersonal relations. So although, in the next chapter and the one following, there is more to be said about self-regarding virtues, we will also focus on the evaluation of other-regarding actions and traits. We must see whether common-sense virtue ethics has enough, and enough that is plausible, to say about the ethical assessment of our relations to others.

# Notes

1. In "Involuntary Sins" (*Philosophical Review* 94, 1985, pp. 3–31), R. M. Adams seems to hold that blame is appropriate in cases where an agent hurts only himself and where we would criticize him, say, for the negligence that led to his being hurt. And he points out that we would naturally say that such a person was

"to blame for" the damage he had caused himself. Even so, it would not be natural to call such a person blameworthy or reprehensible for what he had done merely to himself (in the absence of other-affecting obligations, etc.). Just as "responsible" can be used in an ethically neutral causal way (the hurricane was responsible for the damage), so can "to blame for" (the hurricane was to blame for the damage). Adams's examples therefore give us no reason to hold that serious ethical criticism of a person's intentional actions always commits one to an ascription of blameworthiness.

2. The following places in the *Ethics* are relevant to our discussion of Spinoza: Part 1, Appendix; Part 3, Prop. LIX; Part 4, Props. XVIII, XX, XXIII, XXIV, XXXVII, LXVII, LXXIII and Appendix XXIX; Part 5, Prop. XLII.

For another attempt to separate ethical criticism from ascriptions of blameworthiness, see L. Blum's *Friendship, Altruism, and Morality* (Routledge and Kegan Paul, 1980, esp. p. 189). Blum's point, however, is that specifically *moral* criticism sufficient to justify one in thinking ill of someone need not entitle one to blame that person (e.g., for her attitudes or values). If this is really so, then it should be all the easier to show that *non-moral* ethical criticism can be separated from blaming and/ or ascriptions of blameworthiness. (For another attempt to disengage moral evaluation from ascriptions of blameworthiness, see my *Goods and Virtues*, Oxford, 1990, pp. 56f. For a dissenting view, see Adams, *op. cit.*, p. 23.)

3. Nagel (*op. cit.*) suggests that the problems raised by moral luck may induce one to replace moral attitudes with "aesthetic or other evaluative analogues of the moral attitudes that are thus displaced."

4. The term "virtue" may not be (quite so) unambiguous. We speak of the virtues of a knife and can say that some characteristic is a virtue *in a knife*, but to say *tout court* that some trait or attribute is a virtue is normally to imply that it is a virtue *of character* (and not of some mere thing). If this amounts to ambiguity, it is like the ambiguity of "soluble," which we use in phrases like "soluble in aqua regia," but whose ascription *tout court* would normally imply solubility *in water*.

5. It is not clear that someone for whom blame seems an inappropriate or incorrect attitude to take with respect to other people and who accepts such a view as a result of adopting an ethics of virtue of the sort I am in the process of proposing need feel that it is inappropriate or incorrect to feel anger or, for that matter, gratitude toward others. The latter are regarded as among the reactive emotions, but different theoretical or personal views may have differing implications for the attitudes to which the label "reactive" has been applied.

6. Although arguments against moral praise- and blameworthiness are most typically based on a denial of freedom of will, we have been arguing here on the basis of the contradictions involved in our intuitions about moral luck that we have some reason to consider discarding the notions of moral praise- and blameworthiness. Note, however, that if one does so in the manner suggested here, there will be less motive in general to defend the existence of free will or its compatibility with determinism (or indeterminism). For more on this topic see my "Ethics Without Free Will," *Social Theory and Practice 16*, 1990, pp. 369–83.

# 8

## Virtue, Self, and Other

I have been saying that the virtue ethics to be developed here will be immune to the paradox, incoherence, and other defects we pointed out in common-sense and Kantian morality. To a substantial extent, we have already made good this claim by showing how a virtue ethics based on common-sense views (but ignoring the claims of common-sense *morality*) can use various evaluative notions to assess both self-regarding and other-regarding actions and attributes, without falling into the paradoxes of moral luck that arise within our common-sense *moral* thinking. The price we have to pay—if at this point we are really convinced it is a price—is an inability (at least theoretically) to justify the claims of blameworthiness, reprehensibility, etc., that discussants of moral luck have seen as primarily responsible for its paradoxes.[1]

But earlier, in Chapter 3, we discussed some other difficulties of common-sense morality that must finally be dealt with. And it is also time to make good on the claim that what is acceptable in the common-sense ethics of the rational and the moral can be generated from common-sense virtue-ethical foundations that lack the asymmetries that exist within each of these two areas of common-sense thinking. Despite its agent-favoring self-other asymmetrical character, we have been given no reason to suppose that common-sense practical rationality is subject to the *incoherences* of our ordinary moral thinking, and I propose to turn first to the challenge of deriving our intuitive ideas about self-regarding rationality—or at least some of the most important of them—from within a virtue-ethical framework. Thereafter, we will examine just how much of our ordinary moral thought can be covered—in its own way, using its own vocabulary—by virtue ethics without generating all over again the difficulties that undercut common-sense morality in the first place. But what we are now embarking on is more than an exercise in completeness, and our (at first) separate discussions of self-regarding and other-regarding virtue(s) will in the course of the present chapter enable us to see that these two "sorts" or areas of virtue are more closely related,

126

more of a piece, than they are usually thought to be (even by defenders of virtue ethics).

## Virtue Ethics and Self-Regarding Rationality

We implicitly think of traits such as prudence, providence, judiciousness, far-sightedness, circumspection, policy (the trait of being politic), patience, consistency, self-control, and moderation as virtues of a largely, though not exclusively, self-regarding kind.[2] (Carelessness, imprudence, impolicy, impatience, etc. are similarly self-regarding.) These virtues all naturally fall under the rubric of practical rationality; they are all virtues of practical reason, and failures to act in accordance with or to possess some measure of these traits are typically criticized as irrational. Since, however, what we ordinarily regard as irrational can be criticized and deplored as such, the fundamental terms of virtue-ethical evaluation, "admirable," "deplorable," "strongly criticizable" all clearly apply to what are commonsensically regarded as instances of self-regarding practical rationality or its opposite.

However, it is worth noting that there are at least two general forms of rational criticism available in our ordinary thinking about rationality. We can criticize some disposition or action as irrational or rationally unacceptable[3], but it in some sense also counts as criticism if one says that some disposition or act, while not irrational or rationally unacceptable, falls short of some ideal of practical rationality or is less than the rationally best a person could have had/done in her particular circumstances.[4]

Someone might, for example, exhibit what we would call self-control, moderation, far-sightedness, or providence about her personal affairs in such a way as to justify us in calling her self-controlled, moderate, provident, or far-sighted and even admiring her for her possession of these traits. Yet we might not regard that person as being every bit as moderate or self-controlled as Socrates or as provident or far-sighted as Bernard Baruch before the 1929 stock market crash. So if she has the virtues mentioned above, she doesn't have them to the highest possible degree, in the most ideal possible way we can envisage, and in the light of the comparisons just mentioned and, indeed, independently of those comparisons we may recognize that the woman herself could possess, or could have possessed, moderation, providence, far-sightedness, self-control to a higher degree than she actually does. And similar points hold for actions, so that a particular act that we think of as admirably provident or self-controlled needn't, intuitively speaking, be regarded as the most provident or self-controlled act the agent could have performed in the circumstances, much less as ideally provident or self-controlled.

In allowing ourselves to think in this manner, we are in a most unAristotelian way making room for supererogatory degrees of virtue or admirability. We are saying that an act or person may exemplify a virtue or be admirable even though certain relevant alternatives would have exemplified the virtue to an even greater extent, would have been even more admirable. And indeed it is perhaps easiest to recognize the common-sense force of this idea if we consider how we would have regarded Bernard Baruch if (like few enough others, certainly) he had sold only two-thirds of his common stock before the crash, rather than, as legend has it, all of it. Even then he would have been regarded as admirably provident and far-sighted, though he probably would not have represented—as I believe he does—the practically superhuman ideal of providence, foresight, etc., that he actually does represent to many of us. But in the area of self-control there are similar examples to be found: that is, examples of (the virtue of) self-control that nonetheless fail to embody ideal or even optimal self-control. In part, because I have had more to say about such examples elsewhere, I shall not discuss them any further here.[5] But it is well worth noting, in the present context, that Aristotle's failure to make room for supererogatory degrees of rationality makes his views seem distinctly less commonsensical (can ordinary Greek thought really have been so vastly different, in this respect, from our own?) than the picture of practical rationality as a virtue or set of virtues that is being offered in these pages.

According to Aristotle, virtuous acts represent unique solutions to the practical issues offered to given individuals by various situations that present themselves to them, and acts that in any way fall short of (or exceed) what virtue requires are not virtuous (even though there may be no reason to decry or criticize them).[6] And basically the same idea, in a modern guise, is present in Donald Davidson's view (roughly) that it is not rational to act in a given way when one believes that there is some available alternative action that one has, on balance, more reason to perform and which, in that case, it would be better (where "better" is by no means restricted to moral considerations) to perform.[7] So if commonsense ideas about practical rationality and about what is admirable or a virtue call for some notion of supererogation in this area, then such common sense goes against a long tradition of philosophical thinking that has implicitly or explicitly denied the possibility of rational (as opposed to moral) supererogation.

Elsewhere, I have argued at considerable length, using arguments that needn't be repeated, that practical rationality admits of supererogatory degrees. But when we subsume practical rationality under the more general notions of virtue, admirability, and their opposites, we are given further evidence for this conclusion by the very obviousness of the ways in which the latter notions intuitively admit of degrees when applied to the narrower area of practical rationality: to issues of providence, self-control, and the like. And we are also moved in this direction by the way, with respect to the attribution of particular rational virtues, our ordinary thinking accepts the idea of supererogation. Self-control, patience, providence, and the other virtues we mentioned earlier on in this chapter can all be ranked under the genus: virtue of practical reason. And this may well allow us to treat practical rationality as a "generic virtue" under which self-control and the like rank as specific virtues (species of virtue). But in that case it seems as natural to allow rationality and admirability to admit of supererogatory degrees as it seems natural to think of self-control, patience, and other rational virtues as admitting of such degrees.[8] Since it seems entirely reasonable to say things like "John is patient (or self-controlled or prudent) but Jill is *even more* patient (or self-controlled or prudent)," we have still further reason, therefore, to question and perhaps discard the age-old (implicit) theoretical assumption that practical rationality does not allow for supererogation. (Indeed, most philosophers automatically take the term "supererogation" to refer to moral supererogation.)

However, at this point one might begin to wonder whether all (primarily) self-regarding virtues fall under the genus practical rationality (or, if you prefer, practical wisdom). I think not.

Consider fortitude, the ability/disposition (roughly) to remain unperturbed or at least active in the face of adversity. We admire fortitude, for the most part, but I wonder whether we have any reason to think of people with that trait as more *rational* than they otherwise would be. Certainly, one may be better off for having fortitude in certain circumstances, but one may also sometimes be better off being happy-go-lucky, yet we hardly think of that trait as a form of rationality. Perhaps the best argument for the rational status of fortitude is that that trait embodies, indeed must embody, an attitude of hopefulness, as opposed to despair, that is an absolute condition of practical rational effectiveness in salvaging whatever good one can from otherwise adverse situations. But I find this argument less than totally convincing, and, more important, even in the absence of convincing proof that fortitude is a form of practical rationality, we can admire fortitude and treat it as a virtue. We admire the ability to bear with and toil on through hardship, turmoil, and adversity, rather than be undermined, demoralized, or incapacitated by such factors, but it is unclear whether fortitude thus understood is valued under the general rubric of rationality rather than, perhaps more straightforwardly and simply, as a kind of personal strength or resilience.[9] And yet fortitude is a primarily self-regarding virtue, admired more for what it does for or demonstrates about its possessors than for its beneficial effects on other people. So not all self-regarding virtues need count as forms or species of practical rationality.

But neither, in addition, must we regard all self-regarding virtues as beneficial to their possessors or treat all self-beneficial traits of character (that allow for other-regarding virtue) as admirable, as virtues. Consider the numerous authors who have recommended (irrational leaps of) faith as a salve to men's minds and have also said that if God didn't exist, it would be better for the generality of mankind not to know it.[10] Such talk implies that in the relevant circumstances the noble, brave, strong few ought to face the truth about God's non-existence, and the high estimation of truth implicit in this judgment seems incompatible with claiming that the beneficial tendency to ignore, or deceive oneself about the evidence for, God's non-existence should be regarded as a virtue. And indeed it intuitively makes very good sense to distinguish in this way between what benefits us or makes us better off, on the one hand, and what constitutes an admirable trait, a virtue, on the other.

Self-deception, for example, may have its *uses*, and an incurable cancer victim may, in a sense we can all understand, benefit from his ability to misread or deceive himself about the evidence that he has terminal cancer (which will often include facts about the ways his friends and relations are treating him, in addition to medical evidence). But we commonly regard such a person as less to be admired than someone who faces similar facts squarely, who has the courage to look death in the face, who is less dishonest with himself, even when or if we are willing to concede that the latter may suffer more and be worse off for the knowledge he refuses to evade.[11] So it seems perfectly in keeping with common-sense notions of virtue and admirability to allow that certain virtues—for example, the courage to face certain very unpleasant facts—may not (even other things being equal) benefit those who possess them and that certain self-beneficial character traits—for example, certain sorts of refusal to face facts—may not count as virtues or be considered admirable.

Since, moreover, the courage to face unpleasant facts is admired neither for its benefits to possessors nor for the benefits it may bring to other people, it should be clear at this point that in common-sense terms at least a trait of character may be admirable independently of its ability to benefit *anyone*. To be sure, the person who faces the facts of his cancer squarely may spare his relations the effort of keeping up a certain deception and to that extent his attitude may benefit other people. But it may also be more difficult to avoid a state of depression or panic if one admits to having terminal cancer, and to that extent, one may cause more hardship or heartache for others if one doesn't deceive oneself or allow oneself to be deceived about one's condition. In any event, it seems clear enough that our comparatively greater admiration for the person who is honest with himself about his condition is not based on supposed facts about the comparative benefits, either to oneself or to others, of facing the facts vs. self-deception. Given the value we place on strength of mind and knowing the truth, we are inclined to *think better of* the person who faces his cancer even while agreeing that he isn't, or may not, be *better off* for being able to do so. And I believe similar considerations can be used to show, at least in common-sense terms, that certain other virtues also lack such a connection, as virtues, to the well-being either of their possessors or of other people.[12]

Take modesty, either in the sense of lacking vanity or in the sense of moderation in one's desires or aspirations. A person who is not boastful is more likely to be admired than someone who is, and clearly we often want to criticize or deplore the self-flaunting self-congratulatory behavior of the immodest. But if such behavior sometimes brings people unpleasant doubts about their own worth, it is also often ridiculous and highly amusing. So I don't think we prefer modesty to immodesty because it brings a greater balance of benefits, and it should be clear that our admiration for modesty is not predicated on the fact that it pleases us. We may get pleasure from the contemplation of the modesty of others and the virtue of modesty can give pleasure to those possessing the trait who find themselves on one or another occasion (easily) able to resist a situational temptation to be vain or immodest. But these pleasures *presuppose* the value, the virtue-status, the admirability of modesty rather than constituting the *basis* of such value, etc. Just as the pleasure an altruist gets from helping others presupposes (on his part) the independent value of helping others, so too the pleasant admiration and the sense of self-fulfillment that naturally or usually attend instances of modesty are based on an independent sense of the value, the admirability, of modesty (in the sense opposed to vanity and boasting). But somewhat similar points can also be made about modesty in the sense of moderation, and these give rise to what may be an even more interesting example of a virtue that is neither self-beneficial or beneficial to other people.

Moderation has sometimes been regarded—for example, by the Epicu-reans—as a purely instrumental self-regarding virtue, as a means by which its possessors have an overall happier or less unhappy life than they would have if they were greedy or inclined in every situation to eke out the most good, the most pleasure, possible. And moderation or a lack of greediness has also sometimes been regarded as a purely instrumental *other-regarding* virtue, as, for example, when Aristotle treats *pleonexia* (sometimes translated as "greed") as the desire/tendency to take more than one's share of goods. Now I have no desire to deny that modesty or moderation in one's desires can be valued for purely instrumental rea-sons, but such considerations do not, I believe, exhaust our reasons for thinking highly of moderation and (other things being equal) of moderate individuals. I think we also have purely intrinsic reasons for admiring moderation, and I think the best proof of this may lie in the fact that we sometimes admire moderation even when it (non-accidentally) leads to less overall good for its possessor and for others.

It is standard in economics, decision theory, and various areas of philosophy to assume that a truly rational individual maximizes his utility, always seeks what is (expectably) best for himself—at least in situations where moral and/or altruistic considerations are not in play. I have, however, elsewhere argued that a certain kind of modesty or moderation we think well of would incline one not to try for one's own greatest good in certain circumstances and perhaps even sometimes to reject what would be absolutely best for one in favor of what is (merely) good and sufficient, or good enough, for one's purposes.[13] This is not the time to review those arguments and go through all the examples enlisted in behalf of the intuitive, the common-sense plausibility of the idea of admirable non-optimizing rationality. But I might, for present purposes, just mention the way we sometimes turn down afternoon snacks (or second or third desserts or cups of tea) because, as we say, we are just fine as we are.

Someone who says such a thing need not, and probably will not, think that she wouldn't enjoy an afternoon snack or that, as a result, taking such a snack wouldn't count for her as a good thing (a small ephemeral good thing in her life). For if one is moderate in one's desires/needs, one will sometimes turn down what one would be perfectly willing to admit to be something good on the grounds that it represents much more than one needs (or cares about) and that one is, in any event, fine as one is (perfectly contented as one is). Moderate individuals may be perfectly, thoroughly satisfied even when they (implicitly) know that they are in a position to do slightly or somewhat better for themselves, and, as I said, I have argued at considerable length that such an attitude is not open to criticism in common-sense rational terms.

But, more relevantly to our present discussion, such a moderate attitude seems admirable to many of us, even though, and perhaps indeed just because, it refuses to optimize or maximize with regard to individual or personal good. The person who always tries to eke out the most or best for herself seems unspontaneous and constrained, as well as needy and lacking in self-sufficiency, by comparison with a moderate individual who (on non-instrumental non-other-regarding grounds) is satisfied with the good and sufficient. (As such, the moderate individual doesn't qualify as an ascetic.) And intuitively we admire self-sufficiency and spontaneity. Our admiration for the latter tends to some extent to dampen our esteem for the virtue of prudence, and self-sufficiency (though the Stoics exaggerated its claims and treated it as practically the whole of virtue) is a quality we tend to admire in people quite apart from the good it does for them or for others. Of course, someone who turns down a good thing because he feels he is (doing) just fine as he is may gain a pleased sense of self-sufficiency from doing so, but that pleasure need no more overbalance the goods the moderate person forgoes than the pleased sense of having done one's duty in defending one's country need be regarded as overbalancing the losses sustained by a soldier who dies in battle. The soldier may well lose in terms of overall personal good—we have no good reason to suppose he does not; and the very same thing can be said about someone who deliberately turns down greater heights of well-being or personal good—she doesn't automatically some-how gain, overall, by doing so.

Self-sufficiency of the sort we find in the attitude of non-instrumental moderation seems admirable apart from the overall benefits (if any) that it brings. (Our admiring attitude toward fortitude—as well as equanim-ity— may also in part depend on the self-sufficiency these traits appear to exemplify.) Though a fuller argument—of the kind I have attempted to provide in *Beyond Optimizing*—may be necessary to present a convinc-ing case for the admirability of moderation quite apart from any benefits it brings the moderate individual or other people, I think the reader can see in outline how such an argument would proceed. So the virtue status of modesty in the sense of moderation in one's needs or desires is arguably independent of the benefits that character trait brings either to its possessors or to other people, and we have yet another (potential) example of the ways in which, commonsensically at least, a character trait may be seen as a virtue and be highly regarded and admired in the absence of explicit or implicit assumptions about the overall benefits of having or being around people with that trait.

By contrast, utilitarianism, like epicureanism, makes no room for (purely or predominantly) non-instrumental virtues—treats character traits as admirable only to the extent that they further the good of their possessor (as in epicureanism) or the overall good of sentient beings (as in utilitarianism). But for ordinary ways of thinking, there are other sorts of sources or bases for virtue status, and it is therefore more difficult for a common-sense virtue ethics of the sort described here to be explicit about the ways in which acts or traits can be admirable. As with common-sense morality, a common-sense virtue ethics doesn't seek to impose a single pattern or principle on all the forms of value it acknowledges. It does not say that all virtue is due to benefits for the possessor of virtue or is to be accounted for in terms of the general good of humanity (or sentient life)—and precisely because it denies itself such a simple or systematically unified view of the sources of admirability or virtue status, it leaves itself appealing to a seeming plurality of intuitions and quite possibly unable to divide those intuitions into a finite number of distinct classes that can confidently be said to exhaust our intuitive sources of virtue and anti-virtue status. I am certainly not willing to claim that the sources of admirability and its opposite that have been or are to be mentioned in these pages exhaust all our intuitive bases for ascribing these attributes—virtue ethics has a long way to go beyond the sketch and general defense of it offered at such already considerable length in the present book. But I do want to remind the reader of the stand taken earlier in regard to plurality and system-building in ethics.

The paradoxes and difficulties that beset common-sense and Kantian morality may give us reason to reject these approaches to (aspects of) ethics, but they do not, I believe, call into question the validity of proceeding in an intuitive, pluralistic, and (if you insist) sloppy—as opposed to theoretically neat—way *as long as we remain free of inconsistency, paradox, and similar difficulties.* So as long as a common-sense virtue ethics can remain free of the difficulties found in common-sense morality and Kantian ethics, I can think of no reason why we may not continue developing such an ethics along the present lines. (But we have still, of course, to see whether our virtue-ethical approach can avoid *all* the problems of common-sense morality and Kantianism.)

It is also worth mentioning that our reliance on intuition precisely allows us here to avoid the sort of underdetermination that led us in Chapter 4 to develop, even prefer, a scalar form of utilitarian consequentialism. Because utilitarians typically are reluctant to place much reliance on considerations of intuitiveness, we saw it to be difficult for utilitarianism either to defend its more familiar optimizing/maximizing formulations of the principle of utility over satisficing versions or to defend satisficing over optimizing. And for similar reasons the utilitarian is unable to defend any one form of satisficing over all others, so if we restrict ourselves to fundamental utilitarian motivations and assumptions, it is difficult to avoid going scalar. But common-sense virtue ethics does rely on intuitions, and, as we saw above, our intuitions tell us that virtue can exist in non-optimizing embodiments. Furthermore, I am inclined to believe that, allowing for a certain degree of vagueness, our ordinary sense of what is rational and moral can help us to answer complex questions about how much virtue is enough—that is, about how much is enough to count as an instance of one or another particular virtue in one or another set of circumstances. Virtue ethics certainly can make scalar judgments over different dimensions and on balance as between different dimensions, but at this point I see no reason to doubt that it can intuitively make the full range of positive, that is, non-scalar, non-comparative, judgments as well. It is time for us now, however, to consider some important ways in which the present approach allows an interesting and, I believe, desirable degree of unification in the way we understand self-regarding and other-regarding virtues.

## Connecting Self-Regarding with Other-Regarding Virtues

Ordinary moral thinking deals with questions concerning honesty, loyalty, and trustworthiness toward other people, and considers dishonesty, deception, disloyalty, and untrustworthiness to ground conclusions about moral wrongness somewhat independently of the badness of consequences. However, we have now argued that certain mainly self-regarding characteristics may be valued and admired independently of their effect on people's well-being, so even if some other-regarding character traits (like benevolence and sympathy) are admired (in part) for their links to the well-being of others, there seems to be no reason why other such traits shouldn't be esteemed to some extent independently of their good effects on people other than the trait-possessor.

Thus there is nothing particularly odd about the fact that we tend to deplore and strongly criticize (instances of) dishonesty, deception, untrustworthiness, disloyalty, inconstancy, and unreliability even though our intuitive sense of what is deplorable about them cannot be cashed out in completely consequentialistic or utilitarian terms. And our ability to criticize such actions and traits, as well as others, like meanness, with a more thoroughgoing connection to the interests of other people, means that common-sense virtue ethics can cover much of the ground that essentially other-regarding common-sense morality covers. But it does so without use of a specifically moral critical vocabulary and so has a chance to avoid the theoretical/ethical difficulties that infect our common-sense *moral* thinking. Virtue ethics is capable of criticizing many of the things which, from a standpoint within ordinary morality, we want to criticize and recommend against, but it does so with terms like "deplorable" rather than with "blameworthy" or "reprehensible." To that extent common-sense virtue ethics is less colorful, perhaps more "bloodless," than common-sense morality. "Reprehensible" definitely seems stronger, more forceful, as a term of criticism than "deplorable" or even "*utterly* deplorable." And since, other things being equal and perhaps being even to a substantial extent unequal, we want to be able to use the strongest possible negative language to express our absolute horror at or condemnation for the behavior, for example, of a Hitler or Stalin, the common-sense ethics of virtue defended here is asking people to make a considerable sacrifice in their powers of criticism.

However, other things may be sufficiently unequal so that such a sacrifice is (at least theoretically) justified, worth it. I have argued that the paradoxes and problems that beset common-sense morality seemingly from every side—and that most excruciatingly arise in connection with terms like "reprehensible" and "blameworthy" as they are applied in putative cases of moral luck—justify us in looking for a form of ethical view that can avoid those paradoxes and problems. And if, as we have seen, utilitarianism can avoid, for example, the problems of moral luck by gerrymandering or rethinking the notion of blameworthiness, then there may be equal justification in attempting to develop a theory, an ethical view, that avoids such problems by abandoning the concept of blameworthiness altogether in favor of a theoretically less problematic vocabulary of criticism and commendation.

But it is also important to remember that virtue ethics is concerned with self-regarding traits and actions in a way that common-sense morality distinctly is not and to recognize, further, that (as the reader may well already have realized) the (non-consequentialistic) other-regarding traits mentioned above all have self-regarding analogues. Although some philosophers have denied the very possibility of self-deception, our common-sense thinking clearly believes there is such a thing and also that there is such a thing as the deception of other people. But dishonesty with oneself is also intuitively regarded as being in a different moral boat from dishonesty or deception toward others. And a similar opinion surfaces when we compare other commonsensically moral phenomena with their self-regarding analogues. One can be considered untrustworthy not only for deception in regard to the truth or falsity of certain claims or propositions, but for being unreliable and/or untrustworthy in ways that do not so centrally focus on the issue of truthfulness, and a person who blows hot and cold toward his friends or is erratic in the performance of his other-regarding duties can quite naturally be the target of moral criticism made from a common-sense point of view. But there are self-regarding analogues of such unreliability and untrustworthiness toward others, and one nice example emerges from an examination of frequent or repeated weakness of will. A person who through moral or other weakness often fails to act on his (best) intentions displays a kind of self-regarding untrustworthiness or unreliability that doesn't exactly amount to self-deception or a disregard for truth, and he may appropriately criticize himself and be criticized by others for (acting from) such weakness of will. Indeed, a person who has vowed to stop drinking may be deeply chagrined and shaken by his own frequent backslidings, and he may deplore his own self-regarding untrustworthiness (or inconstancy or unreliability) in terms as bitter as those with which he would castigate instances of other-regarding untrustworthiness either on his own part or on the part of others.

Or take another example. Both common-sense morality and common-sense virtue ethics will be highly critical of the disloyalty of someone who betrays his friend or lover's secrets (as, e.g., Robert Lowell apparently did with things Elizabeth Hardwick had revealed to him in letters), or who betrays his friend or lover to the Gestapo, or who refuses to help a friend or lover when she most needs help. Such people would normally be considered to have behaved badly or deplorably toward other people, but it is interesting to note that self-regarding betrayal or disloyalty can also easily give rise in us to a belief that someone has acted badly or deplorably. When Wordsworth, later in life, said that he would be willing to give up his life for the (established) Church of England, many people regarded him as having betrayed his own earlier social and political ideals, and such betrayal is also naturally regarded as a kind of disloyalty to the person one once, so desirably, was, to one's better, but earlier self. In this example, the intrapersonally intertemporal runs parallel to (issues raised by) the interpersonal, but unlike most other cases of this sort, the present pairing of intertemporally self-regarding and interpersonally other-regarding examples involves a comparison of virtues, of admirable features, rather than a comparison with respect to rationality or life's goods.[14]

However, the connection between kinds of self-regarding honesty, trustworthiness, and loyalty and different kinds of other-regarding honesty, trustworthiness, and loyalty is frequently unnoticed in moral-theoretic discussions of the latter. In such discussions, self-regarding honesty, trustworthiness, and loyalty are either (largely) ignored or treated as special (or degenerate or irrelevant) cases, and the reason may lie in the pervasively self-other asymmetric character of common-sense morality.[15] Honesty or dishonesty, trustworthiness or untrustworthiness, loyalty or disloyalty, toward oneself alone (and with no implications for how well one treats other people) are intuitively not regarded as bases either for moral praise or moral criticism.

But once one drops the agent-sacrificing approach to ethics and allows oneself to notice, or dwell on, the fact, for example, that frequent weakness of will can understandably give rise to the accusation, or self-accusation, of self-regarding untrustworthiness, one may come to see the latter as more closely related or analogous to other-regarding untrustworthiness than one had previously imagined. And the same can be said for other pairings of self-regarding traits and their other-regarding analogues. Because a virtue-ethical approach uses similar vocabulary for other-regarding and self-regarding cases/traits/actions, it tends to make cases of other-regarding deception, etc., and cases of self-regarding deception, etc., appear to be in the same boat, rather than in different boats, appear to be parts or aspects of a single phenomenon of deception, etc., rather than widely disparate phenomena. Self-regarding and other-regarding deception, etc., can be deplored and criticized in the same common-sense virtue-ethical terms, and their self-regarding and other-regarding opposites will both be highly regarded and deemed admirable from the standpoint of such self-other symmetric ethical thinking. And so the kind of ethics we are proposing not only tends to make us focus more on self-regarding virtues than other approaches to ethics would tend to do, but also brings self-regarding and other-regarding phenomena closer together, making them appear more similar, more of a piece, than I believe is possible under utilitarianism, Kantianism, and common-sense morality.[16]

That resultant unity is desirable, moreover, in a way or to an extent that the kind of unity and system utilitarianism gives rise to is not, because it is largely *based in* our ordinary ethical intuitions rather than running counter to—or existing at the expense of—such intuitions. Indeed, the just described unification that virtue ethics brings about depends also on our having denied the foundational status (at least) of specifically moral forms of ethical judgment. But relative to that assumed rejection, the above unifying process works largely, if not entirely, on the basis of (often-ignored connections between) our intuitions. Once agent-sacrificing self-other asymmetry is deemphasized or left behind, we are in a position to pay (more) attention to our intuitions and ideas about self-regarding character traits and to notice how fully or widely they run parallel to our intuitions about what is admirable or deplorable in other-regarding cases, and the closer relation between the self-regarding and other-regarding that is so distinctive of (morally silent) common-sense ethics is in large measure, therefore, the natural product of an accretion or accumulation of intuitions, rather than, as with utilitarianism, the result solely or largely of a clash between ordinary ethical thinking and a desire for systematic unity (and, in the present context, for freedom from paradox and incoherence). In at least one sense, our virtue ethics is produced by tapping our intuitive ethical sense of things more deeply than we have done previously, and nothing like this can be said, I think, of the utilitarian approach to ethics (whatever its other merits—and of course we will be critically comparing utilitarianism and virtue ethics in the final two parts of this book).

I should mention, however, that the present emphasis on the similarities between certain self-regarding and other-regarding virtues should not or need not be taken to undercut another intuitive distinction between (self-regarding or other-regarding) virtues and (self-regarding or other-regarding) talents, pleasing personality traits, and the like. In the *Enquiry Concerning the Principles of Morals*, Appendix IV, Hume notably treats both self-regarding and other-regarding traits as (moral) virtues, but also refuses to grant any fundamental distinction between virtues, on the one hand, and a class of pleasing/admirable traits that are not commonly thought of as virtues, on the other. Thus wit and charm may please us and are even admired, but it would sound odd to call them admirable traits of character, and that may explain why we are not inclined to regard them as virtues. Rather, we quite naturally distinguish between desirable personality traits and desirable character traits, and it is only the latter that are ordinarily treated as virtues. But Hume, for reasons we needn't consider here, will have nothing to do with such a distinction.

However, in the present book I want to remain neutral on this issue. Even if we don't differentiate between moral and non-moral virtues, and even if—like Hume, but for different reasons—we choose to emphasize what is common to various self-regarding and other-regarding virtues, we still needn't deny that there is a distinction between virtues/admirable traits of character and admirable personality traits. That issue can be left open to future investigation although in what follows (see especially Ch. 14), I will play down or ignore the distinction between character and personality when I feel that an insistence on the distinction would not substantially affect the course of the argument.

And there is a further issue I would like to remain neutral on. In the present chapter and previously, I have discussed the relation of various specific virtues (and vices or anti-virtues) to larger-scale issues of rationality and benefit to oneself or others and to questions of overall admirability or virtue status, and it might well be wondered, therefore, whether I wish or need to use Bernard Williams's recent distinction between "thick" and "thin" ethical concepts in developing common-sense virtue ethics. Williams's distinction is supposed to approximate in some measure the distinction between (more) specific and (more) general ethical concepts, and I have certainly been relying on some sort of distinction between more and less specific notions. But Williams's particular distinction is also made by reference to somewhat controversial epistemological theses. Williams holds, for example, that thick/specific ethical terms/notions are more "world-guided" and thus can be applied more objectively than thin/general ethical terms/notions, and he also makes some novel claims about what can be known by those inside and by those outside the cultural community where a certain thick concept flourishes. In the light of those commitments, I prefer *not* to rely on Williams's distinction between the thick and the thin and shall proceed on that basis.[17]

It is now time to turn to a problematic area of common-sense and Kantian morality we have not yet considered in relation to our ethics of virtue. We must see whether such ethics can evade or resist the sorts of difficulties with deontology raised by Scheffler in *The Rejection of Consequentialism*.[18]

## Deontology and Virtue Ethics

The discussion of the last section indicates how attributions of admirability, deplorability, and the like can be applied in a fairly uniform fashion across the distinction between self and other—and not only in regard to benefiting and harming, but also in regard to such less consequentialistically evaluable relations as deception/non-deception, honesty/dishonesty, loyalty/disloyalty. To that extent it should be clear how virtue ethics can avoid the incoherence, paradox, odd results that arise in common-sense and Kantian morality out of their respective agent-sacrificing asymmetries.[19] We have also seen how virtue ethics can avoid the most acute difficulties of specifically moral luck. But there remain, however, the problems and paradoxes—emerging from Scheffler's discussion of deontology—that surround the question whether it is permissible or obligatory to kill or harm others to prevent a greater number of killings or harmings from being done by someone else. Common-sense morality tends to hold that this sort of killing in order to minimize the overall number of killings that take place is impermissible or at least highly suspect.[20] And, of course, standard act-consequentialism holds, by contrast, that it is not only permissible but morally obligatory (other things equal) to kill in such circumstances. Where does virtue ethics stand?

Certainly, a virtue ethics commonsensical enough to take all its cues from common-sense morality is likely to run into grave difficulties in this area. To the extent we firmly believe it is wrong to kill to prevent more killings (and assuming for purposes of argument that common-sense morality takes such an unequivocal stand on the matter), we could simply translate this opinion into morally neutral, but otherwise equivalent virtue-ethical terms and say that such killing is greatly to be deplored, highly deplorable. The question will then open up whether or how it can really be deplorable to act in such a way as to minimize deplorable actions and all the problems mentioned earlier in this connection will then come crashing down upon us. But there may be a more benign option.

Earlier, I mentioned the view of Sidgwick (and others) that common-sense morality is incomplete, in the sense of not (yet) having an answer to every casuistical or situational moral problem that can arise; I also urged that such incompleteness, while hardly an ideal state of affairs, is neither surprising nor unacceptable. Why should we hold that intuitive but critical moral thinking has already yielded up its full harvest of moral solutions to practical or abstractly conceived moral questions. Over the centuries, even the decades, our views about the morality of slavery, or of unequal job opportunities for men and women, have undergone radical emendation, and (forgetting, for a moment, its other difficulties) common-sense morality might well and justifiably maintain that it shouldn't at present be expected to have an answer to all issues of right and wrong, etc. And I can see no reason why common-sense-based virtue ethics shouldn't claim the same privilege of modesty.

Recent discussions by Scheffler and others have criticized the common-sense belief that killing to prevent killings is wrong or at least questionable, in terms of theoretical considerations powerful enough, I believe, to attenuate or weaken the common-sense intuitions in this area of those who find those considerations powerful. And in the light of such criticisms, we may well, therefore, find ourselves less than committed to maintaining the virtue-theoretic analogues of what common-sense morality is supposed to say about multiple-killing-preventive killing. A common-sense ethics of virtue that is critical enough to be mindful of the difficulties inherent in other approaches to ethics might (in relation to its own closest analogues of common-sense moral judgment) wish to oppose common-sense morality here or at least to suspend judgment and claim that it cannot be expected, at this point, to have an answer to every issue. In other words, virtue ethics may be incomplete and, in the light of recent discussions, have nothing, for the present, to say about the deplorability or admirability of killing to prevent more killings. (Notice that such an admission doesn't automatically put virtue ethics in an inferior position relative to utilitarianism. For one thing, *scalar* act-utilitarianism also has nothing to say about the permissibility or impermissibility of killing to prevent a greater number of killings. But what remains to be said on this score is best left to the final part of the book.)

However, for the sake of completeness it ought also to be mentioned that an ethics of virtue might wish to regard the issue of killing to prevent killings as presenting the virtue-theoretic analogue of a moral dilemma. We have yet to spell out what it would mean for virtue ethics to allow for dilemma, but, speaking roughly, we can think of it simply as a case where an agent can't avoid acting deplorably. Applying this idea to the case at hand, there may be certain advantages in holding that it is or may be deplorable to kill an innocent person for the sake of preventing some greater number from being killed, but likewise deplorable, through a refusal to kill, to let such a greater number die.[21] So although I don't want to opt for a particular way of handling the problems that emerge from Scheffler's discussion of killing to prevent killings, I hope I have made it clear that (at this point at least) common-sense virtue ethics—perhaps I should instead speak of our approach as a form of *critical* commonsensism—is not totally at the mercy of the problems that arise in this area.[22]

And in that case, I think we have made good on our earlier promise to show how virtue ethics, shorn of specifically moral concepts, can undercut or avoid the difficulties with Kantian and common-sense ethics that we described at such length in Part I. In the next chapter, I would like to focus on some of the advantages of a virtue-ethical approach to two important areas of other-regarding morality/ethics. I hope to show that it can give a better, a more intuitively plausible account of friendship and citizenship than what specifically moral approaches to these topics—quite apart from problems of the sort raised in Part I—are capable of offering. We spent time in this present chapter considering some of the ways in which virtue ethics brings together the self-regarding and the other-regarding, but it is worthwhile to spend some more of our time on certain largely other-regarding issues that various moral theories discuss and a virtue-ethical approach can distinctively illuminate.

## Notes

1. See, e.g., Nagel, "Moral Luck," in *Mortal Questions*, Cambridge, 1979.

2. For attempts to downgrade or limit prudence as a virtue, see my *Goods and Virtues* (Oxford, 1990, Ch. 2) and the references contained therein.

3. "Irrational" seems stronger, more negative, than "rationally unacceptable," and this may make a difference in the applicability of these terms/notions. Certain moral offenses may be morally unacceptable, yet not serious enough to count as immoral, and something similar may hold in the area of practical rationality. I am indebted here to Shelly Kagan.

4. If (self-regarding) rational dilemma is possible (on this see my *Beyond Optimizing*, Harvard, 1989, Ch. 5), then a situationally optimal choice may be rationally unacceptable and thus hardly ideal. Even without dilemma, there are many choice situations where one's best choice is far from ideal.

5. See *Beyond Optimizing*, esp. Ch. 5.

6. See the *Nicomachean Ethics* 1109b 14–27; 1126a 31-1126b 5.

7. See Donald Davidson, "How is Weakness of the Will Possible?" In J. Feinberg, ed., *Moral Concepts*, Oxford, 1969.

8. Perfection may admit of degrees in the sense that one thing can be more (nearly) perfect than another, but it pretty clearly doesn't admit of supererogatory degrees: nothing can be even more perfect than another.

9. I assume one can display fortitude even in grief at the loss of a loved one.

10. See Voltaire's Letter to Charles Augustin Feriol comte d'Argental, in T. Besterman, ed., *Voltaire's Correspondence*, Geneva: Institute et Musée Voltaire, 1962, vol. LXXI, pp. 246ff.; and Tillotson's *The Works of Dr. John Tillotson*, Dublin, 9th edit., 1726, Sermon I.

11. Cf. Mark Johnston, "Self-Deception and the Nature of Mind," in B. McLaughlin and A. Rorty, eds., *Perspectives on Self-Deception*, California, 1988, esp. p. 85.

12. The above is compatible with holding that knowledge is *some* sort of personal good and ignorance a personal evil (bad thing). Such (non-moral) goods and evils, I presume, can sometimes be more than counterbalanced by other factors.

13. See *Beyond Optimizing*, esp. Chs. 1–3.

14. The parallel between the intertemporal and the interpersonal is an important theme in Sidgwick's *Methods*, in Rawls's *A Theory of Justice*, in Parfit's *Reasons and Persons*, and elsewhere.

15. Even in explicit treatments of the virtues, trustworthiness, honesty, loyalty, reliability, and the like are often deemed to be *moral* virtues, and given the common association of the moral with the other-regarding, this means that the self-regarding instances of these virtues remain entirely out of the picture. For an example of such a treatment of the virtues, see Edmund Pincoffs, *Quandaries and Virtues*, University Press of Kansas, 1986, esp. p. 85 and Ch. 5 generally.

16. Defenders of common-sense morality also speak of other-regarding issues as moral and of self-regarding issues as prudential (or rational), and this difference of nomenclature also serves to keep self- and other-regarding matters separate.

17. See Williams's *Ethics and the Limits of Philosophy*, Harvard, 1985, and, for criticism of the epistemological assumptions attendant on the thick-thin distinction, S. Scheffler's "Morality Through Thick and Thin," *Philosophical Review*, 96, 1987, pp. 411–34.

18. See *The Rejection of Consequentialism*, Oxford, 1982.

19. Recall, from Chapter 3, that the asymmetry involved in Kantian morality has a somewhat different profile from that involved in common-sense morality. But both give rise to problems and paradox.

20. In "A Critique of Utilitarianism," in Smart and Williams, *Utilitarianism: for and against*, Cambridge, 1973, Bernard Williams hesitates to say that it is actually wrong to kill one person to prevent the killing of a large number of people. Williams's example involves killing one member of a group in order to prevent everyone in the group from being killed. Clearly, however, Kant regards such killing as wrong.

21. In "War and Massacre" (in *Mortal Questions*), T. Nagel proposes a similar treatment of a larger-scale case where one must choose between killing the innocent and letting a much larger number of innocent people be killed.

22. Common-sense morality has similar maneuvering room with respect to its analogues of the problem under discussion, but this doesn't help it evade the problems that arise around self-other asymmetry and moral luck.

# 9

## Virtue in Friends
## and Citizens

### Some Problems about
### Interpersonal Relationships

A great many philosophers and others have subscribed to the idea that there are moral duties or obligations of friendship (more generally, of personal relationship) and moral duties or obligations of citizenship (more generally, of group membership). Indeed, anti-utilitarian ethicists frequently claim that certain relationships to individuals and institutions represent an aspect of the moral life where utilitarian impersonality is especially clumsy or inept and where we have every reason to posit special moral obligations that cannot be cashed out in utilitarian or standard deontological terms.[1]

Now one of the best descriptions we have of the putative moral obligations specific to friendship, in particular, is provided by Sidgwick in the *Methods of Ethics*, where with characteristic carefulness he includes in his discussion of common-sense morality a description of the obligations one is sometimes supposed to have to one's friends simply in virtue of their being friends.[2] But there is also common-sense plausibility and a long-standing tradition behind the notion that citizens are under special obligations to obey the laws and support the political institutions of *their own countries* (at least when those institutions are reasonably just and beneficial). Defenders of such a view typically invoke very general moral considerations—that is, considerations not limited to the political or social sphere—in order to argue for such particular obligations to one's own country, and although utilitarian considerations are sometimes brought forward in this context, the discussion has usually proceeded in terms of wide-ranging moral principles that are not purely or strictly consequentialistic. The idea has been, rather, that obligations to one's own government/society/nation/country are supported by considerations of fair play or by tacit or implicit consent or by factors that morally demand certain sorts of gratitude, and in all these cases there is an attempt to understand political/social morality in terms that (also) apply within the sphere of personal or private morality. (That the distinction between public and private is vague and context-relative almost doesn't need saying.)

Since Sidgwick and others who have discussed the (common-sense) morality of friendship, parenthood, marriage, etc., have also argued from considerations that apply more widely than in these special relationships, it is not surprising that the arguments used to ground certain special personal or "private" obligations often parallel—or are even exactly the same as—those mustered on behalf of certain political or social obligations. And the idea, for example, of gratitude for what other people have intentionally done for one—an idea that easily applies between people who are neither compatriots nor bound by any intimate relations—has been taken as the basis of obligations to friends (and spouses and family) no less than it has been taken to ground obligations to one's own government/country, etc. By the same token, the idea of tacit or implicit consent to be helpful and/or cooperative has been invoked as a defense both of narrowly personal and political obligations, though, of course, this idea can also be applied more widely to the relations of individuals who are (otherwise) unconnected by any form of intimacy or a common past.

In recent years, a good deal of scepticism has been raised about the validity of such a moral picture either of friendship or of citizenship. The scepticism I have in mind comes, not from the usual and expectable direction of utilitarianism, but from non-utilitarian, even anti-utilitarian, philosophers who question whether considerations of fair play and the like—together with plausible factual assumptions—can provide an intuitively acceptable or successful argument for the existence of special obligations existing in virtue of special relationships (here "special" at the very least means "not obtaining between every two people, etc., on this planet").

For example, in a thoroughgoing critique of traditional and recently familiar attempts to ground political obligations in intuitively appealing moral principles, A. John Simmons has argued—to my mind convincingly—that none of the arguments that have been presented—and no plausible variations on them—will allow us to justify obligations of obedience to the (just) laws or government of one's own country (I am characterizing Simmons's position very roughly here). And others, like Larry Blum in *Friendship, Altruism, and Morality*, have not directly countered the arguments that have been used to defend special moral obligations of friendship, so much as offered a perceptive, alternative picture of the phenomena of friendship from which it emerges that we cannot properly treat friendship—its characteristic concerns, feelings, and ways of seeing things—as solely or primarily a matter of (special) moral obligations between friends.[3]

Given the fact that we are already, on other grounds, discarding (our intuitions about) common-sense moral obligation, there is perhaps no need for us at this point to review the specific discussions of either Blum or Simmons. I will assume, with them, that we cannot justify obligations of friendship or of political obedience (or cooperation) in the usual, the familiar ways. But I also want to go further than either Blum or Simmons apparently wishes to go. For having played down or denied our right to speak of obligations of friendship or of political obedience, both Simmons and Blum draw the conclusion that we can best understand the phenomena they are dealing with in terms of *certain other sorts of moral notions and relationships.* According to Blum, even if we needn't or shouldn't stress the moral obligations of friendship, we ought to focus on the ways certain forms of friendship are morally superior to others and certain kinds of action and feeling on the part of one friend toward another morally preferable to certain others. And for Simmons the natural alternative to understanding citizenship in terms of moral obligations is to understand it in terms of *less stringent* moral notions like moral goodness, moral justification, and moral worthiness.[4]

But from the standpoint of the present book, we have reason to resist these further, positive moves on Blum's and Simmons's part. Blum's lengthy and Simmons's brief discussion of the applicability of less stringent moral notions to the phenomena of friendship and citizenship are equally subject to the sorts of difficulty, oddness, and incoherence that were earlier found to pervade our intuitive understanding of morality. For we earlier uncovered problems of asymmetry and luck in regard both to the "deontic" notion of moral obligation and the "aretaic" notion of moral goodness, and from there it is but a short step to ideas like moral worthiness or justification. But any criticism we might make of a common-sense moral approach to friendship, citizenship, and other interpersonal relationships might lose some of its force, if a common-sense ethics of virtue (not to mention utilitarianism) proved incapable of providing a reasonable and reasonably detailed or full ethical picture of such relationships.

I believe, however, that virtue ethics is capable of providing a reasonable account of friendship, citizenship, and other "special" relationships, and in what follows I will argue, moreover, that its intuitive picture of friendship, citizenship, and the like is, for reasons having nothing to do with the problems of Part I, preferable to any sort of moralizing approach. What virtue ethics can say about friendship and citizenship is in fact more intuitively satisfactory than the sorts of judgments that emerge from a treatment in deontic or aretaic moral terms. And though we will keep the actual discussion limited to the specific issues of friendship, by the end it should be fairly clear that what we have said about friendship can be generalized to the political sphere and to other kinds of interpersonal relationships.

## Are Friendship and Citizenship
## Moral Relationships?

I would like to offer reasons for a negative answer to the question that heads this section that are quite independent of the critical arguments of Part I. And I think it would be best to begin with an examination of Michael Stocker's seminal example of someone visiting a friend in the hospital.[5] Certain recent writers on the morality of personal relations have opposed the Kantian ideas that there is moral merit only in acts done from a sense of duty and that acting from benevolent or friendly feeling toward a given individual is entirely lacking in such merit. And in an attempt to turn the tables on Kant some of these philosophers have argued not only that there can be moral value in helping someone from friendship or sympathy, but also that actions thus motivated may be and typically are morally superior to actions done strictly from a sense of duty or from other sorts of moral considerations.

Stocker, in particular, asks us to consider a person, Smith, who visits his friend in the hospital and whom the friend is happy to see. The hospitalized friend tells Smith that it is very nice to see how much Smith cares for him (or shares his feelings of friendship), but the visitor soon brings a halt to such grateful talk by contradicting his hospitalized friend. "Oh, no," he says, "I came because I thought it was my duty, not because of any feelings or emotions I might have toward you."

The first response of the hospitalized man might well, however, be to assume that his visitor didn't really mean what he had said, but was, rather, displaying a more or less misplaced modesty about revealing and/or hearing about feelings. But as Stocker makes clear, if the hospitalized man were to press the point and, to his surprise, discover that Smith really, literally, meant what he had said, then he would quite naturally feel dejected or disappointed at the thought that Smith probably lacked the warm feelings he had originally thought to be motivating his visit. And philosophers who have recently used examples like Stocker's have tended to conclude that in many or most cases it is morally better to act from feelings of friendship (or benevolence or sympathy) than out of a sense of duty.[6]

But I think there is every reason to ask whether such claims are really consonant with our intuitive responses to such examples. Larry Blum and others have pointed out that most of us would prefer to be helped from sympathy, or from strong feelings of friendship, rather than from duty,[7] but it hardly follows that we either do or should regard help of the first kind as morally superior to help of the second.[8] For what makes us like a person and what pleases us about (the actions of) a person need not make that person (appear) more admirable or morally better. However, defenders of the greater (moral) merit of (a friend's) acting from sympathy or feeling may at this point reply that there must be something wrong with anyone who generally acts (toward his supposed friends) from a sense of duty rather than from friendly feelings.[9] And surely we all agree that there is something wrong with such a friend *as a friend*. We do, I think, tend to think less well of (the friendship or capacity for friendship of) someone who tends to act from duties of friendship (or from a consideration of the *moral superiority* of helping one's friends). Given such a coldblooded attitude, we would probably want to say that such a person is no true friend, even that he or she lacks the capacity for friendship.

But even if the sympathetic, feelingful person is, or is capable of being, a better friend than someone who acts only from duty, the notion of a better (or truer) friend may not be a specifically *moral* one and may be more accurately, more intuitively, understood as belonging to the sort of virtue-theoretic approach that focuses on what is admirable without the use of distinctively moral notions. In any event, it clearly begs important questions to assume that "better friend" is a moral notion of such a sort that, other things being equal, a person who is a better friend than someone else is morally better or a morally better friend (whatever that means) than that other person.

Furthermore, those, like Hume, who have emphasized the sympathetic underpinnings of morality have also stressed the need for moral dispositions that can outlast flagging sympathies and overcome outright antagonisms, and surely the man who acts from duty may evince steadier tendencies to do (what we regard as) the right thing than someone whose acts were primarily motivated by sympathy.[10] So perhaps our lower regard for the visitor who acts self-consciously from duty is a matter of finding the man less admirable as a human being and even in some sense less human than the friends we hope to have, rather than a matter of finding him *morally* defective. It is thus not at all clear that Stocker's hospital visitor really is less morally virtuous or meritorious than the simpatico person who acts from sympathy. But it does seem reasonable to claim that the visitor is (ceteris paribus) less admirable as a friend and as a human being than someone more capable of acting from sympathy and friendship (or, for that matter, love). And these are precisely the sort of terms to which our virtue-theoretic approach restricts itself and in which it most naturally, and even canonically, expresses itself.

If the above is correct, then there is a certain irony in the fact that Blum himself insists that we not, like Kant, overmoralize personal relations. Even if one doesn't speak of moral *obligations* in connection with friendship, friendship may be overmoralized when seen as a source of special forms of *moral* goodness and betterness rather than of the sorts of positive or comparative admirability or virtue-status that our virtue ethics can speak of. And it would appear, in fact, that both Blum and Simmons have altogether ignored the possibility and the possible strengths of a virtue-theoretic approach to friendship and citizenship of the sort I am suggesting here. Nevertheless this is not, in fact, true of every previous attempt to come to grips with the ethical issues involved in personal relationships like friendship. For as Blum himself has noted, Kierkegaard thinks (acts of) love and friendship have no moral value as such.

However, Blum goes on to claim that the "tradition of which Kierkegaard is a representative places sole emphasis on altruistic attitudes towards strangers, or towards others in abstraction from the special relationships in which we stand to them." And Blum has previously characterized Kierkegaard as holding that concern based solely in one's friendly feelings toward a particular individual is "deficient precisely because it is not a universal form of concern."[11] And I think these statements do a serious injustice to Kierkegaard's views, or at least to the views he expresses in the book *Fear and Trembling* (which Blum does not cite). Those views in fact strike me as very much in line with, and some sort of anticipation of, our virtue-ethical approach to special personal relationships.[12]

I have no wish to deny that Kierkegaard follows Kant in assigning no moral merit to acts done from friendship or love for a particular individual. But that doesn't mean that Kierkegaard has a lower regard for such personal relations or commitments than for the realm of morality. In *Fear and Trembling* Kierkegaard speaks of the "teleological suspension of the ethical" involved in Abraham's willingness to sacrifice his own son at God's command, and he expresses great admiration for Abraham's great faith in/devotion to God. But at the same time he accepts the Kantian view that the ethical is "the universal" (that is, operates through universally applicable rules), and he says that what Abraham does, he does by virtue of his particular relation to God. What Abraham does thus cannot, he says, be formulated or enjoined in terms of universal rules, and as such it is beyond the sphere of the ethical (or the moral).

How are we to interpret these perplexing remarks? We must first get clearer on Kierkegaard's terminology, which is different, I believe, from that adopted here or currently in the field of ethics. I am using the term "ethical" as broader than "moral," so that, for example, moral philosophy counts as but one branch or aspect of ethics. On such usage, our present version of virtue ethics is not a form or theory of morality proper, even if it clearly counts as one kind of (approach to) ethics. But Kierkegaard seems to accept not only Kant's views about the specifically moral, but Kant's terminological equivalence between "ethical" and "moral" as well. And this terminological agreement covers over a substantive disagreement with Kant that Kierkegaard himself clearly recognizes.

Kant refuses to recognize any form of worth other than (or independent of) the moral, and that is why such virtues as foresight have value, according to Kant, only if and when they are used for good, that is, moral, purposes. But for Kierkegaard there is something praiseworthy and admirable about an Abraham who (he thinks) transcends morality in the name of a special commitment or relationship.[13] However, because he follows Kant's narrow usage of "ethical," he cannot describe Abraham's devotion as an ethical suspension of the moral, so he employs the term "teleological" and the phrase "the teleological suspension of the ethical" to convey his sense of the admirability of Abraham and his substantive disagreement with Kant on this topic.

Given our own, more standard usage, however, we can interpret Kierkegaard as holding that non-moral and even anti-moral human action and emotions may be admirable—or as holding that there can be non-moral and even anti-moral *virtues*. But we shouldn't attribute to Kierkegaard the total virtue-theoretical conception of ethics that we are adopting here, for he is perfectly willing to make specifically moral attributions. Nonetheless, Kierkegaard is also interested in exploring avenues of admirability and virtue that Kantian ethics explicitly denies. And what he has to say about one particular (kind of) personal relation seems quite close to things we have been saying, in a virtue-ethical mode, about certain related personal relationships. Of course, the cases of friendship we have spoken of involved no hint of running *counter* to morality, but once one holds, with Kierkegaard, that certain strongly felt personal commitments are admirable in an anti-moral way, it may be easier to follow the lead of virtue ethics and claim that what is distinctively admirable and deplorable about such commitments and the relationships that embody them is in no way a matter of morality.

In addition, Kierkegaard seems to hold that certain personal commitments and relationships are *more admirable* (though less moral) than certain more universalistic attitudes and the acts and relationships *they* give rise to. And it is worthwhile at this point to ask whether there is anything of greater or of special ethical value in particularistic attitudes and relationships.

## Is There a Special Ethical Value in Relationships?

Given our present approach and canonical terminology, this question resolves itself, in the first instance, into a question about the greater admirability of being a good friend (I want to hold questions about good citizenship in abeyance). But, it may well be asked, greater admirability as compared with what? A good friend is presumably more admirable as such than someone who is a poor or bad friend to people (this seems to hold even if the person one is a friend to is a bad or deplorable person), but this comparison seems somewhat irrelevant to the question whether there is special or greater value in particularistic attitudes and relationships. What seems relevant, rather, is some sort of comparison between friendship, for example, and actions toward strangers that are in relevant ways analogous to what friends are or are not moved to do in relation to their friends. The favors that a friend does for a friend out of loyalty and out of concern and love appear to have natural parallels in what a benevolent person may do for a stranger out of sympathy, a feeling of common humanity, or indeed benevolence. We may therefore say that many of the things a friend is likely to do out of friendship, a stranger may do out of sheer humanity (or general benevolence), and so the question we wish to ask may perhaps be regarded as focusing on the issue whether there is anything more admirable about acts of helpfulness motivated by (feelings of) friendship toward a particular individual than there is about similarly helpful acts stemming from a more impersonal or generalized form of concern for people.

However, I think even this resolution of the question before us is somewhat unsatisfactory. It asks us to compare two differently motivated single acts, rather than the dispositions or character traits that presumably underlie such acts, but I think we have a much better chance of understanding, much less answering, the issue before us if we instead allow ourselves to consider it "writ large" in terms of a comparison between two sorts of human character traits, two sorts of general disposition toward feeling and action.

In that case we must consider and compare our intuitive evaluations of the disposition to (form friendships and) act from friendship toward particular individuals and of the disposition to act from a more generalized sense of common humanity or of benevolence. The issue before us is then most naturally regarded as involving the comparison of two ideal (or extreme) types: on the one hand, the person who tends to form close relationships and to act on behalf, but only on behalf, of those individuals with whom he is intimate; and, on the other hand, the person who lacks close relationships but who tends to act helpfully toward non-friends out of a strong, generalized sense of human sympathy. And put even in this relatively clear-cut way, it is not easy to resolve the question we have been trying to ask.

For consider, to begin with, how unlikely it is that someone with a generalized sense of benevolence will do as much for particular individuals as someone motivated by friendship. But even when the helpfulness of the former is more thinly spread among humankind, the latter may nonetheless do less overall good than a person who is ready to help strangers and acquaintances, and in comparing the two sorts of individuals, we must also consider how much more unexpected and unusual the disposition to help strangers is. We expect people to have friends and to love certain people, and it comes as no surprise to us when someone acts helpfully toward those who fall into this category. Of course, there are enough cases around of neglectful behavior toward friends and family to make us think at least well of someone who is good to his (putative) friends and loved ones. But people devoted to mankind more generally are harder to find, rarer, than people devoted to friends and loved ones; and relative at least to this factual assumption, someone with the tendency to be helpful toward people generally may well seem more admirable than someone with the more run-of-the-mill tendency to form friendships and help her friends.

There is, however, another side to this issue. For the person whose devotion to common humanity we tend to admire for the reasons (or in the way) just mentioned is also supposed to have an incapacity for forming close attachments. And we surely have a strong tendency to deplore such an incapacity and think less well of (at the same time we may also feel sorry for) someone incapable of love and intimacy. As far as I can tell, therefore, the deplorable and admirable aspects of the disposition (merely) toward general helpfulness seem counterbalanced by those of the disposition to form friendships and act (only) on behalf of one's friends.

So if we ask whether there is any special ethical value or admirability in close personal relationships, we can answer "yes" if we mean simply to be asking whether there is something distinctively admirable about (the capacity for) close relationships, including friendships, and about the actions typically performed on behalf of those to whom one is closely tied. That is, if we are asking whether what is admirable about (the capacity for) close relationships is different from what is admirable about (the capacity for) general benevolence, then our just-concluded discussion points clearly toward an affirmative answer. But if our question, rather, is whether either tendency, either sort of behavior, is more admirable overall than the other, then our previous discussion seems to move us in the direction of a negative answer. The sense we have been able to make of the question whether being a good (or admirable) friend is more admirable (or more important?) than being good (or admirable) in one's behavior toward people in general leads us to deny that either kind of admirability or goodness ranks intuitively ahead of the other, and even if we may be disappointed by this conclusion, it may in retrospect be unsurprising that we should have reached it.

The question whether being good to friends is better or more admirable than being good to people generally is very much like a more familiar question that sometimes arises within (common-sense based) moral theory, the question, namely, whether private virtues have greater or less moral weight/importance than public ones. And this question is hard to answer even apart from the difficulties with ordinary moral thinking that were raised in Part I. Utilitarianism may be able, in its own terms, to provide some sort of answer to questions of this sort—and we will later discuss how utilitarianism resolves such issues and how that resolution puts it into conflict with some of our most deeply felt common-sense intuitions. But it is not clear that intuitive or common-sense morality would tend to favor public over private morality, nor that a reverse preference is intuitively defensible, and this absence, in common-sense morality, of any definite sense of the superiority either of the public or of the private corresponds, it would seem, to what we have unearthed, or failed to unearth, in discussing the relative merits of friendship and of generalized benevolence from a virtue-ethical perspective.

However, this *aporia* may allow us to say something further about the relative (non-moral) admirability of acting from (feelings of) friendship and acting out of a sense of duty-toward-one's-friends. Someone who visits his friend in the hospital out of a sense that such action is morally obligatory or meritorious shows signs of altogether lacking the capacity for friendship, whereas someone who visits his friend out of strong affection and a desire to see him may not only have the capacity for friendship, but also be beneficent and kind toward people other than his friends. When we are given Stocker's example, I think we tend to hold other things equal between the person described by Stocker and the more "normal" person we imagine who would visit a friend out of friendly feeling; Stocker gives us no reason to assume that the morally punctilious individual who acts from a sense of duty toward his friend is any more likely to be helpful to non-friends than the person who visits a friend out of personal concern.

In that case, these two hypothetical individuals differ only with respect to the dispositions toward (putative) friends that they are naturally taken to exemplify, and there is no obvious defect in the attitude and actions of the sympathetically concerned friend that can be said to counterbalance the obvious deplorability of an incapacity for friendship such as the conscientious visitor seems to exemplify. So considered overall, the conscientious friend seems less admirable, or more deplorable or open to criticism, than an otherwise analogous sympathetic and loving friend, but this comparative judgment, while it takes in other-regarding aspects of the individuals being compared, requires no specifically moral attributions or assessments. It derives entirely from the sorts of concepts and considerations we are allowing ourselves in pursuit of a full-fledged ethics of virtue.

Now, the discussion we have just been engaged in focuses almost entirely on one sort of close personal relationship, and it ignores, for example, the sorts of virtues that can attach to (the behavior of) citizens as citizens. Parallel to the question whether being a good friend is more admirable (is a greater virtue) than being kind to people generally, there is the question whether being a good, a loyal and helpful, citizen is more admirable or praiseworthy than being good to people generally, to compatriots and non-compatriots alike, more admirable or praiseworthy, in other words, than being a good citizen of the world. But I think the difficulties of showing a clear superiority in one direction or the other would emerge just as clearly in regard to this new question as they emerged in connection with the earlier comparison between being a good friend and being kind to people generally, and for that reason I don't propose to go into it further.

In any case, we have seen that our version of virtue ethics is better able to deal with a wide range of issues about friendship than common-sense morality appears to be. And given the rather similar doubts that exist about the relevance of morality either to (the evaluation of) friendship or to (the evaluation of) citizenship, I think we have reason to think that both good citizenship and good friendship are best understood in terms of non-moral admirability and its opposite. Loyalty and devotion in a friend can be prized, admired, and highly regarded for reasons which, like common-sense moral reasons, are based in other-regarding phenomena, but which, unlike common-sense morality, avoid specifically moral concepts altogether. And the same, I believe, can be said about loyalty and devotion in a citizen.

However, even if we can be said to have dealt with the issues of good citizenships and good friendship in differing degrees of specificity, we can hardly be said even to have touched upon certain other interpersonal phenomena. We haven't spoken of what it takes to be a good father, or husband, or spouse, or daughter, nor of what is or is not admirable about certain ways of being a member of groups smaller than the class of one's compatriots: for example, what is involved in being good or admirable as a member of a residential or academic community. Some of these topics raise interesting issues we haven't at all considered—for example, being a good mother involves a relation to legal rights and duties of a sort that seems irrelevant to issues concerning the goodness of a friend. So the reader can perhaps best treat it as a promissory note—based, I hope, on good credit—when I say that I believe a virtue-ethical approach can also successfully deal with these other interpersonal relationships.

In *Moral Principles and Political Obligations*, John Simmons argues against specific moral duties of citizenship, in particular, and takes this to show that we are not in any special way tied to our own country. And by eschewing moral notions altogether, our virtue ethics has arrived at a position which, while disagreeing with Simmons about whether any moral characterizations weaker than obligations are relevant to citizenship and political life as such, seems to agree with his view that, in the absence of moral obligations to the state, "political theory cannot offer a convincing general account of our political bonds."[14] But this appearance is in fact deceptive. If, like Simmons, one understands the notion of political bonds, and of being tied to one's country, in terms of the deontic notion of obligation, then virtue ethics has no cause for disagreement with Simmons on the point just mentioned. But there is another possibility Simmons ignores, but that virtue ethics may well wish to take advantage of: the possibility that virtue ethics may be able to make sense of or give significance to a non-moral, fundamentally aretaic, and clearly ethical notion of bonds and ties. Since the notion of a tie or a bond is somewhat metaphorical even in its standard deontic moral usage, we may be encouraged to think that this notion may find sufficient analogy within the aretaic sphere so as to be able to get a (metaphorical or partial) foothold there as well. And we may therefore hope to find some (fundamental) notion of virtue ethics that can allow us to formulate a virtue-ethical equivalent or analogue both of moral obligation and of the idea of ties or bonds. We will turn to this issue in the coming chapter.

# Notes

1. For the idea that special obligations to family and friends are somewhat different in character from typical deontological obligations like the obligation not to kill the innocent, see S. Scheffler, *The Rejection of Consequentialism*, Oxford, 1982, pp. 22n, 23n.

2. See *Methods of Ethics*, pp. 257–59.

3. See Simmons, *Moral Principles and Political Obligations*, Princeton, 1979, *passim*; and Blum, *Friendship, Altruism, and Morality*, Routledge and Kegan Paul, 1980, *passim*, but esp. pp. 160ff.

4. See Simmons, *op. cit.*, pp. 198ff.; Blum, *op. cit.*, Chs. 4 and 7.

5. See his "The Schizophrenia of Modern Ethical Theories," *Journal of Philosophy* 73, 1976.

6. See, for example, Philippa Foot's "Virtue and Vices" in the book of that title, California, 1978, p. 13.

7. *Op. cit.*, p. 168.

8. We needn't make and don't want to make the moral or virtue-ethical superiority of acting from friendship over acting from duty depend on the fact that the latter would often be misunderstood (as in Stocker's example). Relevant cases can be described in which no such misunderstanding occurs.

9. A person, as in Kant's famous example, who acts from duty because he is momentarily too grief-stricken to be able to muster much human sympathy or fellow-feeling needn't be supposed to have any *general* tendency to deal with his friends on the basis of a sense of duty. Blum interestingly questions Kant's assumption that a sense of duty is a more reliable source of altruism than benevolence, sympathy and other such feelings.

10. However, for interesting criticisms of the idea that self-consciously moral

motivation is likely to be steadier or longer lasting than feelings of sympathy, friendship, and love, see Blum, *op. cit.*, esp. Ch. 2.

11. See Blum, *op. cit.*, pp. 77, 81.

12. Larry Blum has pointed out to me that the work of Kierkegaard he cites, *Works of Love*, appeared after *Fear and Trembling* and may be seen as a retraction of the moral existentialist ideas of the latter. The purely philosophical points being made in the main text can nonetheless stand.

13. On the idea of admirable immorality and for further discussion of Kierkegaard, see my *Goods and Virtues*, Oxford, 1990, Ch. 4.

14. See *op. cit.*, p. 192.

# 10

## Virtue Ethics, Imperatives, and the Deontic

I earlier said that we would eventually have to consider how a fundamentally non-moral aretaic approach to ethics can accommodate general ethical recommendations of a sort sometimes expressed in the (grammatically) imperative mood; and it is high time for us to take on this task. A common-sense ethics of virtue can quite naturally be expressed in terms of precepts (re)commending concern both for oneself and for other people, and I hope to show that such precepts and even the imperative mood are right at home in an aretaic context. But I also want to argue that close analogues of deontic notions like wrongness and obligation can be developed on a purely aretaic (non-moral) basis, and this in turn will allow us to formulate a virtue-theoretic equivalent of the idea of personal or political ties or bonds.

Virtue ethics as we have described it cries out for some sort of familiar, imperatival formulation, and thus conceived we can express our common-sense approach at least partly in terms of the (roughly formulated) bipartite principle or precept: act on behalf of your own concerns, and act on behalf of the concerns of others. We must now consider whether such precepts can be understood (purely) aretaically or whether (at least) they can be given sense and substance through the explicit introduction of virtue-theoretic analogues of common deontic notions.

It is perhaps first worth noting that an aretaic term like "good" is standardly usable to commend and recommend. We needn't be committed to Hare's imperatival analysis of "good"-statements to see that phrases like "this is a good one" are typically usable to perform the speech act of recommending, for example, the purchase of a particular melon or the reading of a particular Agatha Christie mystery. But one may ask with how much force such an aretaic recommendation/commendation is issued and wonder, in particular, whether such a (re)commendation ever has as much force as an ordinarily used imperative.

Here, however, I think we have got the wrong end of the stick. The most helpful question is not, assuming the forcefulness of imperatives, whether statements/claims using "good" or "bad" can ever be issued with equally great force; but rather whether we should assume that imperatives are always employed with the great force, for example, of commands. The etymology of "imperative" shouldn't be allowed to mislead us on this issue by preventing us from seeing the great variety of grammatically imperatival uses of language, and in fact any sort of close attention to that variety should make it quite clear that some, or many, uses of the grammatical imperative are much less forceful than commands.

When we tell a friend "get well soon!" or "have a nice summer," we are not commanding and we don't even seem to be recommending. For example, someone uttering the first expression need not be urging us to take our medicine, but simply expressing a wish that we should (some-how) speedily recover from illness, and such uses of the imperative mood may in fact remind us of what is sometimes said about so-called "ideal" uses of "ought."[1] It has often been noted that when we say such things as "we all ought to love one another" or "we shouldn't have to die," we don't suppose that it is within any person or group of persons' power to bring about what we are saying ought to be done or simply be, and such uses of "ought" (and "should") are then contrasted with certain specifically or situationally moral uses where "ought implies can" applies or seems closer to applying.[2] The ideal "ought" expresses a wish and an ideal rather than a command or even a recommendation; yet in sentences like "you ought to come home right away," "ought" does express a recommendation and even, potentially, a command. And I want to say that a similar split exists within our normal usage of the imperative mood.

"Concern yourself with others" can be used and treated as a command, but there is no reason why it should not, on other occasions, be used simply to express an ideal of behavior that the speaker endorses. Since aretaic terms like "admirable" and "deplorable" are clearly capable of giving expression to a person's ideals or deepest values, there would seem to be no problem about accommodating aretaic virtue ethics to at least some standard uses of the imperative mood. So there is no reason why we shouldn't express the virtue-ethical ideal or standard of human behavior in grammatically imperatival terms, and, given what was said about the ideal "ought," there would also appear to be no reason not to use "ought"s and "should"s when stating the bipartite principle or precept that provides us with our most general (and admittedly somewhat vague) statement of the common-sense virtue-ethical point of view.

But how can I at this point still be using the word "precept" in describing the sorts of things a purely aretaic approach is capable of saying? If the "ought" and imperatives of the latter simply articulate values and ideals, can we be justified in talking of "precepts" or, for that matter, of "recommendations"? However, I have already pointed out that "good" can be used to make recommendations, so surely there is no problem about using aretaically understood imperatives and "ought"s with the force of recommendation. And in the light of what has already been said, I think a similar usage of "precept" makes sense within an aretaic context. Precepts are general in what they urge or recommend, so "this is a good knife" is certainly no precept. But "open marriages are best" is general enough to count as a precept, and it too employs only aretaic evaluative concepts.

So-called descriptivists have been pointing out for decades (I was almost going to say years) that it is difficult or impossible to separate so-called evaluative, emotive, or prescriptive force/meaning from non-evaluative or "descriptive" force/meaning. And such discussions may be added to what has already been said in order, perhaps finally, to make us accept the idea that aretaic value judgments can constitute or appropriately give rise to recommendations, precepts, commendations, and even rules. But more can be said, because it can also be argued that aretaic notions can have a force of requirement or prohibition similar to that of standard deontic concepts like "(moral) obligation" and "(morally) wrong." Let us see how.

Terms like "(morally) right" and "(morally) wrong" are frequently said to have a practical force and be action-guiding, at least for someone who takes morality seriously, and it might therefore be thought that nothing so strong as this can possibly exist in the aretaic realm. The aretaic in general includes both moral and non-moral concepts, and it seems plausible at first glance to suppose that "deplorable" and "morally bad" cannot have the action-guiding force of deontic moral concepts like right and wrong. But let's consider the latter two concepts. Have we automatically told someone to perform an act if we call it morally right? Surely, not. In given circumstances two or more (mutually incompatible) acts may be equally right, and where such a fact is known or expressed, a claim about the rightness of a particular action may not count as a recommendation or constitute telling the appropriate hearer to perform the action in question. But notions like moral obligation and wrongness (and I will simplify matters by discussing only wrongness) may in that case seem more definite than rightness in their action-guiding capabilities. For it would at least seem that we absolutely prohibit (i.e., tell someone not to perform or require the non-performance of) any act we call wrong, even if, because of ties, we may not want to require any and all acts we say are right.

But even this statement has to be qualified in the light, for example, of the possibility of moral dilemmas. In a putative dilemmatic situation where every act is morally wrong and thus in an appropriate sense morally prohibited or forbidden, closer inspection of one's options may reveal a lesser or least moral evil among one's options; and since it is clearly possible to recommend an act as the least, or the lesser, of evils, the claim/admission that an act is morally wrong need not constitute an absolute prohibition on performing it and is therefore not as purely or perfectly action-guiding as we are sometimes inclined to assume.[3]

Moreover, in the light of this last conclusion, I wonder whether we really have any reason to take deontic claims, for example, of (moral) wrongness, as any stronger (as prohibitions or requirements-not-to-do) than aretaic claims of (moral) badness or high deplorability. Is there any reason to suppose that "$x$ would be a (or the) wrong thing to do" speaks or recommends more strongly against $x$ than "$x$ would be a bad thing to do"? Well, consider non-moral contexts where "bad" and "wrong" are used to convey distinctly prudential advice. In such circumstances how does "it would be a mistake to do $x$" compare in strength with analogous statements using "wrong" and "bad"?

It is very difficult, I think, to say. Yet if "$x$ would be a/the wrong thing to do" really has greater emotive-prescriptive force than "$x$ would be a bad thing to do," then we could reasonably expect a "mistake" statement to seem equivalent in force to one, but not the other, of these or else to appear to lie somewhere *between* "wrong" and "bad" judgments in regard to its force. And yet I can find no intuitive reason to identify the force of "it would be a mistake to do $x$" with one rather than the other of our original statement-forms; nor does it feel particularly right to place "mistake" statements at some more or less definite point between "wrong" and "bad" statements. In fact, and quite to the contrary, I think all three statements or statement-forms seem roughly equivalent in force, and so once "mistake" statements are brought into the picture, it may become easier to recognize that the above "wrong" and "bad" statements lack any substantial or intuitively noticeable difference in force.

Of course, in order to make "mistake" statements seem relevant, we examined these statements as they might be made in a prudential rather than a moral context. But if prudential usage of "wrong" and "bad" is indistinguishable in regard to practical force, it would be gratuitous, in fact implausible, to suppose, as it were, that adding the word "morally" created differentially strong prohibitions out of equally strong non-moral prohibitions.

But aside from this abstract consideration, we might just look at those cases where deontic moral prohibitions are most abundantly in evidence—namely, dilemmatic situations where every possible action is said to be wrong—and see whether the force of particular prohibitions or the resultant force of the dilemma is lessened by the substitution of aretaic moral concepts. Having told someone that every act available to her is morally wrong, do I effect any sort of lightening of the moral burden if I retract that statement in favor of saying that every available action is at any rate morally bad or evil? Surely, this doesn't *sound* like a lightening or retraction. And I think that is because however bad it sounds to be in a situation in which one cannot avoid acting wrongly, it sounds no less bad to be in a situation where one cannot avoid doing morally bad things (cannot avoid acting morally badly). If our moral sensibilities are initially, and perhaps permanently, offended by the very idea that through no fault of her own, someone can be in a situation where everything she can do is morally wrong, it seems no less offensive to suppose that, again through no fault of her own, someone can be in a situation where everything she can do is (condemnable as) morally bad.[4] And so I believe that the force of negative aretaic concepts may well be no weaker than that of negative deontic concepts, and this would seem to apply equally to the moral and to the extramoral employment of terms like "wrong" and "bad."

Once we see, therefore, that the deontic terms "right" and "wrong" are not as closely bound to action or action-recommendation as they are often assumed to be, and once (or if), moreover, we become accustomed to the utilitarian distinction between the valid standard of right and wrong and principles that are suitable for the practical regulation of human actions (and see that this distinction also has a place within common-sense morality)[5], it becomes easier to accept the possibility that aretaically based ethical views may constitute our most fundamental ethical standards while lacking certain sorts of action-guiding force and everyday practical usefulness. And, furthermore, in the light of Part I, the intuitively based aretaic approach that appears to have the best chance of such validity is one in which moral concepts/intuitions are avoided and judgments of virtue-status and of admirability treated as basic.

None of the above, however, is incompatible with one obvious fundamental difference between the deontic pair right/wrong and the aretaic pair good/bad. Good and bad seem contraries, right and wrong contradictories, when "right" is taken in its philosophically standard sense of "acceptable" rather than as ascribing positive worth or goodness. But this structural difference fades into insignificance, I believe, when we consider that aretaic ethics can easily express its own equivalent of rightness by speaking of what is "not deplorable (or criticizable)." To be sure, aretaic ethics requires two words at least to express its equivalent of rightness, but the important fact, for our purposes, is that it is capable of expressing an equivalent or analogue both of deontic rightness and of deontic wrongness. Once this is seen, we are well on our way to understanding how analogical or ersatz deontic notions can be derived from aretaic ethical concepts.[6]

The virtue-ethical analogue of (moral) wrongness is deplorability or (some appropriate degree of) criticizability, and to the extent rightness is conceived simply as the contradictory or negation of wrongness, that is, as permissibility or acceptability, it would appear that non-deplorability or non-criticizability is the virtue-theoretic equivalent of (moral) rightness. In that case, we are now in a position to define virtue-analogues of "ought" and "should" and of statements in the imperative mood.

To the extent that claims of moral wrongness are thought to justify "ought" claims and imperatives,[7] we are entitled to claim that someone ought not to do something and to use a grammatical imperative to tell her not to do that thing, once the claim that it is wrong has been justified; likewise, within the aretaic realm, the claim that something is deplorable can at the very least justify imperatives and "ought" claims that stand to more familiar, deontic imperatives and "ought" claims as deplorability stands to wrongness. Where a given act would be deplorable, we can say "don't do it" or claim that one ought not to do it, and such utterances will be derivatively or analogically deontic, if we insist that aretaic notions are fundamentally non-deontic. Such an insistence may possibly be warranted even in the face of the earlier-given arguments for the equivalent force of (morally) aretaic and (morally) deontic claims, respectively, of badness/deplorability and of wrongness. But in fact I am not sure how one can uphold the aretaic/deontic distinction while granting the equivalence in force of aretaic and deontic judgments, and so, although there is more, much more, that needs to be said on this issue, I think we should at this point at least mention the possibility—relative to what has been argued above—that there may be no significant fundamental distinction between aretaic and deontic notions.

Of course, if there is, then derivative, analogical deontic notions can be defined and used as we have been suggesting. But if the distinction is not significant or at least not fundamental, then aretaic judgments may well give rise to full-fledged (so-called) deontic claims about what one ought or ought not to do and to full-fledged "deontic" imperatives. Either way, the earlier mentioned idea that virtue ethics *tells us to be concerned* about our own interests and virtues and also to be concerned about the interests and virtues of others has now been given underpinnings, and it can be seen that even imperative sentences like "Be concerned with others; and be concerned with your own well-being too" are justifiable on a virtue-theoretic, aretaic basis.

Furthermore, if imperatives and "ought" statements are either derivable from or basically at home with aretaic notions, then there is perhaps a more general moral to be drawn about the usage of imperatives and of "ought"s. It may well be that *any* set of evaluative concepts that permits a sufficient range of positive and negative judgments about actions can also accommodate derivative or analogical "ought"s and imperatives and may even in fact allow for its own endemic imperatives and "ought" judgments. For example, in an area of aesthetic evaluation like ballet, a claim that some way of dancing is deplorable or bad can as naturally give rise to the imperative "don't dance that way!" and to the statement "one shouldn't dance that way" as we earlier saw our virtue-ethical attributions of deplorability and admirability naturally slide into imperatives and "ought"-statements. Whether, however, this is a result of the easy derivability of imperatives and "oughts" or is a testimony, rather, to their *fundamentally free-floating evaluational character*, I have not attempted to decide—although it seems to me to be a question well worth pursuing in its own right. But at any rate, given all that we have been saying, I think I should at this point at least offer a final, canonical or foundational statement of the "rules" of common-sense virtue ethics that were introduced, with promissory notes, in Chapter 6.

The virtue-ethical analogue of a perfect duty is a kind of action that is always deplorable, but since, unlike Kant, I have not tried to argue, for example, that lying is always wrong, the deplorability of lying—just to take one example—must be understood as the deplorability of certain kinds of lying done in certain kinds of circumstances. And since, moreover, common-sense moral intuition about the morality of lying—about when it is or is not morally justified—*may not be* codifiable in any long, complex, qualified statement, there is no reason for us to assume that our intuitions about deplorability *have to be* formulable in such a way. What remains, in any event, is our intuitive sense that certain sorts of actions—like lying—raise issues of deplorability (or moral wrongness) case by case whereas others—like charity or beneficence—typically raise such issues *en masse* (as it were). The virtue-theoretic analogues of perfect duties are actions or kinds of actions that raise the issue of deplorability (but not, typically, of admirability) on a case by case basis, and thus, for example, to say that there is a virtue-theoretic equivalent of the perfect duty not to lie is to say (very roughly) that it is, in every instance of the right kind, deplorable (of one) to lie. From such a canonical statement one can then derive the virtue-ethical claim that one *ought not* to lie in such cases and any virtue-ethical imperative with similar import.

By contrast imperfect duty's virtue-ethical equivalent will have to involve the en masse notion of a sufficient number of sufficiently weighty actions of the right kind. Thus virtue-ethics can and, intuitively, should allow for an analogue of the imperfect moral duty to help needy others and can claim, therefore, that it is deplorable for a person who is well off not to give enough and not to give frequently enough to people in need. But the notion of an imperfect duty also allows for a sufficient amount of beneficence to make one morally praiseworthy, and so a plausible virtue-analogue will also want to say that enough giving, sufficient beneficence, is positively admirable. In that case, the "imperfect" virtue rules of Chapter 6 can be fundamentally or canonically (albeit roughly) stated in the form: It is deplorable for one not to actively concern oneself to a sufficient extent with one's own well-being and ethical development, but admirable if one does sufficiently do so; it is also deplorable for one not to actively concern oneself to a sufficient extent with the well-being and ethical development of other people, but admirable if one does sufficiently do so.[8]

Having said as much, I think it should also now be clear how an ethics of virtue can ground—or perhaps even immediately allow for—a notion of ties and bonds. A good or admirable friend, on our account, is, roughly, one who would (almost?) never do the things it is always deplorable for a friend to do, the things a friend ought never to do. But such a friend is also one who not only does for his friend(s) a sufficient (weighted) number of the things it is deplorable for a friend not to do enough of, but also sufficiently often does for his friend(s) what it is positively admirable for a friend to do (thus often). He does, in other words, what he (imperfectly) ought to do vis-à-vis his friend(s) and avoids what he (perfectly) ought not to do vis-à-vis his friend(s), and since a notion of ties and bonds is immediately derivable from such "ought" claims, it should be clear that virtue ethics is capable of grounding a notion (its own distinctive notion) of personal ties. Analogous reasoning would also allow it to ground an equivalent idea of political bonds or ties, though I think there is no reason at this point to grind out the details.

We have now seen that a common-sense approach to ethics that avoids specifically moral judgments and intuitions is capable of avoiding the paradox, incoherence, and other difficulties we say Kantian and common-sense morality/ethics get into in Part I, and we have seen that by use of the notions of a virtue and of admirability we can ground our overall ethical thinking in an economical (i.e., non-redundant) self-other symmetrical way. The present approach gives intrinsic consideration to the good and virtue of others, and as such it comes closer to Aristotelian ethics than, say, to the sort of egoistic foundations one finds in the arguably virtue-ethical approach of Spinoza, the Epicureans, the Stoics, or Nietzsche. Thus we have taken a more conservative tack than would be taken by throwing over Kantian and common-sense morality for an egoistic form of virtue ethics, and I have in fact been assuming, since no one I know seems willing to defend egoism, that egoism need not concern us here.

However, what is not implausibly regarded as a kind of generalized or universalized (Epicurean) egoism, namely, utilitarianism, still very much concerns us, and having at this point discarded Kantianism and common-sense morality, we still have the task of considering the relative merits of utilitarianism and virtue ethics. From now on I will assume that our main goal is to decide between these two approaches to ethics, and we will confront that task head-on in Part IV of this book. First, however, I want to spend some time comparing utilitarianism and virtue ethics. Having previously characterized utilitarianism and virtue ethics in relative separation, I think we can learn a great deal more about each of them if we now, in Part III, spell out some of the most important differences between them. This, in turn, will prove to be of great help when we come to judge their respective merits as philosophical/ethical views in Part IV.

## Notes

1. See, e.g., Sidgwick's *Methods of Ethics*, 7th ed., p. 33.
2. I am not assuming that "ought" is ambiguous or that there is a specifically moral *meaning* of "ought."
3. I assume that what allows for recommendation of $x$ doesn't absolutely prohibit $x$. But we have barely scratched the surface of a complex topic. Cf. Chs. 9 and 10 of Bernard Williams's *Moral Luck*, Cambridge, 1981.
4. Similarly, it seems no less risky to deny a version of the overridingness thesis that uses "bad" than to do so in reference to the standard version using

"(morally) wrong." It is as hard (but no harder) to imagine being overall justified in doing what is morally bad as to imagine having such justification for a morally wrong action.

5. In *Common-sense Morality and Consequentialism* (Routledge, 1985, Ch. 4), I have argued that the common-sense or intuitive permissibility of killing in self-defense needn't be and shouldn't be expected to be taken into account by someone who legitimately kills in self-defense. Where one's life is in imminent danger, it may be entirely acceptable for one just to respond effectively to the danger rather than (at any level) appealing to the justifiability/permissibility of doing so. Thus an appropriately qualified principle about the permissibility of self-defense killing may represent a valid standard of right or permissible action but not an appropriate or inevitable action-guiding rule/practical precept.

6. Robert Louden (in "On Some Vices of Virtue Ethics" in R. Kruschwitz and R. Roberts, eds., *The Virtues*, Wadsworth, 1987, p. 69) mentions, but is not very specific about, the possibility of deriving deontic from aretaic concepts.

7. Those who think moral claims are not automatically reason-giving and who believe appropriate uses of "ought" imply the existence of reasons for action can relativize what I am saying to contexts/individuals where wrongness—or deplorability—is automatically taken to be a reason against doing something. What is taken to be a reason need not, in any event, be taken as an overriding reason for or against action.

8. I have simplified somewhat by not distinguishing between what is enough to undercut claims of wrongness, badness, or deplorability and what is enough to justify claims of goodness or admirability.

# III

## BETWEEN VIRTUE ETHICS AND UTILITARIANISM

# 11

## Reduction vs. Elimination

### The Consistency in Virtue Ethics and Utilitarianism

In Parts I and II I have given an outline, respectively, of utilitarianism and virtue ethics. Both these substantive theories or approaches were formulated with one eye on the partially overlapping paradoxes and difficulties attending common-sense ethics and Kantian ethics. However, I have not attempted and do not now propose to analyze the ethical notions or terms we have been working with. Recent critics of common-sense deontology have not, for example, based their criticisms on particular analyses of wrongness or obligation, nor have they claimed that progress in substantive ethical theorizing requires us to formulate analytic definitions of the terms we use while engaged in such theorizing. And I can see no reason to dispute their methodology or their assumptions in this regard.

What many recent critics of common-sense morality *have* been doing is formulating methodological criticisms of the overall shape or the underlying structures (either metaphor is usefully suggestive) of common-sense morality: criticisms based on charges of inconsistency, asymmetry, incompleteness, oddness, and the like that are somewhat analogous to the sorts of methodological criticisms relevant within other kinds of theorizing. And we have followed this practice both in criticizing Kantian and common-sense ethics/morality and in defending the merits, or at least the relative merits, of both utilitarianism and virtue ethics. However, the ways in which virtue ethics and (direct) utilitarianism seek to avoid the problems of Kantian and common-sense ethics/morality are really very different and need to be spelled out at greater length and more explicitly than we have so far found time to do. Each is in fact internally consistent in the way it learns from or at least avoids the difficulties encountered at such length in Part I, but these separate consistencies in fact contribute to large and striking overall differences between utilitarianism and virtue

ethics, and these larger differences will be the main focus of the remainder of the present chapter.

On the conception of utilitarianism offered in Chapter 4, the utilitarian
proposes similar conditions of application for all moral and rational/
prudential notions. And in doing so the utilitarian smooths out the
varying asymmetries that in common-sense or Kantian thinking attach to
the use of these notions. In addition, however, the solution utilitarians
offer for the difficulties that arise (in part) from such asymmetries is quite
similar to the solution utilitarianism offers for the problem of moral
luck—and this further similarity requires our attention.

The further similarity doesn't simply lie in the fact that utilitarianism
applies the principle of utility to the notions of blameworthiness, praiseworthiness, culpability, etc., just as (though in a somewhat different way)
it applies that principle to notions like wrongness, rationality, and obligation. By employing the principle of utility, utilitarianism clearly clashes
with common-sense intuitions about the applicability of notions like
blameworthiness and also clashes with such intuitions about the application conditions of wrongness, rationality, and the like, but the similarity I
have in mind and wish to emphasize in what follows more closely
concerns the way in which utilitarianism attempts to resolve the problem
of moral luck and the way it seeks to avoid the paradoxes and inconsistencies engendered by self-other asymmetry and the differing degrees (or
strengths) of obligation both Kant and common sense ascribe to our
relations with (socially) nearer and further others.

In both areas, utilitarianism seeks to avoid difficulties, not by simply
eliminating one or another term or concept, but rather by offering its
own distinctive conception of the application conditions of the concept(s)
or term(s) that give rise to the difficulties, and this strategy stands in
marked contrast with the way virtue ethics deals with the very same
original difficulties. Assuming that blameworthiness, (moral) praiseworthiness, and culpability—rather than the class of moral notions
generally—are the concepts that give rise to the inconsistencies inherent
in common-sense thinking about moral luck, the utilitarian offers a new
conception of blameworthiness, etc., that—as we saw in Chapter 4—
attempts to take the sting from the idea of moral luck, whereas virtue
ethics, as we have also seen, proposes simply to eliminate the concepts
that give rise to moral-luck difficulties, rather than to rework them in
terms specifically its own. And this same difference between reworking
and eliminating is also to be found in utilitarianism's and virtue ethics'
respective treatments of the paradox and inconsistency that arise in
connection with self-other asymmetry and with our intuitively stronger

obligations to closer other people. By reworking notions like obligation and wrongness, the utilitarian smooths out the self-other asymmetries and differential obligations to others and thereby avoids the problems facing common-sense and Kantian uses of these notions. But once again, rather than rework the terms that give rise to the difficulties, the virtue theorist eliminates or avoids those terms—and since, unlike the problem of moral luck, the paradoxes connected with asymmetry and differentially strong obligations to others seem to arise for all moral terms without exception, the latter difficulties lead the consistent virtue ethicist to eliminate or abandon all specifically moral terminology in favor of language which, even in its everyday intuitive employment, succeeds in avoiding the difficulties that face Kantianism and common-sense morality (or a common-sense ethics that includes moral notions).

So at least with respect to the problems I have mentioned here, common-sense virtue ethics is consistently eliminative, whereas utilitarianism consistently reworks the concepts that give rise to common-sense difficulties. (We will see later that this distinction may be less absolute than it presently seems, but for our immediate present purposes it can stand.) But these differing consistencies can be further characterized in a way that ultimately should prove extremely useful to our present enterprise, and this further characterization concerns, in particular, the seemingly *reductive* character of the utilitarian approach.

In reworking the notion/term "blameworthiness," for example, the utilitarian also reduces it to (more) empirical terms: the blameworthiness, say, of an act is reunderstood as the existence of a moral obligation to blame the act; that obligation is in turn accommodated to the principle of utility; and the resultant fact that it would produce better results to blame, rather than not to blame, the act is then, and finally, formulated in terms of the fact that blaming the act would produce a greater balance of pleasure over pain (or of desire-satisfaction) than not blaming it. Since this final claim makes no use of evaluative notions and arguably has nothing but "strictly empirical" implications, it is possible to conclude at this point that utilitarianism offers a reductive account of blameworthiness, reprehensibility, and the like and this stands in marked contrast with virtue ethics' eliminative treatment of these notions.

But in its response to self-other asymmetry and differentially strong obligations to others utilitarianism also offers a reductive account of rightness, wrongness, obligation, permissibility, as well as of rationality, prudence, and justice. Obligatoriness (in non-scalar utilitarianism) is reduced to (conduciveness to) the production of maximum pleasure (or happiness or preference-satisfaction) via the identification of this latter with maximally good (i.e., best) results or effects. And it takes no particular ingenuity to see how scalar utilitarianism allows a similar reduction of the comparative terms "morally better," "juster," "more rational," etc. to fundamentally empirical (at least in the sense of non-evaluative) concepts. So utilitarianism is consistently reductive in its attempts to evade or resolve the difficulties that arise from the ordinary usage of moral terms, and by the same token, virtue ethics takes a consistently eliminative stand with regard to the same difficulties and the same terms.[1]

The contrast between morally reductive utilitarianism and morally eliminative virtue ethics assumes a special significance in light of the more general and indeed almost universally applicable contrast between theoretical reduction and theoretical elimination. For example, in past decades as well as currently, the issue of the reduction vs. the elimination of mental entities or concepts has been one of the central issues in the philosophy of mind, and the relevance of methodological or theoretical ideals to that issue has been widely acknowledged and acted upon by those participating in the debate. Similar issues of reduction vs. elimination occur in many, many other areas of philosophy (in the philosophy of mathematics, e.g., as well as in social philosophy, where opponents of social holism may seek either to reduce or eliminate the commitment to such things as societies). But the main point in the present context is that the rivalry or disagreement between utilitarianism and virtue ethics is readily subsumed under the larger contrast between reductive and eliminative theories or approaches. Whatever we eventually decide to say about the relative merits of these two (remaining) ethical theories will possibly have implications for the issue of reductionism vs. eliminationism as it applies in those other areas of philosophy (or scientific theory) where we are more accustomed to finding it. But, by the same token, methodological or other considerations that have seemed relevant to the choice between reductionism and eliminationism in other areas may turn out to be relevant to the choice between utilitarianism and virtue ethics, and so once we recognize the reductionist character of utilitarianism and the eliminationist tendencies of virtue ethics, we may be better able to find ways of adjudicating between them, and what might initially seem to be an intractable problem may turn out to yield (at least partly) to methodological/theoretical considerations of a sort that are fairly familiar from the long-standing debate between common sense and utilitarianism, but are relatively unfamiliar in any application to virtue ethics.

Above, I said that utilitarianism is reductive, while virtue ethics is eliminative of the moral and, although the statement can stand, I think it is important to point out that it does less than full justice to the differences between utilitarianism and virtue ethics. The utilitarian reduces *all* ethical and evaluative concepts to mental/causal empirical terms, and virtue ethics, while it certainly eliminates specifically moral notions, is clearly *not* universally eliminative with respect to ethical notions or entities. There is no reason why an ethics of virtue that has no room for morality proper cannot accommodate notions like prudence and rationality and treat them as virtues and admirable, and it may well turn out that virtue ethics can eventually reduce rationality and prudence to the notion of admirability (or of a virtue) taken together with non-ethical (i.e., non-evaluative) concepts like the self-regarding, the other-regarding, and the causal/counterfactual. So virtue ethics and utilitarianism assume their starkest contrast with respect to moral facts and moral concepts, and the idea that the one is eliminative and the other reductive becomes unfounded and misleading when one speaks more broadly of their theoretical tendencies.

## Reduction and Elimination in Ethics and the Philosophy of Mind

At this point, I think there is more to be learned from turning once again to a comparison between the issue of reduction vs. elimination that arises in connection with utilitarianism and virtue ethics and that which arises in the philosophy of mind between reductive and eliminative materialism (or physicalism).

Two main types of materialism in the philosophy of mind, or metaphysics, have been reductionist identity theory and eliminativism. The former says that mental states, processes, and events can be reduced to states, processes, and events in the brain or central nervous system; the latter eliminates the mental in favor of purely physical or material entities and concepts, denying the existence of anything mental or psychological and claiming that human behavior, or bodily motions, are to be explained in terms of physical phenomena that realize or exemplify no mental or psychological predicates.

In recent years, new kinds of materialism have been defended that fall into neither of the just-mentioned categories: for example, Davidson's anomalous monism and various forms of functionalism. But, for the purposes of our comparison with ethics, we need not consider the latter views.

However, it might at first appear to be a mistake to compare the choice between reduction and elimination in ethics with the choice between reduction and elimination in the ontology/ideology of the mental, because of what appears to be a major difference between the options available in these two areas. Both in the philosophy of mind and in science reduction occurs through an identification of different kinds of higher-level entities with different kinds of lower-level entities: pain, for example, is identified with c-fiber stimulation and joy with some different kind of physical state or process. But utilitarian reductionism seems to be quite different from such models, because it apparently desires to reduce various kinds of ethical predicates, applying to various sorts of entities, to a single natural property: conduciveness to the greatest (or a great or greater) overall balance of pleasure over pain (or of preference-satisfaction over non-satisfaction). And it may therefore be thought that I have perhaps confused reduction with unification, in speaking as I have, of utilitarianism's reductionist tendencies. By making a variety of evaluative characterizations applicable in terms of a single criterion—namely, that embodied in one or another specific form of the principle of utility—we may have provided for a desirable systematic unity in ethics, but since different predicates are presumably not being reduced to different empirical properties, the situation is not like that encountered in the philosophy of mind or in familiar cases of scientific reduction. So perhaps we shouldn't say that utilitarianism is reductionistic and should limit ourselves to claiming that it has unifying tendencies.

But why shouldn't we insist, instead, that in utilitarianism reductionism is *combined* with a strong kind of unificationism? After all, some forms of mind-body reductionism are more unifying at the reducing level than certain others are, and one can, for example, imagine a form of such reductionism that regarded certain smells and certain tastes as identical (at the physical level) and that thus treated two phenomenological kinds as closer than either common-sense or other mind-body reductionist views would consider them to be. Furthermore, in various of its forms, central-state materialism is in a significant sense already both reductive and unifying by comparison with earlier forms of mind-body reductionism. Democritean mind-body materialism identified different senses and mental functions with different bodily organs, whereas modern reductionism regards all mental and sensory functions as centered in a single organ or system of the body. And this represents more than a *spatial* unification, because the location of all forms of psychological functioning in a single place (more easily) allows us to account for the interdependencies of different psychological activities and states and thus helps us to come up with a (more) unified, systematic explanatory account of mental life.

In the cases just mentioned, unification goes hand in hand with reductionism, and to the extent utilitarianism identifies everything moral and ethical with a single natural or empirical property, it would seem appropriate to regard utilitarianism as a form of reductionism, even if it also represents a limiting case where unification is so total or extreme that the reductionistic aspect of the theory is left utterly lacking in variety or complexity. In addition, however, we ought to question whether utilitarian reductionism really is as unified or unvaried as we have until now been assuming for the sake of argument. Does utilitarianism really reduce everything ethical to a single empirical property? I think not, and at this point it is important to see why.

To begin with, and most obviously, the claim that everything is reduced to a single property ignores the distinction utilitarians have always insisted upon between what is good or bad in itself and what is good or bad because of (in virtue of) its consequences or effects. If utilitarianism reduces rightness to *conduciveness* to as great a net balance of pleasure, happiness, or preference-satisfaction as any of an act's alternatives (where "conducive" is understood as remaining neutral as between actual-consequence and expectable-consequence versions of act-utilitarianism), then utilitarianism clearly reduces intrinsic goodness—or goodness in itself—to a *different* property, the non-causal (non-probabilistic) property of *containing* (overall) a positive net balance of pleasure (or whatever) over pain (or whatever). Of course, these two properties are conceptually related (how closely depends on how close *any* causal property and non-causal property can be to one another), but they are importantly different.

Utilitarianism can be broken down into a (maximizing) consequentialistic thesis and a (non-maximizing) thesis about the character of the intrinsically good (this blurs a distinction whose importance will emerge for us in our next chapter, but it will do for the moment). In its consequentialistic aspect, it says that rightness is a matter of (reduces to) maximal conduciveness to consequences of a particular kind: pleasure as opposed to pain, happiness rather than unhappiness. But utilitarian consequentialism picks out consequences of that particular kind because of its hedonistic view of the good, its acceptance of the thesis that only pleasure (or happiness, etc.) is good in itself, its reduction, then, of the intrinsically good to the on-balance—rather than the maximally—pleasurable (or to the containing of a positive—as opposed to an ideal—balance of pleasure over pain, etc.). And so we can already see that utilitarian reductionism is less unified and monotonous than our earlier accusation would have it.

However, there are different and additional reasons for denying that utilitarianism, if it reduces at all, reduces everything ethical and evaluative to a single property, and we ought to mention them.

Utilitarianism may, as we have been suggesting, reduce prudence, rational acceptability, moral rightness/permissibility, and justice to exactly the same empirical property, but there is at least a slight difference, for example, between the property to which it reduces rightness and/or rational acceptability and that to which it reduces moral obligation and/ or rational requiredness. The latter, as we have already seen, are reduced to conduciveness to a *greater* balance of, say, pleasure over pain than any alternative action (would be conducive to); the former, as we have also seen, to conduciveness to *as great* a balance of pleasure over pain as any of an act's alternatives.

Moreover, according to Bentham and other utilitarians, the goodness of a trait, motive, or disposition is a matter solely of how overall good its consequences are for humans (or sentient beings).[2] And even if such motive/trait-utilitarianism and act-utilitarianism are both best treated in scalar or comparative fashion, the former still distinguishes between the evaluation of general motives/traits and the evaluation of particular motives and reduces these two forms of evaluation to slightly (somewhat?) different empirical properties. The betterness of a particular motive (e.g., of the desire for water felt on a given occasion as compared with the desire for wine felt on the same or a different occasion) is, for a utilitarianism of motives, a matter of its being conducive to a greater overall balance of pleasure over pain, whereas, for such utilitarianism, the betterness of some general motive or motive-kind (e.g., of the desire for water compared with the desire for wine) is a matter, rather, of *its instances over all time* being conducive to a greater overall balance of pleasure over pain.

Furthermore, we have still not mentioned the distinction even scalar utilitarianism will presumably wish to make between the (greater) praiseworthiness or blameworthiness and the (greater) moral goodness or badness of an action. Whether one act is morally better than another reduces, as we know, to the act's being conducive to a greater balance of happiness over unhappiness, but for a utilitarian, the greater praiseworthiness of an action would consist in the somewhat different empirical property of its being such that *praising it* would be conducive to a greater balance of happiness over unhappiness than *not praising it*. And finally, since Bentham and other utilitarians have distinguished acts and pleasures or pains with regard to their purity, their fecundity, and their extent, one can easily see how a utilitarian might wish to specify and reduce the notion of an act or other entity's being *good* (or *better*) (over the long run) *for some particular individual* to its being (more) conducive in the long run to that individual's happiness (or balance of happiness over unhappiness).[3]

Now of course in making the above reductive distinctions, various (though not all) terms occur again and again in different combinations, but so far from this counting against the status of utilitarianism as a reductionist view, it tends to highlight and illuminate its reductionist character by sending us toward various comparisons with historically or presently well-known forms of (scientific) reductionism. The Democritean form of atomism treats all psychological and molar physical notions as reducible to descriptions of the motions and natures of atoms in the void, and one of the aims or accomplishments of such a theory is to reduce the variety of descriptions it requires, so that everything it says can be viewed as a particular way of combining a certain smallish number of recurring conceptual elements (e.g., shape, size, position, time). And what we have been seeing and saying about utilitarianism allows us quite comfortably and with a certain amount of insight to compare its unity-inducing form of reductionism to that of ancient atomism or of more recent well-known attempts to reduce everything to a limited number of physical elements or concepts.

However, at this point I think we should consider another objection that could be used to distinguish scientific or mind-body reductionism from ethical reductionism and to cast doubt on the very possibility of the latter. The objection claims that evaluative/ethical terms have an emotive force or meaning that factual, non-evaluative terms lack and so are irreducible to the latter terms even if terms in science or the philosophy of mind *are* reducible to *other factual or non-evaluative terms.*

I mention this objection, not because I think it is particularly forceful, but rather because it will occur to some readers and is probably, therefore, worth responding to, even if only in a brief or sketchy way. In recent philosophy, the distinction between factual and evaluative has seemed less rigid and exclusive than it did, say, forty years ago, but even if we grant that ethical terms possess some sort of emotive/evaluative meaning absent from the terms that occur in more familiar forms of reduction, I can see no reason, in the light of what we have already said, to doubt or deny the possibility of reducing ethical concepts/judgments to fundamentally non-ethical, empirical, natural concepts/judgments that lack emotive or evaluative meaning. If the reduction of terms doesn't require synonymy—and cases like "water is $H_2O$" and "pain is c-fiber stimulation" clearly allow for such a possibility—then why should a particular aspect or feature of the meaning of ethical terms, namely, their evaluative/emotive meaning, have to be preserved in every attempt at reducing such terms, so that we can reduce ethical terms (like "right") to more basic ethical terms (like "conducive to as great a balance of good over evil as any alternative"), but not further to purely naturalistic or empirical terms that are assumed to lack emotive/evaluative meaning (like "conducive to as great a balance of pleasure over pain as any alternative").[4]

Moreover, it is possible to frame an account of evaluative/emotive meaning that plausibly allows sentences using terms with such meaning to have truth conditions, and surely once one has gone this far, it makes no good sense to rule out the possibility of *reductive* truth conditions for such sentences using such terms.[5] And so once again and finally, I think we can see that objections to the idea of utilitarian reductionism melt away under the fire of counterargument, and it seems, therefore, that we have every reason to accept the contrast we have defended between the reductionism of the utilitarian approach and the kind of eliminationism inherent in virtue ethics as we are developing it here.[6]

However, having said as much, I can't resist adding a somewhat non-philosophical observation. If utilitarianism is a form of reductionism rather than eliminationism, and if it is appropriate to compare, as we have, reductionism in the philosophy of mind and reductionism in ethics, then a further fact, a curious fact, seems to stare out at one from the antipodes. Most Australians have preferred reductionist to eliminative materialism and such Australians have also typically been utilitarians, and thus, if all the above is accurate, also reductionists in ethics. Is this more than a coincidence? Is there some reason why Australian (or other) utilitarians should choose reductionism rather than eliminative materialism? Because it is a better account of the mind, some of them will say, hoping to leave the matter at that. But many Americans are eliminative materialists without being utilitarians. And all this seems to suggest some sort of rational or evidential connection between reductionism in ethics and reductionism in philosophy of mind. One may wonder, for example, whether consistency might not require someone who is a reductionist about the one to be a reductionist about the other. So perhaps, in addition, to the merits of reductionism in the philosophy of mind and in ethics taken separately, the preference for reductionism in both together represents a laudable form of consistency for Australian philosophy.

But then shouldn't consistency favor being an eliminativist about mind-body if one accepts a form of virtue ethics that eliminates the moral? Not necessarily. The Australian may be able to claim an additional virtue of consistency in holding reductionism in both the philosophy of mind and in ethics, if he has independent reason for each form of reductionism taken on its own. But in that case, if there is no reason to be an eliminativist about the mind, then there is no special merit in being consistently eliminativist in the philosophy of mind and in ethics.

In any event the eliminativism of virtue ethics is only partial, only the moral is eliminated, whereas mind-body eliminationism standardly denies every kind of mental entity and idea. By contrast, utilitarian reductionism reduces all ethical terms in the way that mind-body reductionism reduces all mentalistic or psychological notions, so the move from either kind of reduction to the other represents a more thoroughgoing or ideal example of consistency than what can be attributed to the move either from mind-body eliminationism to eliminative virtue ethics or in the reverse direction. The complete or ideal parallel of mind-body eliminationism would be a view that denies validity or applicability to all ethical concepts, not one that discards moral concepts for more broadly ethical notions. But this is certainly not the eliminationism advocated by defenders of virtue ethics—and, although it may represent an intriguing, indeed even an important possibility, this is not the time to consider it. Virtue ethics is selectively, not totally, eliminative, and at the present moment we have our hands quite full enough attempting to understand the contrast between such (justifiably) selective eliminativism and a direct scalar utilitarianism that reduces all ethical terms to empirical or non-evaluative terms.

However, before we leave this topic, let me just point out one rather tricky ancillary issue regarding our just-drawn contrast between utilitarianism and the present virtue ethics. We have said that our virtue ethics eliminates all specifically moral concepts/terms and makes use only of broadly ethical notions like admirability, but after our description of the unifying way in which utilitarianism tampers with and/or reduces specifically moral (as well as other ethical) concepts, we might well wonder whether the latter understood in its own terms really makes any use of specifically moral notions. Concepts like the morally good and the morally wrong count as *specifically* moral by or through *contrast* with prudential/rational notions (and perhaps certain other evaluative notions as well), and ordinary admirability, which applies in a single sense *across* these areas of evaluation, for that reason can be said not to be a specifically moral notion. But utilitarianism reduces our divergent ordinary notions of prudence, rationality, moral rightness, and justice to a single agent-neutral criterion of application, and unless we insist even more strongly than we have so far on the distinction between concepts and conceptions, there may be no reason to claim that utilitarianism preserves the specifically moral (or, for that matter, specifically prudential) concepts that ordinary thinking employs.

If, for example, the utilitarian reduction of "rightness" and "prudence" changes the meaning of each and leaves them with a single meaning in common, then utilitarianism gives us a new concept, not merely a new theory or conception, of rightness. In that case, unless one stresses essentialistic origins more than is obviously necessary here, the concept of rightness employed within utilitarianism will not be specifically moral. And although it is not obvious that utilitarianism alters the meaning of "right," etc., in the just-mentioned way, I can see no reason to *insist* that utilitarianism retains (our ordinary) specifically moral concepts while our virtue ethics eliminates them. The differences between virtue ethics and utilitarianism—especially regarding the issue of reductionism—are salient enough even without that particular assumption. But it is time now for us to take the comparison between utilitarianism and virtue ethics in a somewhat different direction, one that opens the whole issue of reduction vs. elimination to a much broader spectrum of considerations. Indeed, our whole treatment of virtue ethics and utilitarianism will now widen considerably, but for this to happen, we will first have to recognize that we have all along been guilty of a certain ambiguity, or possibly vagueness, in our talk about intrinsic goodness.

## Notes

1. Earlier ethicists and others tended to assume that reduction requires synonymy between reducing and reduced terms or expressions: see, for example, W. D. Ross, *The Foundations of Ethics*, Oxford, 1939, p. 8. But more recent accounts of reduction deny the need for the preservation of meaning across reductions: see, e.g., Hempel's *Philosophy of Natural Science*, Prentice-Hall, 1966, pp. 101–10; Stephen Ball's "Reductionism in Ethics and Science: A Contemporary Look at G. E. Moore's Open-Question Argument," *American Philosophical Quarterly* 25, 1988, pp. 197–213; and Putnam's *Reason, Truth and History*, Cambridge Press, 1981, pp. 141, 206ff. (Putnam argues that the utilitarian may wish to identify moral goodness with conduciveness to maximizing total utility on an empirical basis, but also holds that utilitarianism is totally unacceptable as a view of morality or of human flourishing.)

To the extent the ordinary usage of "(morally) right" contains strands the utilitarian wishes to criticize and do away with, the utilitarian view that rightness is nothing more than conduciveness to overall best consequences is already reductive. Certain aspects of the ordinary criteria for applying "right" are pared away, leaving the (from the utilitarian perspective) valid core that is tied to the production of good consequences, to the goals of benevolence. But this can occur before any attempt is made at a further reduction to strictly empirical or non-evaluative terms, of the sort that occurs when the production of good consequences is identified with the production of pleasure/happiness (or when the intrinsically good is identified with pleasure/happiness). Note further that the earlier stage of reduction (before naturalism sets in) would be accepted even by non-utilitarian act- or direct-consequentialists, and, further, that the latter might well seek their own kind of identification (possibly anomalous) of the ethical with the physical/empirical/natural.

2. See Bentham's *An Introduction to the Principles of Morals and Legislation*, J. H. Burns and H. L. A. Hart, eds., London: Methuen, pp. 89, 100, 114f., 125.

3. A question worth considering: if utilitarianism accepts a scalar view of (greater or lesser) moral (or extrinsic) value, is there any reason for it also to hold a purely scalar view of (greater or lesser) intrinsic value, hold, that is, that pleasures and pains can be compared as intrinsically better or worse, but cannot properly be regarded as intrinsically good or bad (evil)? The question obviously ties in with issues of consistency and with questions about ordinal vs. cardinal measures of utility, but there is no space to pursue it further.

4. For criticism of the claim that "factual" or "descriptive" claims must lack emotive/eliminative meaning, see Putnam, *op. cit.*, pp. 208ff.

5. For a view of emotive meaning that treats it as a Grice-type conventional, but non-logical implication of the assertoric use of certain terms, see my "Value Judgments and the Theory of Important Criteria," *Journal of Philosophy* 65, 1968, pp. 105ff. But the idea that emotive meaning doesn't affect (the existence of) truth conditions goes back (surprisingly enough) to Charles Stevenson's *Ethics and Language*.

6. The possible further objection that reduction makes sense for value judgments only if such judgments and/or such reduction serve some useful explanatory purpose can at least partly be answered by reference to the explanatory uses to which utilitarian and other value judgments have recently been put by defenders of utilitarianism and others. See, e.g., N. Sturgeon, "Moral Explanations," in D. Copp and D. Zimmerman, eds., *Morality, Reason and Truth*, Rowman and Allanheld, 1984, Ch. 2; Peter Railton's "Moral Realism," *Philosophical Review*, 1986, pp. 163–207; and my "The Rationality of Aesthetic Value Judgments," *Journal of Philosophy*, 1971, pp. 821–39.

# 12

## Two Kinds of Intrinsic Goodness

We know that the term "good" is (something like) ambiguous across the many domains of its use, and when we are told that the use of "good" in "Eva is a good person" is very different from its use in "his actions have had good consequences," we are not likely to object too strenuously (even if on theoretical grounds we may be inclined to hold that "good" has a single meaning), because we recognize a clear difference between goodness as admirability (moral or otherwise) and goodness as some sort of (intrinsic) desirability. A good and admirable man may also be desirable (to have around in given circumstances or more generally), but good consequences are, standardly, desirable consequences, not admirable consequences (whatever that may mean), and when we say, in virtue of the pleasure produced for all concerned, that a certain decision had good or desirable consequences, it would be at the very least odd to speak of the decision's having had admirable consequences, because we don't usually regard (feelings of) pleasure as (morally or otherwise) admirable. Even utilitarianism, with its penchant for unification acknowledges the conceptual difference between moral or instrumental good, on the one hand, and intrinsic good, on the other, with only the latter sort of good usually being relevant to the discussion of the goodness of consequences.

However, there is a distinction between what makes for personal well-being and what makes states of affairs good whose importance may be underrated if one regards everything from a utilitarian perspective. Utilitarians are hedonists who hold that (intrinsic) personal good or well-being is exclusively a matter of desire-satisfaction, pleasure, or happiness. But they are also (in Sen's sense) "welfarists" who claim that facts about personal good determine the relative goodness of states of affairs, and they hold, even more strongly, that the *net sums* of personal good existing in states of affairs determine the relative goodness of those states of affairs. This last thesis Sen calls "outcome utilitarianism," and I have expressed it only in rough terms.[1] But what is important for our purposes here is that it is possible to be a hedonist without holding welfarism, much less outcome utilitarianism, for the recognition of this possibility will force us to recognize that there are two kinds of intrinsic goodness or desirability.

Thus for all their deep disagreements about other matters, Kant, for example, seems to agree with utilitarianism in holding a fundamentally hedonistic view of personal well-being or happiness. Kant famously distinguishes, of course, between *das Gute* (the good) and *das Wohl* (well-being, welfare, happiness), but he treats the latter at least as fundamentally a matter of pleasure vs. unpleasure or pain, and even if Kant and the utilitarians (and the Epicureans, to bring in those whose views on pleasure and well-being Kant seems most immediately to have in mind) formulate hedonism differently and end up with slightly differing views as a result, the similarities here seem far more striking than the differences.[2] However, none of this means that Kant is a welfarist about what makes states of affairs, or states of the world, good. Although Kant doesn't explicitly, much less self-consciously, speak of good states of affairs or their determinants, it is easy enough to understand him through the prism of such terminology. So when Kant distinguishes personal good from what an impartial observer would approve and tells us that such an observer or judge would not approve a person's well-being or happiness if it were totally unaccompanied by any moral merit, we can naturally read him as saying that it is not (a) good (thing) that personal good, happiness or well-being should exist in the absence of any worthiness to be happy, and when (elsewhere, but very much in the same vein) Kant distinguishes between *das Gute* and *das Wohl* and ascribes the former to situations where individuals have the latter proportionately to their moral deserts or merit, there is every reason, I think, to understand him to be distinguishing, sharply, between facts about the personal *well-being* that exists *in* a given situation or history of events and the *goodness of* such a situation (history or state of affairs). And in that case, while (coming close to) being a hedonist about personal good, Kant's views about what makes situations or states of affairs good is clearly incompatible with welfarism and with a utilitarianism that implicitly or explicitly accepts welfarism.

I mention the possibility of implicit welfarism here, because, even if it is somewhat anachronistic to attribute welfarism to those utilitarians, like Bentham and Sidgwick, who didn't explicitly talk about good states of affairs, it seems fairly clear that, if asked, such utilitarians would never have said, like Kant, that the goodness of situations/states of affairs can be influenced by factors other than personal welfare.[3] On the subject of welfarism, there is a radical divide between utilitarianism and Kant, however close they may come with respect to hedonism, and this historical/analytical observation should help to illustrate the difference between two major notions of ethics that ethical theorists often fail to distinguish or actually confuse. The idea of good states of affairs has up to now in this book been kept fairly well in the background, but once we have that notion clearly in view and clearly differentiated from the idea of personal well-being or good, the issue of reductionism vs. eliminationism widens in significance and requires our attention as a topic of more thoroughgoing study than we have as yet been able to devote to it. For the moment, however, I think we have our hands full just with making the distinction between personal good and goodness in states of affairs, so let us, in somewhat greater depth, make sure we know what we are doing as we sail off under the assumption that there is a philosophically important distinction to be made here.

To begin with, we might ask ourselves how the distinction interacts with or is affected by that between intrinsic and extrinsic or instrumental good or value.[4] Can our supposedly new distinction not in fact be subsumed under the latter, familiar one and the whole previous discussion be demystified—even rendered otiose—by insisting on the difference between what has value or is good in itself and apart from its effects and what is valuable (only) in virtue of (potentially) leading to or resulting in valuable consequences? I believe not, and it can be shown, I think, that the failure of these two distinctions to coincide or be reducible to one is actually responsible for some of the tendency to confuse the goodness of states of affairs with the personal well-being of those who are in various states of affairs.

Although in some, even many, cases the distinction between intrinsic and instrumental personal goods may be vague or difficult to apply, some personal goods are typically regarded as merely instrumental to a good life, others as part of, elements in, personal well-being or a good life, and the distinction, for example, between money and what it brings is clearly considered relevant to differentiating intrinsic from instrumental/extrinsic personal good. According to many, the mere possession of wealth is not even partly constitutive of a good life or personal well-being, and is merely a means to living well, merely an instrumental personal good; and although this last assumption is probably more difficult to defend than is usually conceded,[5] its point is clear enough and should help to make us clear or clearer on the difference between intrinsic and instrumental personal goods.

But, unfortunately, this gets us nowhere in any attempt we may wish to make to reduce the distinction between good states of affairs and personal goods to the distinction between intrinsic and instrumental/extrinsic good(s). For the same distinction between intrinsic and instrumental can also be applied to the assessment of states of affairs. The existence of a proportionality between moral merit/desert and happiness is not valued by Kant on instrumental grounds, but rather, quite clearly, for its own sake. But once one acknowledges that certain states of affairs or courses of events are good in themselves, it is clearly possible to consider other states and events as valuable means to the latter, and if, for example, it is considered intrinsically good for morally bad people not to prosper and actually to be punished for their wrongdoings, then one can easily regard the fact that a certain evil person is being tried for his crimes—regard that total situation, event, or state of things—as an instrumentally good means to the just-mentioned inherently valuable end.[6] So the evaluation of states of affairs, etc., allows of an intrinsic/instrumental distinction that seems no less valid than that between intrinsic and instrumental personal goods and, as a result, it seems clear that the distinction between good states of affairs and personal goods cannot be equated with or reduced to the familiar distinction between the instrumental and the intrinsic. In fact, given our interests as ethicists, the distinction between good states of affairs and personal goods is effectively or most importantly a distinction between two kinds of intrinsic goodness.

Indeed, the fact that the intrinsic/instrumental distinction cuts across the distinction between personal goods and good states of affairs helps to explain how and why the latter is so frequently ignored or a source of confusion. The idea that there are two kinds, even two concepts, of intrinsically good things doesn't naturally or easily occur to one after one has already taken the trouble to differentiate intrinsic from instrumental goods, and the further fact, as it appears, that a philosophically clarified and distinct concept of intrinsically good states of affairs first begins to emerge in Kant's ethics and, within the utilitarian tradition, in the writings of G. E. Moore, shows how recently clarity about the distinction I am focusing on has become possible. Nonetheless, it is an important distinction from the standpoint of general ethical theory and even, in addition, as a means to settling quite particular issues that have often been a source of controversy and confusion.

Consider, for example, the long-standing, familiar question whether the pleasure a sadist takes in the suffering of an innocent person is an intrinsically good thing, and thus, somewhat more generally, whether all pleasure is good apart from its (possibly beneficial, possibly deleterious) effects. Some philosophers treat this question as (fundamentally equivalent to) the question whether such pleasures can correctly be regarded as intrinsic personal goods (or as good for those who enjoy them if one leaves any and all intrinsically bad causes and effects of such pleasure out of the picture). Notably and notoriously, the classical utilitarians wish to regard such pleasures as good taken in themselves, but something in most of us rebels at such a view and, to the extent the distinction between personal goods and goods states of affairs is not explicitly available, that feeling is likely to emerge as some sort of opposition toward the utilitarian/hedonistic assumption that sadistic pleasures are an element in the personal well-being or good of sadists.[7] And it is at the very least difficult to defend such opposition when the utilitarian insists that in calling the sadist's pleasure intrinsically good or good in itself, he is ruling out of consideration the bad character that may cause and the bad effects on himself and others that may result from sadistic pleasure, that is, is ascribing goodness only to the pleasure considered in itself and apart from its causes and effects. For it is in terms of its causes and effects that common sense most readily objects to calling sadistic pleasure good, and the utilitarian may therefore seem to win the day here by making distinctions that common-sense seems to be confusing or failing to attend to.

But intuitive opposition to calling the pleasure of sadists (intrinsically) good can get a second wind from the distinction we have been insisting upon between good states of things and personal goods. For even if it is granted that the pleasure of a sadist is intrinsically good for the sadist, an element in his personal well-being or good, the *existence* of such pleasure is (typically)[8] not a good thing (in itself or in its effects or causes). That is, it is not intrinsically or inherently (a) good (thing) that sadistically derived pleasure should exist, so the state of affairs consisting in some sadist's feeling sadistic pleasure is (usually) an intrinsically bad, rather than a good one, even if the sadist derives personal good or benefit from or in having such pleasure. Of course, one may wish to insist that there is nothing *in any sense* good about sadistic pleasure, and the distinction between good states of affairs and personal goods clearly does not help one to make this stronger claim. But even Kant, I think, would shy away from disallowing sadistic pleasure as an element in someone's Wohl (well-being), and once the distinction is made in the above manner, I think most of us would, on or relative to intuitive grounds, be happy to conclude that it is (usually or often) a bad thing (state of affairs) for a sadist to derive personal good or pleasure from inflicting pain on other people. So it is a good deal easier to say what one wants to against sadistic pleasure if one distinguishes between good states of affairs and personal goods in a way that many utilitarians and others who have discussed this issue have failed to do.

Moreover, this same example also helps us in avoiding some further confusions that derive from the *attempt* to make the distinction between good states of affairs and personal goods, rather than from *failure* to be aware of that distinction. After all, the pleasure that a sadist feels is reasonably regarded as a psychological/physical state of that person, so if we say that it is intrinsically good for the sadist, aren't we talking about an intrinsically good state of affairs, rather than, as we earlier claimed, about an intrinsic personal good (only)? And isn't (the taking of) a good hot bath a train of events in the life of some individual whose goodness is operative at the level of good trains of events, rather than (merely) at the level of personal good? Obviously, we need further support for the distinction I have been attempting to make, if we are to be confident of its existence and its import, and I believe this further support is forthcoming from some of the locutions we have already been making use of in characterizing the difference—as well as from one or two other points that have as yet not really been made.

Above, we effectively equated the intrinsic non-goodness of the state of affairs consisting in somebody's feeling sadistic pleasure with the idea (1) that the *existence* of such pleasure is not an intrinsically good thing and with the further idea (2) that it is not (an) intrinsically good (thing) that such pleasure should exist. These latter locutions may help us distinguish between what we have wanted to call good states of affairs and personal states like sadistic pleasure that we have insisted represent only personal goods. (We can make good the distinction between events-as-personal-goods and the goodness of trains or histories of events in similar fashion, but to keep things simple(r), I will talk only about states of affairs and the example of sadistic pleasure.)

The sadistic pleasure felt by a sadist may be a personal good (that most of us would be incapable of feeling or sharing), but (in most cases) intuitively the fact or existence of such pleasure is not a good thing in the sense of (2) above. And "that"-clauses of the general type exemplified by (2) can serve as our canonical way of expressing evaluations (intrinsic or otherwise) of states of affairs. The pleasure felt by the sadist may well count as an (intrinsic) personal good and, since it constitutes a state of that sadist, as a personally good state of the sadist; but even so that state of pleasure doesn't count in our present terminology as an intrinsically good state of affairs because it is not good that the state of pleasure in the sadist should exist, that is, more simply stated, not good that the sadist should feel such pleasure (even if the sadist derives personal good from or in doing so).[9]

Thus if in one sense sadistic pleasure may be the desirable result of arrangements the sadist himself may make, if, that is, that pleasure may count as a personally good thing that the sadist has managed to arrange for himself, still in another sense/way something undesirable also seems to result from these arrangements, and in common-sense terms it seems quite plausible to say that it is undesirable, or bad, that such pleasure should be felt. However, from a utilitarian perspective not only is the sadist's pleasure an (intrinsic) personal good, but it is also in no way (intrinsically) undesirable that the sadist should feel sadistic pleasure (i.e., pleasure at the very thought of someone's suffering as a result of her own doings). For utilitarians, to the extent they accept any view about the goodness of states of affairs, accept welfarism and outcome utilitarianism and thus hold that the source and even the character of pleasures felt make no difference to the intrinsic value of states of affairs involving such pleasures except by affecting how much pleasure is felt in the states of affairs under evaluation. It doesn't matter whether the pleasure derives from pushpin or from poetry or whether it is inherently (i.e., in its intentionality) sadistic or innocent—it is only the net amount or sum of pleasure or happiness or personal good that determines, for the utilitarian, how (comparatively or non-comparatively) good a certain state of affairs is, and this stands in marked contrast with our ordinary intuitions about the goodness of states of affairs and with Kant's views on this topic, as well.

In fact, by contrast with utilitarianism, Kantian views about the goodness of states of affairs or histories of events seem quite close to those most of us would naturally espouse if we were asked appropriate leading questions, and the idea, for example, that it is not a good thing (and is even a bad thing) for evil to go unpunished and/or for happiness to be "disproportionate" to virtue or moral merit seems as much to be part of common-sense thinking as to belong to Kant's distinctive view of ethics.[10] To be sure, if you ask a non-philosopher whether she thinks it is better or worse for people to be happy—and she is not put out of sorts by being asked such an obvious question—she will probably without ado say that it is better; but far from supporting the utilitarian idea that only (amount of) personal well-being or good is inherently relevant to the evaluation of states of affairs, such an answer at best shows how charitable people are in dealing with such questions. Implicitly or explicitly, such an answer presupposes—even if the person has never thought of it—that the people whose happiness is at issue are deserving of happiness, or at least not wicked or deserving of punishment or unhappiness, and if one explicitly asks, for instance, whether it is good for people as bad as Hitler to be happy, the principle of charity is given no foothold and one will get a very different answer.

So common-sense thinking and Kant come rather close to one another in the way they assess goodness and badness in states of affairs—and this should come as no surprise when one considers how much closer common-sense and Kantian moral judgments are to each other than either is to the particular moral judgments utilitarianism espouses. Although I wouldn't want to say that Kant has in effect captured our common-sense thinking about the intrinsic character of states of affairs or even that the two forms of thinking are close in every important respect, they seem at least to have the following in common: both treat common-sense, non-consequentialistic moral judgments as if they were immediately relevant to judgments about the goodness or badness of states of affairs, situations, etc. And this is something utilitarianism clearly and deliberately refrains from doing (to the extent it makes explicit judgments about the goodness of states of affairs).

We morally disapprove of sadistic pleasure and of the idea of the evil going unpunished or being supremely happy/contented, and it seems reasonable to suppose that these common-sense and non-consequential-istic moral judgments influence or are relevant to our judgment that it is (usually) not good for sadistic pleasure to be felt or for morally bad people who have, say, harmed and killed many other people to lead subsequently happy lives. (Canonically, this is equivalent to saying that it is not good *that* sadistic pleasure should be felt or that bad people should . . . be happy.) But utilitarianism considers (the net sum of) personal good(s) to be the only factor(s) relevant to the assessment of states of affairs, and so subscribes to the theses of welfarism and outcome utilitarianism in a way that neither Kantianism nor common intuition is willing to do. Interestingly enough, however, there is at least one respect in which Kantianism and utilitarianism seem closer to one another than either is to common-sense ethical thinking. For if we limit ourselves to what is intrinsically desirable in life, to the question what things count as intrinsic personal goods, then both classical utilitarianism and Kant seem committed to (something like) hedonism, whereas common sense appears to allow for a number of elements of well-being that cannot be equated with or reduced to pleasure or happiness.[11]

But having made these distinctions and comparisons, I would like to revive the main issue of the preceding chapter and consider how all the above relates to the issue of reduction vs. elimination. And perhaps we had better first talk about reductionism, because the relation of what we have just been saying about utilitarianism to the generally reductive character of the latter is fairly easily demonstrated.

For a utilitarianism in which the notion of a good state of affairs is explicit, the idea of one act or motive's being better than another reduces to the idea of conduciveness to an overall better state of affairs than alternatives would lead (or would have led) to; this notion in turn is reduced via the thesis of outcome utilitarianism to the idea of conduciveness to a greater net sum of personal good or benefits; and the latter, finally, is reduced via hedonism to the idea of conduciveness to a greater net sum of happiness or pleasure.

This more complicated process/thesis of reduction has an interesting side benefit, because it indicates how a utilitarianism that accommodates or insists upon the notion of a good state of affairs or history of things can reduce that notion to the notion of a personal good or benefit, taken together with various other notions that seem strictly non-evaluative and non-ethical. And this adds a further dimension to utilitarian reductionism that we are only now, I believe, in a position to explore. The last chapter made it clear that moral/instrumental notions like goodness of motive or action are reducible by the utilitarian to the notion of a net sum of benefits or personal goods. But what emerges in the present chapter is that utilitarianism is capable and desirous of reducing more than the evaluative/ethical notions of instrumental (or moral) goodness or betterness and of intrinsic personal good or well-being. In addition, the utilitarian can reduce the notion of an intrinsically good state of affairs, but instead of first reducing it, as with moral goodness, to *conduciveness* to (a positive or greater net sum of) intrinsic personal good or benefit, the utilitarian reduces it to some notion of *containing* or *including* (a positive or greater net sum of) intrinsic personal good or benefit, and this adds further complexity and a new dimension of interest to what we have previously said about the character of utilitarian reductionism. (Nor is our picture of utilitarian reductionism even now completed.)

In the previous chapter, moreover, we compared utilitarian reductionism vis-à-vis the moral to a proposed virtue-ethical elimination of moral notions, and we ought therefore to consider whether this parallelism continues into the topic of good states of affairs. Can anything we have said, can anything we may be able to say about the idea of a good state of affairs give us similar reason to eliminate the notion of a good state of affairs from a virtue ethics that wishes to remain free of the earlier-mentioned difficulties of common-sense moral thinking? What may make us hope for and pursue this further parallelism is the previously noted fact that moral considerations seem to enter into our criteria for goodness in a state of affairs. For Kant it is (intrinsically) bad or at least not good that happiness should not accord with moral virtue or merit or that (and it is probably easier for us to get an ordinal grip on these notions) certain people who are more morally virtuous than others should have less happiness than those others.[12] And Kant has clearly here picked up on an element of ordinary moral or ethical thinking: what he says here is intuitively plausible or at least doesn't seem totally counterintuitive to most of us. So to the extent that Kant and ordinary thinking treat moral notions like moral virtue or goodness as inherently relevant to the goodness or badness of states of affairs, a virtue ethics that suspects and stays clear of specifically moral ideas will presumably have some reason to stay clear of the concept of a good state of affairs as well.

But why shouldn't virtue ethics just treat good states of affairs along utilitarian reductive lines, making (net total) personal good the sole criterion of goodness in states of affairs and thus removing all distinctively and intuitively moral considerations from the evaluation of states of affairs? Even virtue ethics isn't always eliminative in regard to ethical concepts, so why should it have to be eliminative about all, rather than just some, specifically (or implicitly) *moral* notions? Well, perhaps it doesn't have to be eliminative about all moral concepts and could somehow find a way to preserve and give a satisfying account of goodness in states of affairs, but that doesn't mean that it makes sense, in this one instance, for common-sense virtue ethics to follow the *utilitarian* path of reduction. For we earlier saw how commitment to certain forms of direct utilitarianism gave one reason, in all consistency, to espouse certain other forms of direct utilitarianism (e.g., with respect to the concepts of prudence and rationality). And once we let the utilitarian foot in the door by accepting a utilitarian reductive account of good states of affairs, the alert utilitarian will be all over us asking why, in all consistency, we shouldn't also accept a utilitarian reductive account of moral wrongness or betterness, rather than eliminating these notions, as our present approach to virtue ethics proposes. So if virtue ethics wishes to survive and remain free of the charge of inconsistency, the foot shouldn't be let in the door and goodness in states of affairs should be eliminated, rather than reduced in utilitarian fashion. Of course, this leaves open the possibility of some other form of reduction with less devastating consequences—but I have no idea how such a thing would work, and until we have a better idea of this possibility I think we had better stick with the approach to virtue ethics I am here working out in some detail.

In doing so, and, in particular, in allowing virtue ethics to escape the charge of inconsistency by simply refusing to give a utilitarian reduction of goodness in states of affairs, I am not, however, giving virtue ethics any sort of unfair advantage in its theoretical competition with utilitarianism, and I am certainly not freeing virtue ethics from the need to answer strong criticism. The point, rather, is that virtue ethics' only chance of success requires it to avoid inconsistency just as we earlier pushed utilitarianism to avoid inconsistency, but the total or larger ethical picture that a consistent virtue ethics eventually arrives at still needs to be measured against direct utilitarianism, and nothing we have yet said prejudices the issues involved in that ultimate critical comparison. So I think virtue ethics has reason at this point to eliminate the morally colored notion of a good state of affairs rather than attempt a reduction of it in utilitarian terms.

But there is another possibility we have not yet considered. We might simply leave the notion alone and hope or attempt to show that despite the relevance of moral considerations to its Kantian and its ordinary application, the idea of a good state of affairs has none (or few) of the problems endemic to our ordinary application of notions like moral goodness and rightness. But it is in fact difficult to see how our ordinary or Kantian usage of "good state of affairs" could avoid the problems uncovered earlier. The notion of a good state of affairs is not merely marginally or occasionally affected by moral considerations during the course of its ordinary or its Kantian employment, and though, in the light of previous discussion, this point should be already obvious in regard to the Kantian criteria for goodness in states of affairs, some further attention to our ordinary usage of the notion can make it clear that the latter is thoroughly infiltrated by (intuitive) moral considerations.

For one thing, we normally would hold it to be worse (other things being equal) that someone who has negligently damaged another person should go unpunished (or be happy) than that this should occur with someone who has merely damaged herself, and such judgments clearly indicate how the self-other asymmetry of common-sense moral evaluations of actions influences, or is at least exemplified in, our ordinary views about the goodness (or fittingness or rightness) of states of affairs. But those views also reflect the differentially strong obligations that common-sense morality assigns to us in virtue of our nearer or further relation to other people: that is, it seems morally worse to neglect the health of one's children than to neglect that of one's neighbor's children (other things being equal), and that difference is reflected in a tendency to think that it is worse that a given person should neglect his children's health than that someone, possibly the same person, should neglect the health of children—the same number of children if you wish—living in his neighborhood. So at this point I tend to believe that our intuitive application of the notion of a good state of affairs is subject to paradoxes and difficulties that parallel (at least some of) those uncovered in Part I in connection with the common-sense morality of actions and persons. If we had reason to drop specifically moral concepts relating to acts and persons in an attempt to develop an ethics of virtue, we have reason now to drop the notion of a good state of affairs in our otherwise common-sensical virtue-ethical approach to ethical theory. So in regard to the notion of an (intrinsically or extrinsically) good state of affairs, the same division of labor into utilitarian reduction and virtue-ethical elimination holds good that we previously witnessed in connection with specifically, or more explicitly, moral notions like right and wrong, praise- and blameworthiness, etc. But we are even now not yet finished with our business in this area. I think we need to take a larger view of the issue of reduction vs. elimination than anything we have so far attempted, and the attaining of such a larger view requires us in the following chapter both to take a more synoptic look at the main concepts we have been using and to recognize how completely they cover, or at least touch, the most important perennial problems of substantive ethical theory.

## Notes

1. For a more precise account of these theses, see Sen's "Utilitarianism and Welfarism," *Journal of Philosophy* 76, 1979, pp. 463–89. Like Sen, I will for simplicity's sake assume a constant population and ignore the distinction between average utilitarianism and total welfare utilitarianism.

2. The Kantian views I am describing can be found, e.g., in the *Fundamental Principles of the Metaphysics of Morals* and in the *Critique of Practical Reason.*

3. To the extent that it is somewhat anachronistic to attribute welfarism to Bentham and Sidgwick, it is also somewhat anachronistic to employ the notion of a good state of affairs in defining consequentialism and utilitarianism. And yet this is the way these views are most typically defined/conceived nowadays (see, e.g., Sen, *op. cit.* and Williams, "A Critique of Utilitarianism" in Smart and Williams, *Utilitarianism: for and against*, Cambridge Press, 1983). Although he is not totally explicit about it, G. E. Moore in *Principia Ethica* seems to have been the first utilitarian to evaluate actions by reference to the production of good situations or states of affairs. But, of course, the notion of a good state of affairs may be implicit in the very idea of good or best consequences—which is not, after all, exactly the same as the notion of consequences in which there is the greatest net sum of good or well-being.

4. To keep matters relatively simple, I will not discuss, though I am implicitly

adjusting my account to, the distinction between conditional and instrumental goods. (See C. Korsgaard's "Two Distinctions in Goodness," *Philosophical Review* 92, 1983, pp. 169–95; and my *Goods and Virtues*, Oxford, 1990, Ch. 3.)

5. On this point see *Goods and Virtues*, Ch. 6.

6. I am ignoring here the problems that would be introduced and the complications that would be necessitated by a consideration of the Good Samaritan Paradox.

7. For what I take to be an example of this tendency, see Richard Brandt's discussion of sadistic pleasure in *Ethical Theory*, Prentice-Hall, 1959, pp. 315f., where no implicit or explicit distinction seems to be made between intrinsically good states of affairs and intrinsic personal goods and where the latter are the sole focus of the discussion. By contrast, Sen, *op. cit.*, uses this kind of example *precisely in order to distinguish* between the evaluation of (sums of) personal goods and that of states of affairs.

8. This qualification and those to follow are inserted to allow for the possibility that a sadist's feeling sufficiently *great* pleasure at someone's *minor* pain might on balance count as a good state of affairs. One might (commonsensically?) deny welfarism while granting that (quantity of) personal good always has some force in favor of the goodness of containing states of affairs and even that it can sometimes outweigh the fact of the personal good's being sadistic. I am indebted here to an anonymous referee.

9. The distinction between good states of affairs and personal goods is not easily statable in terms of the person-relativity of the latter, because it is also possible to quantify into a "good that" context, and, speaking *de re*, evaluate the state of affairs consisting in some entity $x$'s being well off. For an example, see the assertion made near the end of note 8, above.

Note too the potential ambiguity in "it is good for the sadist to feel sadistic pleasure" as between "the feeling of sadistic pleasure constitutes a personal good for the sadist" and "it is good that the sadist should feel sadistic pleasure." Such ambiguities are no doubt also part of the explanation of why so many philosophers with a stake in making the distinction seem nonetheless to have ignored the distinction between good states of affairs and personal or life goods (elements in personal well-being).

10. For a preKantian expression of something like Kant's view about the undesirability of failures of correlation or proportionality between moral worth and happiness, see Samuel Clarke's *A Discourse of Natural Religion* in D. Raphael, ed., *British Moralists: 1650–1800*, Oxford, Clarendon, 1969, esp. p. 193.

11. See *Goods and Virtues*, Ch. 6.

12. An ordinal connection between virtue (or moral desert) and happiness would exist if for any two people $x$ and $y$, $x$ was (long-run) happier than $y$ if and only if $x$ was (long-run) more virtuous than $y$. A cardinal connection would exist if absolute numerical values (relative to some standard unit) could be assigned to the virtue and the happiness of different individuals, and if some sort of equiva-

lence or proportionality between the numerical value of happiness and that of virtue could be used as the basis of a general view about the goodness and badness of states of affairs involving the relation between happiness and virtue. Another simpler, but richer than ordinal possibility: the idea of an equivalence between how happy and how virtuous given people are. The complete good or a good state of affairs would exist if everyyone, e.g., who was very virtuous was very happy and everyone slightly bad was slightly unhappy, etc. For a fuller discussion of Kant's ideas here and, in particular, of some distinctions among different notions of the *summum bonum*, see L. W. Beck's *A Commentary on Kant's "Critique of Practical Reason,"* University of Chicago, 1963, pp. 246f., 268f.

# 13

## Reduction vs. Elevation

### Main Concepts of Ethics

The ethical notions we have been working with in the present book can conveniently and usefully be classified into five main categories. To begin with, we have been speaking about and making substantive use of *moral concepts*, and we have also mentioned and employed what can be called *rational concepts*, concepts involved in the evaluation of choices, acts, and other entities from the standpoint of practical reason: examples of the latter include prudence, rational acceptability (or requiredness), (the) goodness, or betterness, of (a) choice, and the idea of reasons for action. Of course, there are a number of ways in which one might criticize any attempt to distinguish between terms of rational and moral assessment. It could be said that moral terms, rather than being separate from the vocabulary of rational criticism, represent a specific subclass of that vocabulary—or one might claim that the truly fundamental divide is not between moral and rational notions, but rather between rational and moral aretaic notions, on the one side, and rational and moral deontic notions, on the other. But rather than join these issues, let me simply say by way of concession that I am not claiming any sort of ultimacy for the conceptual lines I am drawing and that I won't take sides on whether appropriate uses of moral concepts automatically give reasons for action—anyone who thinks moral concepts are a species of rational ones can think of the distinction drawn above as differentiating specifically moral rational concepts from morally neutral or undifferentiated rational concepts.

However, we have also made use of ethical concepts that are neither rational nor moral, and the most important of these have been the notion of a virtue, the notion of admirability, and their opposites (in size and in sign). Since the notion of a virtue is arguably just that of an admirable trait of character and since, on the other hand, anyone suspicious of the distinction between character and other personal traits will presumably still want to equate the virtues with (certain kinds of) admirable personality traits, it would seem that the ethical notion of a virtue can be reduced to that of admirability taken in conjunction with other notions whose identity may be somewhat subject to dispute. So I will say that admirability and kindred concepts represent the third of the categories of ethical notions we have been employing.

The two remaining categories are those, in fact, that we concentrated on in the previous chapter. The notion of personal well-being or welfare, the concept of personal good or of *a* personal good, the idea of things going well for someone or in someone's life, or, finally, of a good or desirable life: all these notions seem to cluster naturally together and can be treated as involved in a common class that can be conveniently referred to as the category of personal good. And as we saw just a little while ago, this category, this set of concepts, is distinct both from the category of the moral and from our fifth major category, the class of notions that can be used to evaluate states of affairs, histories of events, and the like.[1]

One of the main strengths or attractions of utilitarianism is that it allows for a reduction of the five just-mentioned ethical categories to the notions of just one of those categories suitably supplemented by appropriate causal, mereological, and other notions.[2] Utilitarianism as a view of right and wrong, obligation and permission, allows for a reduction of all its moral terminology to the idea of producing or resulting in good states of affairs, and the latter idea and others of its category can in turn be reduced to the category of personal good. (As I have mentioned, the reduction can be effected without going through the idea of a good state of affairs, but the latter, in any event, can be reduced to ideas relating to personal good, according to utilitarianism.)[3] In addition, we saw in Chapter 4 that a consistent direct utilitarianism has reason to treat rational terms similarly to the way it treats moral terms, so notions like "prudent," "rationally acceptable," and "good choice" are also utilitarianly reducible to the category of personal good taken together with nonevaluative concepts.[4] For utilitarianism, the notion of a virtue is equivalent to that of a good trait of character (or of personality), and the latter clearly also reduces to the idea of causing personal good or benefit. And presumably admirability and excellence of character are equivalent to goodness of character, and so represent, for the utilitarian, species of evaluation that can be handled in the way other evaluative notions are. To the degree that the utilitarian wishes to make any use of them, they too will be reducible to the ethical category of personal good.

In addition, however, and as already mentioned, the category of personal good is treated by the utilitarian as further reducible to empirical or non-ethical notions like preference-satisfaction or pleasure/pain, so the above classification into five categories, together with the discussion of previous chapters, shows us how the utilitarian can reduce all ethical notions to naturalistically understandable concepts. Thus the ability to take (the) main concepts of ethics and reduce them to a single kind demonstrates once again, but more impressively because even more generally than we have seen previously, the unifying power of the utilitarian approach to ethics, and as our discussion just now shows, that unifying power is combined, in utilitarianism, with a powerful method of reductionism that enables the whole realm of ethical value or evaluation to be cashed out in naturalistic or value-free terms.

Contrast the approach of virtue ethics. The latter eliminates the specifically moral and evaluations of the goodness, badness, betterness, etc. of states of affairs.[5] And although it may turn out to be able to reduce all rational notions to specific forms of admirability, what we said earlier about the intuitive possibility of virtues or admirable traits whose status as such is not attributable to the (personal) good they do for their possessors or for other people should indicate that the reductive capacities of an intuitive virtue ethics are likely to be far inferior to those of utilitarianism. Even given the possibility of reducing rationality to notions having to do with admirability, the process of reduction comes grinding to a halt once we are left with the category of admirability and the category of personal good; at this point, therefore, and relative at least to the assumptions we made earlier about what intuitively count as admirable traits of character, it would seem that utilitarianism has a theoretical or methodological advantage over virtue ethics. The latter, despite the ethical categories it eliminates, seems to leave us with the two ultimate ethical categories of admirability and personal good, whereas utilitarianism is capable not only of uniting all its ethical categories under a single such category, but also of reducing that single category—and therefore all five main ethical categories as well—to the naturalistic or non-evaluative terms it treats as underlying all valid ascriptions of ethical concepts. So utilitarianism would seem, from the standpoint of theory building, to have distinct advantages over virtue ethics, and unless we can find some counterbalancing consideration in favor of virtue ethics, the latter may not be able to survive comparison with direct utilitarianism.

But counterbalancing considerations I believe there are in plenty, and the first I would like to point out concerns the assumption we have been making that in the absence of further capacity for reduction or elimination, the (at least) two ultimate ethical categories of virtue ethics must remain two and leave the matter to that extent in an inferior position as compared with utilitarianism, with its capacity for reducing everything in ethics to the single category of personal good. There is another way of unifying categories and concepts that we have not yet mentioned, and it will, therefore, turn out that an ethics of virtue may be capable in principle of unifying all its ethical categories into a single such category by some technique other than reduction. In the next section I will clarify this dark saying by making use of some distinctions that most naturally arise in connection with Epicureanism and Stoicism. I earlier claimed some sort of right to treat egoistic views as ethical non-starters, but even if Epicureanism and Stoicism need not be regarded as viable competitors with the larger ethical views we have focused on, there may be other reasons for paying attention to them, and in what follows I hope to show you that certain fairly familiar aspects of the ancient opposition between Stoicism and Epicureanism can enable us to recognize some new possibilities for unification within the present approach to virtue ethics. In fact, if we can properly characterize how these ethical doctrines disagree, we will be in a much better position to see what the choice between utilitarianism and common-sense virtue ethics actually amounts to.

## Stoic Elevation vs. Epicurean Reduction

It is natural to speak of the identification of pleasure with the personally good as a form of reduction, because it is natural to think of value properties as *supervening* upon the *underlying* natural states and relations of things in the world, but of course reduction also occurs outside ethics, and when we speak of reducing the organic to the inorganic or society to its individual members, we seem to have in mind a relation between things and their component parts or underlying structure. In other cases, however, reduction and reductionism have less to do with part and whole and the idea of structure than with some (metaphorical or analogical?) connection between the higher and the lower: as, for example, when Freud is said to have attempted to reduce all higher activities and aspirations to mere sexual strivings (or, as with Adler, when they are reduced to the desire for power). And the idea or metaphor of higher and lower is to some extent, I think, also at work in our talk of reducing certain value properties to empirical or naturalistically understandable ones, since ordinarily, and without the benefit of such proposed reduction, the realm of value is in some sense regarded as higher—more ideal perhaps because involving facts about, or the measure of, what is ideal—than the realm of (non-evaluative) fact.

However, even *within* the realm of value(s) a distinction can in some cases be made between higher and lower, and the issue, for example, and if I may put it thus, between aestheticism and moralism is fundamentally a question of whether aesthetic or moral values rank higher (in some sense, obviously, that needs to be elaborated). Among the five categories or classes of concepts we have been speaking of there also seem to be intuitive differences as between higher and lower, and perhaps the most obvious and forceful of these differences concerns the distinction between virtues and personal goods. Some of the things that make for a good life, or are normally taken to be elements in some forms of happiness, involve no particular virtues on the part of those who enjoy them; in particular there is or need be nothing admirable in the fact that one enjoys or is able to enjoy going bowling, playing golf, taking sauna baths, eating Chinese food—and although, indeed, some of these activities can be performed better or worse, more or less admirably, the fact of enjoyment itself, with respect to such activities, is typically taken to constitute an element in some people's good quite independently of how skillfully or well they engage in them.

Sheer enjoyment, sheer fun is not as such considered admirable or a constitutive element in virtue or particular virtues, and because certain human traits are not only desired, but admired, whereas others are simply desired, we have a tendency to regard certain virtues and other admirable traits (violin-playing ability may be regarded as admirable, but is not treated as a virtue) as higher than certain enjoyments, which, although they constitute personal goods and are desirable as such, are not thought to be admirable in those who experience them. We can put the matter another way: our views about what is admirable or a virtue are among our ideals, and in becoming, say, generous or judicious, we would normally be thought to be realizing certain actual or possible ideals of character or of personhood. But various enjoyments and the achieved capacity for such enjoyments are not typically thought of in this way, and these differences feed a sense that most of us, I think, have that the admirable aspects or virtues of individuals are or represent higher values than those exemplified in merely desirable personal enjoyments.[6]

In that case, when an attempt is made to characterize human virtue solely in terms of causal relations to people's enjoyments (and/or to other personal goods that are not commonly regarded as in any way admirable), that attempt seems reductive, and though clearly, given what we have already said, utilitarianism counts as reductive in this way/sense, utilitarianism has typically focused more on the evaluation of actions than on the characterization of virtue,[7] whereas Epicureanism was to a large extent conceived as an ethics of virtue, and the latter had the same reducing tendencies regarding (the) virtue(s) that one can attribute to utilitarianism, but doesn't find often actually exemplified in the writings of utilitarians. And there is another reason for focusing temporarily on Epicurean rather than utilitarian reductionism. I cannot think of any contemporary ethical view that stands to utilitarianism as Stoicism stands to Epicureanism, but I think the very fact that Epicureanism and Stoicism are in such obvious and total opposition to one another may enable us, in a manner that otherwise might not be available to us, to discover a way in which non-egoistic virtue ethics has the capacity to unify our main ethical categories in as thoroughgoing a manner as utilitarianism has been seen to do.

Let us begin by being somewhat more specific about Epicurean reductionism. We are assuming that in some intuitive sense concepts involving admirability or the virtues are higher than the cluster of concepts that surround the notion of personal good or well-being, and relative to that assumption, Epicureanism reduces the higher to the lower through its claim that virtue and the virtues are nothing more than (more or less effective, etc.) means to pleasure or, more accurately, though I won't be insisting on this, to freedom from pain. Although Epicureanism has a prominent place for what we would call social or other-regarding virtues, it is fundamentally an egoistic doctrine and the ultimate measure, then, of virtue in any given individual is whether some trait or form of action tends to benefit the individual who has the trait or performs the action. But as with utilitarianism, benefit and personal good are cashed out in (very skewed) hedonistic terms, so ultimately individual virtue for the Epicurean is what tends to free the individual possessing the virtue from (more) pain (than she otherwise might/would feel) over the long run.[8]

This constitutes an instrumentalist conception of virtue and the virtues, as opposed, for example, to views that treat certain traits of character as good in themselves and apart from their beneficial effects (on their possessors or others), and just as utilitarians regard even benevolence as having the status of a good motive or virtue because of its effects on general human happiness, rather than (as intuitively may seem to be the case) because of its intrinsic character as a motive,[9] so too does the Epicurean regard such "higher" or "admirable" traits as moderation or honesty as achieving the status of virtues only through their causal relation to the personal good, the freedom from pain, of those who possess them. But here, as with utilitarianism, it is not, or at least it is not solely, the *instrumental* character of the ethical doctrine that makes it count as a reductive view. If one held, for example, that traits counted as virtues to the extent they led their possessors to contemplate the Form of the Good, one would have a causal/instrumental conception of (the) virtue(s)—I am certainly not saying it is Plato's—but the conception would lack the reductive character of Epicureanism and utilitarianism, because it is so natural to think of contemplation of the Good as an ideal or admirable state or activity. It is only when instrumentalism combines with a focus on states/activities/traits/facts that seem lower than the states/activities/traits/facts one is trying to analyze or account for that we have what is understandably regarded as a form of reductionism. But, of course, both utilitarianism and Epicureanism possess this combination of features in a way that makes the attribution of reductionist aims appropriate to both these approaches to ethics.

But what, then, of Stoicism and our sense that it is in fundamental ways the very opposite of Epicureanism? The opposition is clearly not with respect to egoism, which is attributable both to Stoicism and to Epicureanism, so where does it lie? One obvious answer to give at this point is that Stoicism isn't reductive the way Epicureanism is. But this won't quite do, because various common-sense views about the virtues— for example, the earlier mentioned fact that not all virtues seem intuitively to be a matter of producing good consequences (for their possessors or others)—appear to negate or contradict Epicureanism and utilitarianism, but not to be as *antithetical* to Epicureanism (and even to utilitarianism) as Stoicism is felt to be. A commitment not to reduce— but rather to treat personal good and virtue as mutually irreducible categories—is clearly not as antithetical or opposed to reductionism as some process or method of theorizing that moved in the opposite direction from Epicureanism, and a process meeting this description can in fact, I think, be attributed to Stoicism. Just as the Epicurean (or utilitarian) moves from the higher to the lower, the Stoic moves from the lower to the higher in a way I am about to say a good deal more about, but assuming, for the moment, that such a process or method makes intellectual sense, one can see how it might represent more than the negation of Epicureanism and reductionism, but rather a genuinely antithetical approach to ethics.

As far as I can determine, there is no name for the about-to-be-described process of moving from the lower to the higher, but since reductionism seems to imply a going from more to less or from higher to lower, perhaps "elevationism" can be the term we use for any implicit or explicit insistence on going from lower to higher, lesser to greater, and the like. Stoicism can be treated as embodying elevationism because of the way it identifies human well-being or personal good(s) with some intuitively understood idea of human virtue(s). For Stoics virtue or the virtues taken together are the sum and substance of human well-being: nothing beyond virtue (or a life led in accordance with virtue or reason or nature) is required for us to be well off or have good lives, and nothing that fails to improve us in virtue can be, therefore, of any real benefit. A virtuous individual bereft of wealth, friends, bodily pleasure, and good health can be as well off as it is possible to be, and so on a Stoic account human well-being is treated or regarded very differently from the way it is ordinarily or commonsensically. For common-sense, virtue, or various virtues, may constitute elements of (not just means to) a good life, but, for example, certain enjoyments and capacities that seem neither admirable nor means to anything admirable are also seen as constituents of living well, of a good life, of personal good or well-being. But Stoicism denies the intrinsic personal goodness of so-called worldly and sensual goods and doubts even the instrumental goodness of such things, because it questions whether they usually lead to the virtue of those who enjoy them. And so the following contrasts can be drawn between the Stoic and Epicurean treatments of the relation between personal good and virtue.

The Epicurean deflates our ideas about virtue and admirability, by regarding the latter as simply a matter of what is conducive or not conducive to the well-being (or happiness) of individuals. What is normally seen as higher than mere personal well-being (as being, e.g., admirable in a way well-being or enjoyment isn't) turns out, on the Epicurean account, to be of a piece with, at the same level as, facts solely about human well-being and its causes or effects.

But rather than reduce virtue/admirability to personal well-being (or happiness), the Stoic inflates our ideas about personal good (or well-being or happiness) by regarding the latter solely in terms of what constitutes or is conducive to human virtue or admirability. What is normally seen as lower than (ideals of) virtue turns out, on the Stoic account, to be of a piece with facts about virtue. And if, for the Epicurean, virtue is nothing more than a factor in personal good or happiness, then, for the Stoic, happiness and well-being are nothing less than virtue or virtuous living, and these contrasts should at this point make it understandable that Stoicism should be deemed a form of elevationism if Epicureanism is regarded as a form of reductionism.[10]

It is important, however, to be clear about what reduction(ism) and elevation(ism) each amount to. Neither method/process is, I take it, to be regarded as meaning-preserving or as necessarily non-empirical, but I can imagine someone at this point asking why I have bothered to introduce a new name for a relation that is simply the converse of familiar reduction.

The question embodies a confusion, because elevating is not simply the converse of reducing. It is simply not true that by reducing, say, virtue to personal well-being, I am simultaneously, or ipso facto, elevating well-being to virtue or admirability, and we really do need, therefore, to introduce a new name and a new relation if we want to understand the difference between Stoicism and Epicureanism (or utilitarianism). Perhaps I need to be a little more precise.

The notion of reduction, the idea of reducing one kind of entity, say, to another, is sometimes usefully clarified by the notion of certain *distinctions* being reducible to certain others. If the mental is reducible to the physical, then every valid mental distinction can be reduced to (or identified with) some distinction made in physical terms, and where, therefore, no physical distinction obtains no distinction will (be able to) occur at the mental level either. Note, however, that none of this entails that every physical distinction will be accompanied by some mentalistic one. As long as the mental is a function of the physical, the reducing relation can obtain even if no function from the mental to the physical can be found, and so, more briefly, we can characterize typical reductions of the mental to the physical as claiming that physical distinctions are *necessary but not sufficient* for the existence of mental distinctions.

By the same token, when Epicureanism (or utilitarianism) reduces virtue to well-being, it treats all distinctions of virtue or admirability as accompanied by distinctions in (causal, relational, and other) facts about individual well-being or happiness. But it need not claim that every distinction relating to the production of well-being (distinctions, e.g., about *who* certain dispositions benefit) will be accompanied by or give rise to a distinction in regard to virtue. And, of course, none of this would count as an instance of reduction unless the distinctions of virtue that are said to be always accompanied by distinctions with regard to well-being were intuitively regarded as higher than distinctions of the latter sort; we can also speak of reducing the mental to the physical only because the former seems more molar and perhaps higher than the latter.

Then what is it to elevate from one kind of thing or concept (up) to another? Something quite similar, in fact, to what it is to reduce one kind of thing or concept (down) to another, but with the difference, of course, that in elevating one moves from the lower to the higher. That is, in elevating *a* to *b* one does to *a* the very same thing one does to *b* if one seeks to reduce *b* to *a*, with the only difference being that *b* is higher than *a* in both cases. And, to put the matter very briefly, the reason why elevation isn't the converse of reduction is that it is essentially the same relation as reduction, with the only difference being in the "height" of the relata involved.

When the Stoic elevates the personally good (up) to the virtuous or admirable, he or she is committed to saying that every distinction with regard to the former can be treated in terms of distinctions involving only the latter, just as, when the Epicurean reduces the virtues or virtue (down) to matters of well-being, he or she is committed to saying that every distinction with regard to the former can be treated in terms of distinctions involving only the latter. The only difference is in the respective *heights* of "the former" and "the latter" in the two cases. In elevations, distinctions with regard to the lower are always correlated with distinctions in the regard to the higher, but the reverse need not be true. In reductions, distinctions regarding the higher are always accompanied by distinctions regarding the lower, though, again, the reverse need not be true.

And I think this puts us in a position, finally, to see clearly why elevation is not the converse of reduction. If it were, then, for one thing, elevating personal well-being or happiness in the manner of Stoicism would involve reducing virtue and the virtues in the manner of Epicureanism, and every Stoic would be an Epicurean. But aside from the absurdity of this conclusion, we can also see why elevation is not the converse of reduction if we keep clearly in mind the distinction between distinctions that are necessary to the existence of other distinctions and those that are sufficient for the existence of other distinctions. When we reduce higher $b$'s to lower $a$'s, $b$-distinctions must be accompanied by $a$-distinctions, but the reverse needn't hold. So consider, then, the elevation of lower $a$'s to higher $b$'s. Where such elevation has been successfully attempted, all $a$-distinctions will be accompanied by $b$-distinctions, but the reverse may not hold. But where it doesn't hold, not all b-distinctions are accompanied by a-distinctions, and this contradicts the claim that higher $b$'s reduce to lower $a$'s. So it should now be obvious—if it wasn't already—that reduction is not the converse of elevation. In elevation, the lower is "pulled up" (relative to our ordinary intuitions) to the (unchanging) level of the higher, and this clearly doesn't require (or even allow for) the higher to be simultaneously "pulled down" to the (unchanging) level of the lower. Elevation and reduction thus seem to bring together concepts and entities in different, indeed opposite, directions, and our intuitive philosophical sense of the opposition, the antithetical character, of Stoicism and Epicureanism can be understood and further elucidated in terms of the distinction just introduced between elevation(ism) and reduction(ism).

Nor is the usefulness of this distinction limited to this particular issue. It in fact has a wide range of application and can take us far beyond the confines of ethics. Consider, for example, the earlier mentioned reduction of the social, of facts about society, to the individual, that is, to facts about individuals. One name for such a reductionist view of society is individualism, but an opposed view of the relation between individual and society is also conceivable according to which the individual is nothing more than an aspect or minor facet of the organic whole constituted by the society of which he is a member. Understood in this strong sense, organicism is more than the denial of individualism: such organicism involves an elevation of the individual to the social just as its antithesis, individualism, reduces the social to the individual. Here again, elevation is not the converse of reduction; rather they are competing possibilities, competing conceptions of how things are. And just as there can be and has been a dispute between elevationist Stoicism and reductionist Epicureanism, so too there has been and, in social theory, continues to be a clash between elevationistic organicism and reductionistic individualism. And there are many other areas where elevationist approaches clash with reductionist ones. (I can't resist mentioning that if identity theory is a reductionist view of the relation between mind and body, then Berkeleyan subjective idealism, Hegelian idealism, and phenomenalism may all, though perhaps in differing degrees, represent elevationist accounts of that relationship.) There have been many studies of the philosophical bearing of one form of reductionism on others, and a separate study might well be worth doing on how or whether the choice between elevation and reduction on one question has any rational bearing on the same choice as it arises in regard to other questions in different areas of philosophy. But this is not that study, and I shall not pursue the issue of reduction vs. elevation beyond its bearing on the respective merits of virtue ethics and utilitarianism.

We have already said that utilitarianism is a form of reductionism, and in fact we earlier claimed that utilitarian reductionism proceeds in two steps, with moral and other evaluative claims first being reduced (either directly or by means of the notion of a good state of affairs) to claims and distinctions about individual well-being or personal good; and the latter, in turn, being subjected to a further reduction to facts about pleasure and pain, happiness and unhappiness, or preference-satisfaction and dissatisfaction. Clearly if Epicureanism goes from (or with) the intuitively higher toward the lower, so too does utilitarianism, which likewise treats all matters of good character and motive as nothing more than matters of conduciveness to personal well-being, happiness, etc. This many-stage reducing process allows utilitarianism to unify all ethical concepts under the single ethical category of personal good, whereas we also saw that virtue ethics, even by eliminating certain categories and reducing others, seems incapable of any unification beyond the two categories of personal good and admirability (virtue-status).

Does this mean that virtue ethics must accept duality, and that only a utilitarian approach can achieve the sort of desirable unity that results from having a single fundamental ethical category? In the light of our discussion of Stoicism and elevation, we can answer this question in the negative. Elevation allows Stoicism to unify the personally good with the virtuous or admirable, just as Epicureanism allows the unification of these two categories. The methods move, of course, in opposite directions, but they are equally capable of bringing about unity of ontology and/or concept. We earlier seemed to be forced to accept two ultimate categories (concept-clusters) for virtue ethics, because reduction and elimination were the only methods of unification we had available, and indeed elevationism is a far less familiar technique of unification (at least nowadays) than either elimination or reduction. But it is worth remembering it, and giving it a name, and even making use of it, because elevationism as between the personally good and the admirable has intriguing possibilities and possible merits as a way of developing virtue ethics. Nothing we have said thus far about virtue ethics forces us to avoid attempting to unify the personally good and the admirable by the method of elevation, and such a way of proceeding makes sense for virtue ethics to the extent Stoicism still exercises its attractions on us.

To be sure, I am ruling out the possibility that a distinctive ethics of virtue would want to reduce the admirable and the idea of a virtue to notions connected with personal good or well-being. Such a reduction may be possible for utilitarianism and Epicureanism, but we are avoiding egoism in the virtue ethics we seek to develop, and, even if utilitarianism is not egoism, we are also trying to develop a form of virtue ethics that is distinctive and different from utilitarianism and that can be critically compared with the latter. If we allowed virtue ethics to reduce the idea of a virtue to that of personal good, we would end up with a fragment of utilitarianism (or of something in many ways analogous to utilitarianism) and we would, then, have missed out on the opportunity to develop something genuinely different from utilitarianism that might be able to compete with and even surpass the latter on theoretical grounds. Such a possibility is one this book cannot afford to miss. So I will not now consider whether virtue ethics should move reductively in relation to personal good and admirability, but will only consider whether it should

attempt to elevate the personal good and thereby unify the main categories of ethics under the single heading of admirability or should instead
remain content with an ultimate duality between admirability and personal good or well-being that recommends itself at least on intuitive
grounds, if on no others.

## Monistic Virtue Ethics

A virtue ethics that eliminates both the moral and the morally loaded
evaluation of states of affairs, that seeks or hopes to reduce rationality to
admirability and/or personal good, and that takes the additional, final
step of elevating personal good to the concept-cluster that surrounds the
notion of admirability can be termed a monistic virtue ethics. And if we
ultimately reject the idea of taking virtue ethics in a monistic direction, if
we decide that we need separate notions of personal good and admirability to achieve an adequate ethics of virtue, then our virtue ethics will in
the obvious sense be dualist—or perhaps pluralistic, if rationality-notions
also turn out to be intractable in other terms.

I would like now to consider some of the implications of taking a
Stoic-like, elevationist approach to personal well-being and see whether
they are plausible enough to allow a virtue ethics that gives credence to
intuition (when and where it doesn't lead to incoherence and paradox) to
accept them for the sake of the superior unity such monism allows us
to achieve. We will see that such an approach—and this is also true of
Stoicism—has ways of dealing with what we value in life that allow it to
achieve a greater degree of plausibility than the reader might initially
expect (and than I myself anticipated). I don't propose to give a full-
blown account of monistic virtue ethics either of a Stoic or of a non-
egoistic variety; the emphasis will be on the question whether and to what
degree elevating personal good can leave us with a plausible account or
understanding of what is really valuable or good in human life. And let us
begin by considering the place that even a dualist or pluralist virtue ethics
will want to make for particular virtues as part of the/a good human life,
as one element at least of personal good or well-being or living well.

Our common-sense thinking about personal good or well-being does
not run in predetermined hedonistic grooves, but is willing, rather, to treat
a great variety of things as intrinsic personal goods, as inherently desirable elements of a good life.[11] And among the things we implicitly regard
as personal or life goods are various virtues or other admirable traits that

some people have and others seem to lack. The fact that someone has physical courage or the courage of her convictions; the creative musical genius of a Beethoven or a Mozart; the modesty and/or moderation, the objectivity or generosity, the excellence as a father or mother, that some people evince and others lack totally: all these are personal traits or aspects that we not only admire in people, but consider desirable, worth having, as well. And this desirability, in all the cases just mentioned, is not, by our common lights, a merely instrumental one. Even if, for example, we think of courage or objectivity as (sometimes) likely to pay off, for those who possess them, in the familiar coinage of enjoyment, comfort, success, or other worldly goods, that is not the main or only reason why we tend to think of them as desirable, and to a large extent I believe we regard them as things inherently worth having, desirable, largely, for themselves, that is, because they are the traits they are.

There is some evidence for this in the way we envy or easily can envy people their superior objectivity (in daily life or in their official role as judges); their moderation and self-sufficiency as compared with our own voracity for the good things in life; their superiority as parents; etc. For where there is envy, there is or may be admiration for what we lack or have failed to achieve ourselves, but there is also a sense that others possess or have achieved something that it would have been a good thing for us to possess or have achieved. If we envy someone's attainments, we think we would have been better off (or that our lives would have been better), other things being equal, if we had achieved what we thus envy; if we envy Beethoven his musical gifts, it is because, other things being equal, we would have benefited, we think, from having such gifts. And the envy here cannot merely be a sign of admiration, of the admirability rather than the desirability, of what is envied. For that assumption would not allow us, for example, to explain why we envy Beethoven (or Mozart or Tchaikovsky) his genius, but not his total life. Given his general unhappiness or discontent through much of his life, it is quite natural to say that we admire Beethoven but do not envy him. And I think the difference between the envy some of us admittedly feel toward his musical gifts or creativity and our lack of envy in regard to Beethoven, the whole man, is best made sense of if we suppose that envy involves the background assumption that someone possesses (has done, etc.) something that it is desirable to possess, but that we ourselves lack. We envy Beethoven his musical genius because we think we would have been better off (other things being equal) having such genius, and although we admire both Beethoven's genius and Beethoven himself, we won't envy him, or his life, unless we think he was better off overall than we, and in the light, therefore, of Beethoven's reputed unhappiness, we are not likely to envy Beethoven's life or the man himself.[12]

The above seems to entail that certain sorts of contentment are regarded by many or most of us as having a role in making a life good, in making things go well for people, alongside the role that various virtues and admirable qualities or accomplishments also seem to play in constituting or contributing to a good life. If we admire Beethoven more than we envy him, it is because we feel that admirable achievements and the possession of (many) highly admirable traits may not compensate for certain sorts of persistent misery or unhappiness and judge that in Beethoven's (or, if you prefer, Mozart's or Tchaikovsky's) case, the pervasive quality of his unhappiness left him on the whole and over time less well off than much less gifted people often are.

But our most immediate question is not whether, in addition to various admirable achievements/qualities, various (non-admirable) forms of contentment or enjoyment are also part of what makes lives good or better. Rather, we have just been considering whether the things we admire are often or sometimes or ever desirable elements in (a) life, and the answer we seem to be getting from consulting ordinary thinking is that many virtues and many talents *are* intuitively regarded as (to some extent) desirable or worth having in themselves. But the fact, on the other hand, that, in regard to traits or attainments we lack, envy does not always follow admiration indicates, as I have mentioned, that we tend to consider various non-admirable features of human beings or their lives as likewise desirable and, indeed, as sufficiently important elements in a good life, or in living well, that their absence—for example, the absence of contentment or health—can make us doubt or deny the overall goodness or desirability of the lives of certain people we greatly admire (consider admirable). And we must now consider whether and how plausibly we can question or deny such assumptions.

The idea that only (enacted) virtue is necessary to the/a good life, or that despite physical pain, the lack of friends, poverty, and ill health, someone who is and remains virtuous in thought and action will have a good life (or even as good a life as it is possible to have) can be found not only among the Stoics, but in Plato, and even Aristotle comes very close to having such views. Aristotle, at least, considers a lifetime of activity in accordance with virtue—or the highest virtue(s)—to be the main component of a life of *eudaimonia*, of a good life.[13] And although in places he seems to want to argue that being on the rack, or friendless, or poor can make it impossible for one's life, or some part of one's life, to be good, it is possible to interpret this as a claim that the just mentioned features of a life make living well impossible because and to the extent that they make it impossible to act in accordance with virtue. If one is poor and has no friends, and certainly if one is "broken" on the rack, one will lack for opportunities or for the ability to exercise certain virtues like liberality or justice, and such cases, therefore, do not necessarily call into question the equation of living well or a good (or the best) life with living in accordance with (the highest) virtue, with a life full of admirable activities (desires, thoughts, etc. all being included among such activities).

However, a virtuous person will engage in activities with certain goals or ends, and these will typically be goods for the person himself, for other people, or for the larger community. Someone who possesses and continues to possess the wealth, friends, freedom from pain, etc., that enable him to engage virtuously in a wide range of activities may, nonetheless, through bad luck or ill fortune fail to attain some or many of the ends or goals of such activities, and, as John Cooper has pointed out, one can hardly make sense of treating such activities as forms of excellence or virtue, while denying the sensibleness or reasonableness of the goals sought (*ipso facto*) by the virtuous person who is engaged in those activities. But if the goals can be thus characterized, then they are or represent elements of personal good, things that it is good, in life, to have, enjoy or do, and in that case there will for Aristotle be substantive elements of the/a good life or living well whose attainment, even by the virtuous individual, will be subject to luck. On such a view, presumably, there will be desirable things that the fully virtuous admirable individual may fail to obtain or attain, things which, had his activities been successful in the way he hoped or intended, would have made his life better, and even if one can still (barely) hold on to the idea that activity in accordance with virtue can guarantee a good life, the views just mentioned do seem to entail that a full life led in accordance with (the highest) virtue or virtues can fail to be as good as it or a life can be.

If such a view of Aristotle is correct, then Aristotle comes remarkably close to the Stoic idea that only (living in accordance with) virtue is (personally) good and that the most virtuous life is *ipso facto* the best. But he does seem to hold that failure to attain certain goals, even when this involves no lack of or diminution in virtue, can make one's life less good, and to that extent he disagrees with Stoicism and with any monistic view that seeks to elevate personal good (up) to admirability in trait, action, desire, etc. However, Aristotle also seems to leave room for failures of happiness, for failures to have a fully good life, that result, not from bad luck in virtuous activities, but simply from the unpleasant or painful character of one's experience or state of mind. Priam's misery and misfortune at the end of his life deprived his life of blessedness, and marred his total life to a certain extent, not only because they impeded certain virtuous activities on his part, but because of the very painfulness of that later life,[14] and this suggests that things can go worse in life not only because one may be prevented from acting fully virtuously and because one may through bad luck fail to obtain the goods one aims at in acting virtuously, but also for reasons that may lack any essential connection with virtuous activity and its goals. If, as Aristotle at least sometimes seems to suggest, the presence or absence of great pain can be an independent factor in how well one's life goes, then we have taken a further step away from the Stoic view, though that, of course, is hardly a reason in itself to refrain from that step or doubt its validity. To the extent the step(s) Aristotle takes away from the purely Stoic point of view seem plausible, there is pressure on the Stoic position and on elevationist monism about human good. But the moves we have just followed don't foreclose the possibility of Stoic or otherwise elevationistic rebuttal, and at this point we ought to explore some ways in which the Stoic might seek to show the plausibility or tenability of her own view in the face of what we have been describing as Aristotelian disagreements with that view.

The Stoic view of goal-directed activities exemplifying reason or virtue requires a "stoical" attitude toward failures to achieve the ends or goals one aimed at. A self-sufficient Stoic sage is supposed not to care deeply about what happens to him and others as long as it doesn't affect his ability to act virtuously, but, largely unlike Aristotle, the Stoics also tended to hold that virtue (or rationality) is entirely under the control of the individual person (or, at least, of the Stoic sage), and to that extent luck and accident can play no role in determining how good his life is.[15] But, of course, the objection has long been known that a bad cold or a coughing fit can interfere with the rational or virtuous activity even of the most admirable people, and so luck may well, therefore, play an important role in virtuous or rational activity. Even granting this point, however, it might still be maintained that virtuous, rational living was sufficient for the best kind of life, and if, as the Stoic holds, we shouldn't really care about—be emotionally dependent on—what happens to our friends or our own projects, or even (to the extent it doesn't interfere with rationality) about whether we are in pain, then perhaps living virtuously is all there is to a good, or the best possible, life. But the idea that all we ought to care about is our own virtue—and here virtue may be conceived either egoistically or in the self-other symmetric but morally neutral way we have been developing it here—is so repellent that it may well be capable of putting most of us permanently off Stoicism or elevationist monism. However, still more can and ought to be said.

It seems odd that someone should seek goals that he has no reason to really care about, and to the extent that Stoicism thinks that a virtuous individual can and will seek such goals, one may wonder whether Stoicism or a less egoistic form of elevationism shouldn't be discarded on grounds of obvious incoherence. But the Stoics were aware of this kind of problem, and in order to answer it, they introduced a category of external goals and objects which, though not actually good, were "preferred." It is rational, on such a view, to seek preferred things or experiences, because such pursuit can provide an area of activity that we subject to our own rational control. Shopping for and eating food is an activity that sets the stage, primes the pump, for displays of virtue, and the individual who cares about eating or who is immoderate in her appetites thus fails to exemplify the rational virtue that is called for and valuable in such an activity. So for the Stoic an emotionally detached but real pursuit of certain objects gives more play to virtue—to the exercise of self-control and of rational thinking—than a total failure to engage in such activities would allow one. And the Stoic thus wants to encourage the virtuous (i.e., emotionally detached) pursuit of preferred (but indifferent in the sense of not really good) things, because such activity allows one to more fully exemplify virtue and thus improve one's life.

This rather ingenious line of thought may not fully allay our suspicions that there is something conceptually suspect going on here, but on the other hand, it is not immediately obvious to me where the incoherence, if any, lies.[16] Indeed, what strikes me as most criticizable about stoic/ elevationist monism is not any obvious conceptual incoherence, but its failure to capture some of our most irrecusable ideas about what makes lives good, about what things in life are good.

Last summer my wife and I went on a trip to France. We picked up a car at Bordeaux and drove East and South across the entire country, eventually ending up in Nice. Along the way, we saw many works of art, many churches, much beautiful scenery; we also ate very, very well. And all the while we had enough time not to feel the need to rush; our enjoyment was great but also leisurely, and the vacation as a whole was probably the most enjoyable Jenny and I have ever taken together.

But consider how a Stoic or some other monist-elevationist would have to invoke the idea of preferred things as means solely to exercises of virtue in order to accommodate my belief that things went especially well for both of us, that both our lives went well, during the trip. The flattering elevationist could say that our appreciation of French art, architecture, and food displayed admirable taste and discrimination, and that what was truly good about our lives during that trip was precisely the admirable exercises of admirable traits that were called forth and exercised by us during the course of it. He might want to add that we shouldn't have been so attached to realizing our goals as to have been disappointed, as we were, at our failure to realize certain of them (we ended up missing some wonderful Romanesque churches we had hoped to see). But the chief contention of the elevationist view here is that the trip represents a good part of my wife's or my life only in virtue of the excellent discrimination and taste, if any, it enabled us to give play to, to realize in feeling, thought, and action. And for the life of me I cannot understand how anyone could really believe, seriously believe, with respect to trips or parts of lives that go (if one is lucky) as our recent trip went last year, that such arguably admirable features exhaust what is valuable, wonderful, good about them.

When I think back on the trip, I can't help thinking how much we enjoyed our time together and the things we did and saw, and I absolutely balk at the monistic notion that the enjoyment was at best only a means to what was really or inherently good in that part of my life, to what was really good about the trip, namely, the admirable, active realization and employment of certan admirable rational and aesthetic powers. (Here, we are already espousing a version of elevationistic monism with a wider notion of the admirable than Stoicism would presumably allow.) I find I cannot accept this view, and in saying so, I suppose I am exposing the other side of the coin that Aristotle brings to our attention by mentioning Priam's suffering as a factor independent of any interference with exercises of virtue in determining the less than blessed character of his (later) life. If sheer pain can diminish the goodness of life independently of how, if at all, it interferes or must interfere with virtuous or admirable active living, then presumably enjoyment such as Jenny and I shared last year has an independent role in making lives (temporarily) better, and it is on such grounds as these, perhaps more than any other, that I would want for my own part to reject the elevationist monism of Stoicism as well as any monistic development of the non-egoistic virtue ethics I have been developing here.[17]

However, I think I should mention a reply that some elevationists might at this point want to make to what I have just been saying. (I am indebted here to the suggestions of an anonymous referee.) It might be said that certain sorts of pleasure and/or enjoyment are necessary to "complete" various virtuous acts or activities, are even part of what is virtuous or admirable in or about such activities, and, if that is so, then pleasure and enjoyment can count as good things, part of individual well-being, for an elevationist monistic ethics. Do I really have any reason, then, to treat the sort of enjoyment and contentment my wife and I experienced on our recent trip as constituting personal goods that elevationism cannot account for?

I think I do. For the kind of pleasure or enjoyment that completes a virtuous activity is most easily and naturally understood as having a certain sort of intentionality or cause. One is pleased *at* having made such-and-such (excellent) discriminations or, at the very least, one is given enjoyment *by* (what is admirable in) certain admirable activities one undertakes. And although I would not want to deny that some of what was good and enjoyable about our recent trip can be categorized in this way, such an account also leaves out much of what was pleasurable and valuable for Jenny and me on our trip through France. I think it would be unnatural or artificial to connect (all) the leisurely contentment and senuous/gustatory pleasure or comfort we felt with the completion of virtuous or admirable activities, and to the extent, therefore, that what is good about certain parts or moments of our lives is not, in the neat way envisaged above, connected with being admirable or acting/feeling/desiring/thinking admirably, it doesn't seem to me that elevationism can really succeed.

## Eliminative Utilitarianism

Although I am at this point inclined to believe that virtue ethics should not move toward a unitary, elevationist account of personal good and virtue/admirability, the very possibility of such a conceptually monistic form of virtue ethics raises some important issues concerning the relative merits of an overall utilitarian and an overall virtue-theoretical approach.

Since it is possible for one to take virtue ethics in the direction of a unity no less impressive, I think, than the conceptual unity that stands as one of the most impressive features of utilitarianism, anyone who rejects such unity needs to have a good reason for doing so. And in the previous section I claimed, in particular, that the desirable unity that can be attained through elevating the personally good up to the admirable is simply not worth the sacrifice of the deep-seated intuition—an intuition that I have counted on most of us sharing—that there is more to living a good life than simply living *admirably*.

But perhaps I am mistaken; perhaps such unity is worth the implausible consequences, in the same way utilitarianism so frequently claims it to be.[18] If it is, then virtue ethics should be developed in an elevationist, conceptually monistic direction along the lines sketched in the previous section of this chapter, and this will leave both utilitarianism and virtue ethics swallowing implausible conclusions about the relation between admirability and personal good. But because utilitarianism is reductionistic and virtue ethics, to the extent it identifies all its concepts under one rubric, is elevationist, the two doctrines are committed to *different* implausibilities.

As we have just seen, the monistic virtue ethicist holds that being admirable and doing (feeling, etc.) things admirably are the only things that are worthwhile or desirable in life; but, in contrast, the utilitarian (or Epicurean) conceptual monist must assume that there is no more to something or someone's being admirable (in one or another respect) than its or his serving as a means to human well-being, to general happiness. And this strikes me as no more, though also no less, plausible than the implications of monistic virtue ethics.[19] Indeed, in just the way that reduction and elevation oppose one another, the differently implausible implications of monistic utilitarianism and monistic virtue ethics also strike one as complementary opposites. And if we assume that systematic conceptual unity is capable of counterbalancing and even overriding such implausibilities, then the possibility of a monistic virtue ethics to that extent seems, with respect to present considerations, to put virtue ethics in a theoretical position no less satisfactory and desirable than that of utilitarianism. In that case, we can either stay with a monistic form of virtue ethics and, like utilitarianism, reap the benefits of conceptual unity; or, assuming as I have that those benefits are really not sufficient, one can opt for dualist/pluralist virtue ethics which to that extent will be no less satisfactory, and perhaps even superior, to utilitarianism. And either way the position of the virtue ethicist will not suffer by comparison with the constant, reductive monism espoused by the utilitarian.

Unless, of course, there is some reason to prefer the reductive to the elevationist form of conceptual monism, and one may already see how the utilitarian might wish to argue for such a superiority. Reductionism, after all, is in keeping with a general tendency of recent scientific thought; scientific identifications always move (I believe) either in a reductionist direction or else somehow stay at a single level, and the instances of elevationism we find in philosophy are largely out of keeping, therefore, with the impetus toward identification one most often finds in scientific and philosophical thinking nowadays. It may be a form of heedless, needless scientism to assume, on such grounds, that reduction is to be preferred to elevation, but let us make the assumption anyway. For even if we do, I believe it will be less helpful to utilitarianism, either as defended here or in other, more familiar forms, than the utilitarian seeking to refute elevationistic virtue ethics may anticipate.

If there is reason to prefer reductionism to elevationism on grounds having to do with the general tendency and the accumulating impact of scientific practice over the past few centuries, we may be able to push virtue-ethical monism to one side, but at the same time, in all consistency and fairness, we will have to take notice of a possibility we haven't yet considered, the possibility of an eliminativist form of utilitarianism. If on scientific (or scientistic) grounds reductionism is preferable to elevationism, there would appear to be no similar, general reason, in science or philosophy, to prefer a reductive over an eliminative approach to suspect or otherwise dangling entities. And if it makes sense and is possible to formulate a version of utilitarianism that stands to by-now familiar reductive utilitarianism as, say, eliminative materialism stands to reductive materialism, our respect for the method and propensities of science should make us take that eliminative version very seriously, seriously enough, in any event, to consider whether we have any reason to reject it in favor of the reductive utilitarianism we have so far exclusively focused on.

And, of course, when one thinks about it, an eliminative form of utilitarianism is distinctly possible, and the analogy with the choice between reductionism and eliminationism in other areas gives us a pretty clear notion of what an eliminative utilitarianism has to say. Just as an eliminative materialism claims there are no mental entities or (realized) mental properties, only physical entities and properties functioning in certain complex ways; so an eliminative utilitarianism will deny that anything is right or obligatory or intrinsically good, will deny that there are any exemplified ethical (or evaluative) properties or facts. And the reasoning behind such conclusions will in fact, as in other cases where there is a choice to make between reduction and elimination, follow the reasoning for reductive utilitarianism until it reaches a final parting of the ways with it. Like reductionist utilitarianism, the eliminative form will point out the primitive, or at least intellectually unsatisfactory, thinking that lies, for example, behind our ordinary moral thinking. It will hold that when one strips away or otherwise removes the meaningless or unjustifiable elements in our ordinary usage of "right" and "wrong," one will be left with the clear and humanly significant core idea of producing (a net balance of) pleasure or satisfaction for sentient beings. But here parting ways with ordinary reductive utilitarianism, it will argue that the latter is unnecessarily, gratuitously misleading, when it makes the principle of utility the criterion of application for familiar terms like "right" and "wrong." Precisely because of all the confused and unjustified elements that characterize ordinary usage of these terms, it makes more sense, according to the eliminativist, to drop the terms and make do, instead, with talking about what will or will not (tend to) produce (the greatest) overall pleasure or happiness.

Clearly, the issue here between eliminative and reductive utilitarianism is familiar from our experience of other disputes regarding the respective merits of an eliminative and a reductive approach. And since the most familiar of these, probably, is the long-standing debate between eliminative and (one or another form of) reductive materialism, it is perhaps worth mentioning one possible advantage that eliminative utilitarianism (or eliminative ethics more generally) has over eliminative materialism. It is not obvious that sense experience and thinking are merely posited hypothetical entities, and there may be some force to the claim, therefore, that what eliminative materialism eliminates (among other things) are the very data that reasonable abductive thinking must seek to account for. But the idea that we immediately experience certain ethical data or properties is, I believe, an (even) harder thesis to defend than what we have just allowed as a possibility in the area of mind and body, and to the extent, therefore, we have better or more immediate knowledge of our own experience(s) than of ethical facts and properties, utilitarian eliminativism may well be in better shape than (or have at least one advantage over) eliminative materialism.

But even apart from this consideration, it seems difficult to find any reason to prefer reductive to eliminative utilitarianism, once we move decisively in the science-influenced direction that favors reduction over elevation. If the traditional, reductive utilitarian protests, for example, that the eliminative approach does away with ethics altogether and therefore with utilitarianism itself as a form of ethics, it can be pointed out that this pair of claims is either simply false or altogether begs the issue against eliminativism. After all, eliminative utilitarianism, like eliminative materialism, makes a distinctive claim of its own. It doesn't remain silent or somehow render it impossible for claims to be made, but rather comes out openly and asserts that nothing is good or right or obligatory—or, if you prefer, that "good," etc., do not denote any properties of things. To be sure, problems can arise here about how the negative claims of eliminative utilitarianism are most properly formulated, but there are similar problems about how to express eliminative materialism, and there is no reason, in either case, to say that the eliminativist eliminates the philosophical field he or she is supposed to be working in. Just as the eliminative materialist holds a metaphysical position and is naturally regarded as a materialist of one particular stripe, the eliminative utilitarian subscribes to a particular ethical view, and one, moreover, that is for similar reasons naturally regarded as a form of utilitarianism.

On the other hand, what one may mean by saying that the eliminativist does away with ethics is that the eliminativist does away with, in the sense of denying the existence of, ethical properties or facts. But even granting that there is a sense in which this charge is true, it hardly seems to constitute an intelligible reason for preferring reductive utilitarianism over eliminative. In the sense presumably intended, the claim that the latter does away with ethical facts or properties simply points out the essential difference between the two forms of utilitarianism. And one cannot treat that as an argument against eliminativism without essentially begging the question against it.

Certainly, if one denies the existence of good things or right acts in favor of the (mere) existence of pleasure and things conducive to it, that may have an effect on those who hear the denial(s), an effect the reductivist may wish to call bad and that even the eliminativist can say goes against overall human happiness or pleasure. But because the eliminativist may care as much about the advancement of human happiness as any reductionist, he may have equal reason or motive to preserve the esoteric character of his theoretical views about or in ethics. If the reductive utilitarian can defend the validity of his views by disavowing their practical character or usefulness, the eliminativist can do something entirely analogous even without making use of specifically ethical or evaluative notions. And so, just as we earlier saw that the theoretical validity of optimizing utilitarianism is compatible with preference for common-sense morality in everyday life and that a theoretical insistence on scalar utilitarianism can tolerate everyday non-scalar practices, we now see that eliminative utilitarianism cannot readily be undercut as a theoretical option by pointing to the consequences of its being adopted by people generally.

In that case, if the choice between eliminationism and reductionism is as difficult as it currently seems, then utilitarianism is in something of a bind vis-à-vis the criticisms it wishes or may wish to make of elevationism. For if its criticisms of the latter are justified, it may then lack any reason to accept reductive in preference to eliminative utilitarianism, and there will then be no reason for the consistent utilitarian to accept any familiar form of utilitarianism or even the scalar version of it defended in Chapter 4. If the utilitarian wishes to avoid making his (scalar or more familiar) reductive views seem underdetermined relative to his own methodology and underlying assumptions, he had better not criticize elevationism for its anti-scientific character. But, of course, even apart from whether utilitarianism lodges a criticism of this sort against elevationism, the choice between reduction and elimination remains a serious problem for the utilitarian, and I frankly am aware of no easy way to get him out of this difficulty.

At this point, however, I want to drop the issue of utilitarian reduction vs. elimination and return to our critical comparison of virtue ethics with scalar, direct (reductive) utilitarianism. What the possibility of eliminativist utilitarianism shows us is that it is difficult for reductive utilitarianism to attack virtue ethics without raising problems for its own position. But in the next part of this book, I want to bring in a number of other difficulties for the (reductive) utilitarian position. So far our development of utilitarianism has proceeded in large part by reference to symmetry or consistency or uniformity as a methodological desideratum. But in the final section of Chapter 4, we produced, not an argument from consistency or symmetry or uniformity, but an argument from underdetermination, in favor of scalar versions of every form of direct utilitarianism. However, this argument from indeterminacy or underdetermination, relative to familiar founda-tional methods and assumptions, had a benign, as well as a chastising aspect. It told us to stop accepting familiar optimizing (or, for that matter, satisficing) versions of (act-)utilitarianism, but since optimizing utilitarian-ism can be criticized as being too strict or demanding, it is perhaps desirable to have a reason to give up such utilitarianism in favor of a scalar form that easily avoids the criticism of overdemandingness.

But what we will see overall in Part IV is that the charge of underdeter-mination can also be made in a new way we have not yet considered. And it turns out that this new claim of underdetermination—taken together with underdetermination respecting the choice between reductionism and eliminationism—have more unsettling implications than those we drew from our one earlier discussion of utilitarian underdetermination. Utili-tarianism and consequentialism generally will turn out to be in a some-what worse position, and virtue ethics in a correspondingly and relatively better position, than anything thus far has indicated. But before we turn to these issues, I would like to say something more about what I take to be the intuitive superiority of (dualistic) virtue ethics over utilitarianism.

## Notes

1. *Goods and Virtues* (Oxford, 1990, Ch. 5) and *Beyond Optimizing* (Har-vard, 1989, Chs. 1–5) argue in differing ways for an absence of tight intuitive

connection between rational notions and the idea of a personal good, or of a good life. It is worth noting that some concepts with application inside one or another of the five main categories of ethical concepts just described also apply outside the sphere of the ethical. Even if the notion of a virtue *tout court* is strictly ethical, the notion of admirability applies both inside the ethical and outside: e.g., to artistic performances, works of art, meals, etc. But this fact has no bearing on the accuracy or usefulness of our typology, and neither, in addition, does the fact, if it is one, that certain deontic or quasi-deontic notions apply *across* several of our categories and outside the ethical as well. Even if the notion of what ought to be (done)—or what is right or appropriate or fitting—is in some sense free-floating with respect to its evaluative applications and/or is as fundamentally at home, e.g., in moral, virtue-related, and even aesthetic contexts as it clearly is in rational, i.e., reasons-giving, contexts, that notion or notion-schema can be used to make specific judgments/claims only, it would seem, by attaching or lending itself to one of the five ethical categories mentioned above or to some extra-ethical category like etiquette or aesthetics.

2. This is as true for indirect forms of utilitarianism as for direct forms.

3. Some forms of non-utilitarian consequentialism do not permit a reduction of goodness in states of affairs to personal good; but others are welfarist while denying the outcome utilitarian thesis that the goodness of states of affairs is a matter of *total* individual well-being: e.g., some consequentialists tie the goodness of states of affairs to individuals' well-being via a *maximin* criterion.

4. I here ignore the complications that result from adopting a strictly scalar form of utilitarianism. Note too that utilitarianism typically has no use for—and can in some sense be said to eliminate—the notion of a (prima facie) reason for acting or choosing.

5. Note, however, that some evaluations of states of affairs are not ethical and need not be eliminated by an ethics of virtue: e.g., it is amazing (or odd or unlikely) that such and such happened.

6. I am here ignoring or excluding the pleasures that are said to accompany or reflect knowingly virtuous or admirable actions, but I will say something about such pleasures later on.

7. Bentham himself points this out in the Preface to *An Introduction to the Principles of Morals and Legislation*, Oxford, 1982, p. 3. But compare Bentham's later *Deontology*.

8. On Epicureanism, see the very useful anthology, edited by Long and Sedley, *The Hellenistic Philosophers*, Cambridge, 1988, vol. 1.

9. See Bentham's *Introduction*, p. 114.

10. Kant is very clear on the antithetical character of Epicureanism and Stoicism, and some of the things he says about them come very close to the present distinction between reduction and elevation. See *Critique of Practical Reason*, Part I, Book I, Ch. ii.

11. For support of this idea, see *Goods and Virtues*, Chs. 1 and 6.

12. The fact that someone has deliberately chosen something on non-instru-

mental grounds needn't show that he regards it—or that we should regard it—as a personal good or (at least temporary) improvement in his life. Some people sacrifice their own well-being, their lives even, in the name of various ideals or out of a sense of duty/obligation. And the fact, e.g., that someone would prefer to have—or have his children have—a creative but troubled life like Beethoven's doesn't show that he thinks, or we should think, that the person having such a life is *better off* or *more fortunate* than he would be with some more ordinary, less troubled existence. We may choose (for our children) to be admirable rather than happy.

13. Here and in what follows, I am indebted to John Cooper's "Aristotle on the Goods of Fortune," *Philosophical Review* 94, 1985, pp. 173–96.

14. See the *Nicomachean Ethics* 1100b 28–1101a 4.

15. On some of the ideas of Stoicism I am mentioning, see Long and Sedley, eds., *op. cit.* On Stoic views about being free of emotional dependence, e.g., on material goods or people, see my *Goods and Virtues*, Ch. 6.

16. For an argument against the Stoic account of preferred goods, see C. C. W. Taylor's review of a volume edited by Schofield and Striker, in *Oxford Studies in Ancient Philosophy*, vol. 5, 1987, pp. 235–45. But I remain unconvinced.

17. If, in something like the manner discussed earlier in Chapter 7, one allows attributions of admirability or virtue to be subject to the luck of consequences, one may be able to rule out cases where, as Cooper at least assumes, one acts as admirably or virtuously as possible but fails to achieve the goals/goods one aimed at. But this still leaves cases where enjoyment or suffering occur independently of rational or other purposive activities, and these alone I think, suffice to make Stoic or other forms of elevationist monism untenable.

18. Obviously, utilitarianism imposes or recognizes other kinds of unity and levels of unity than we have just been describing, but these aspects of utilitarianism and their bearing on the relative merits of utilitarianism and virtue ethics have either already been mentioned or will be taken up in Part IV.

19. Here I have in mind a monistic virtue ethics that allows for more forms or sources of admirability than presumably ancient Stoicism would have acknowledged or been comfortable with.

# IV

## REASONS
## FOR PREFERRING
## VIRTUE ETHICS

# 14

## The Main Issue
## Between Utilitarianism
## and Virtue Ethics

In the last chapter, I spent a good deal of time discussing the intuitively implausible implications of Stoic and other, more catholic or permissive forms of monistic virtue ethics, where, if you remember, the monism in question is one relating to the categories of personal good and of admirability/virtue. I also mentioned the implausible aspects of monistically reductive generalized utilitarianism, but I spent less time on that issue, making only a fairly brief reference to the way in which the admirability of certain individual traits of character seems to involve something more than or different from a tendency to contribute to overall human well-being. In the present chapter, however, I spend more time discussing the implausibilities that follow from an acceptance of utilitarianism, and because it helps bring to a head the conflict between virtue ethics and utilitarianism, I chiefly focus on their respective views about what makes individual traits and what makes people or total lives admirable or excellent. The people and personal characteristics for which utilitarianism has the highest regard are very different from those a common-sense non-moralistic virtue ethics thinks best of, and we will see in particular that the differing *comparative* value judgments that the two approaches make in this area are also so different in fundamental plausibility as to call utilitarianism further into question and give us another positive reason for preferring virtue ethics.

## What Makes Lives Admirable?

Both utilitarianism and common-sense virtue ethics allow us to distinguish between the desirable and the admirable. For virtue ethics there are desirable but non-admirable things in life and some lives, as we have seen, it will allow us to consider more admirable than desirable. Of course, a larger common-sense ethics that included moral and morality-related judgments would recognize two kinds of desirability: of states of affairs and of what we call personal goods, but the virtue-ethical abandonment of morality as such has also simplified its conception of the desirable—personal good(s) is/are the only thing it calls desirable—though, of course, it allows that what is admirable can also count as personally good and thus as desirable.

Utilitarianism also distinguishes two fundamental kinds of evaluation that correspond well enough for our purposes—though not in regard to every nuance or aspect—to the distinction between the admirable and the desirable. It distinguishes intrinsic from instrumental evaluation, and (making some allowances for the idea of an instrumentally good state of affairs) intrinsic evaluation corresponds, for utilitarianism, to the desirable and instrumental evaluation to the admirable. Utilitarianism allows for both intrinsically good states of affairs and intrinsic personal goods, but the former notion reduces in ways we have seen, on utilitarian assumptions, to the latter, and the latter is therefore—and for purposes of useful comparison with virtue ethics—utilitarianism's idea of the desirable. In an important sense, both utilitarianism and virtue ethics treat personal good as the (sole or ultimate) desirable (thing)—though we must also recognize their potentially large differences about what counts as a personal good.

In regard to the admirable, utilitarianism views obligatory and morally right actions as instrumental goods corresponding or amounting to examples of admirability, whereas our virtue ethics rules out moral categories and leaves no place for moral (as opposed to other-regarding) admirability. Helping another may count, for virtue ethics, as admirable on other-regarding grounds, but that does not allow us to regard such help as *morally* good or *morally* admirable.

We have also seen that virtue ethics allows for non-instrumental virtues, in a way that utilitarianism clearly does not. Whatever counts as a virtue for utilitarianism or for virtue ethics will thereby count as an excellent or admirable trait for the one or for the other, but this agreement should not be allowed to obscure the fact that for utilitarianism there is only instrumental virtue and admirability, whereas for virtue ethics there are both instrumental and intrinsic forms of virtue and admirability. In addition, most utilitarians, following Hume, do not distinguish between virtues and other admirable traits or between acts/ achievements that are ethically admirable and those that are (merely) aesthetically or intellectually admirable;[1] and in order, therefore, to permit a general critical comparison between utilitarianism and common-sense views about what is admirable in human life, I will have to treat common-sense virtue ethics as including intuitive judgments about traits that may ultimately not count as virtues/character traits and about acts/achievements that might turn out to be admirable for other than ethical reasons.

Our previous chapter focused mainly on the differing judgments utilitarianism and virtue ethics make concerning the relation(s) between the admirable, on the one hand, and the desirable understood as the personally good, on the other. And the disagreement between these two approaches came down to two questions: whether the admirable and personally good are fundamentally distinct and whether, if they are not, they should be identified reductively or elevatively. I am now assuming that elevationism won't work for common-sense virtue ethics and that the latter must assume a fundamental dualism between admirability and desirability/personal good. But utilitarianism is irrecusably reductive of the admirable to the desirable/personally good, and it is in these forms that our critical comparison of the two approaches will proceed.

We must not, however, assume that the radical differences between what utilitarianism and what virtue ethics say about what makes lives or traits admirable are a matter simply of the above difference between reductive monism, regarding the admirable and the desirable, and a dualistic conception of their relationship. After all, egoism is also capable of a dualistic conception of the desirable and the admirable, yet egoism yields judgments about what makes lives/traits admirable and about which particular lives/traits are more admirable than which others that are not only at variance with monistic utilitarianism, but differ importantly from the deliverances of a self-other symmetric conception of virtue ethics of the sort defended here.

Moreover, and this is a point easily missed, the differences regarding admirable traits, people, and lives between even *non-egoistic* virtue ethics and utilitarianism are not simply attributable to their disagreement as to whether the admirable can be reduced to the personally good or must remain a separate category. For the differences are also in part attributable to the different ways in which utilitarianism and virtue ethics avoid egoism, or, to put matters more perspicuously, to the differing standards of self-other symmetry each conforms to. Utilitarianism evaluates via a standard that gives equal weight to every individual; it is self-other symmetric *in sensu diviso*. But virtue ethics is self-other symmetric *in sensu composito*, and this means that it gives equal weight to the self/

agent/trait-possessor and to other people taken as a class or category. Both differences as to the reducibility of the admirable to the desirable and differences concerning the proper form of self-other asymmetry to adopt help to create disagreements between utilitarianism and virtue ethics with respect to admirability in lives as well as in other sorts of things. And though I will not harp upon these matters, it will turn out that the differing judgments about admirable lives we are about to unearth turn on differences both about self-other asymmetry and about reducibility—as well as on a fundamental disagreement between the two views about whether there can be non-instrumental virtue or admirability.

For the utilitarian, what makes some traits, lives, or people more excellent or admirable than others are the differing effects they have on overall human or sentient happiness.[2] (We are sticking with comparative judgments because we have tentatively concluded that utilitarianism is best stated in scalar form; but the comparative judgments of virtue ethics clearly conflict, in any event, even with the comparative judgments utilitarianism is committed to.) In effect, utilitarianism instrumentally evaluates lives or people by means of some scalar variant of the principle of utility, but no such single, clearly statable principle is capable of expressing the basis or the grounds of our common-sense virtue-ethical judgments about which lives or people are more admirable than which others.

Thus for utilitarianism it would seem to be possible to compare both different lives and people, as well as different possible lives of the same person, via the principle that one life or person is more admirable (or less deplorable) if its or his overall effect on human happiness is more favorable to such happiness, and I think it can also be assumed here that the effects overall of a person are simply the effects overall of (the events and other relevant aspects of) her life.[3]

By contrast, once again, our common-sense evaluations of greater or lesser admirability in lives or people seem to rely on considerations that cannot easily be unified. Even the principles—perfect and imperfect— that emerged in Chapter 6 as the overarching standard or credo of virtue ethical thinking cannot give us everything that one might wish to have in the way of unifying principles. Since those principles recommend that we improve others and ourselves with regard to admirability or the possession of various virtues (and not corrupt others or allow ourselves to be corrupted in the relevant ways) and say nothing explicitly about what considerations make for admirability and how they combine into overall judgments of admirability, they give us neither a unified standard of admirability nor anything as explicit about the bases of admirability, say, as Ross's hexalogue of prima facie obligations.[4]

I don't want to underestimate the capacities of common-sense virtue ethics for self-systematicization in the manner of Ross's list of prima facie moral principles or in casuistry about actual and possible acts or constellations of character. But I don't think that it is necessary for us here, and given present concerns, to make an attempt in that direction. We have seen examples, earlier on, of the ways in which what counts as admirable or as a virtue for common-sense thinking is not rigidly tied to the well-being or good of the agent who acts admirably or the possessor of a given virtue—much less to the well-being, happiness, or personal good of all mankind (or sentient beings), and we have also seen that certain kinds of personal strength and personal self-sufficiency represent commonplace, but, none the less for that, deeply held ideals of human admirability or excellence. Clearly, and as far as we are proposing to go at the moment, a host of different factors seem relevant to common-sense or intuitive evaluations of admirability, seem capable of making a difference to how highly or well we think of personal traits and of people themselves and/ or their lives, and, indeed, the specific examples now to be mentioned clearly are based on a whole variety of considerations, though the complexity seems in no way to prejudice the firmness of our views in this area. And what is perhaps most relevant at this point to the comparison with utilitarianism is the large role self-regarding considerations can play in our intuitive assessments of greater or lesser admirability.

For example, we greatly admire Alexander's single-mindedness, organizing power, and self-confidence, Disraeli's energy, verve, and composure (or forbearance) in the face of anti-Semitism, Talleyrand's far-sightedness and delicacy in diplomacy—and we admire these people themselves— largely apart from any consideration of the benefits mankind generally reaped from the traits or people just mentioned. (Of course, we don't suppose them, any of them, to be monsters of cruelty or totally selfish or self-centered when we admire them thus.) Even assuming, as we may do, that mankind was no better off or possibly even somewhat worse off as a result of their brilliant careers, we tend to think more highly of these people and be more impressed by their total lives than anything we are likely to find ourselves thinking or feeling about people who are decent and do a positive amount of good within a limited circle of acquaintanceship, but whose personal qualities—whether other-regarding or self-regarding—seem less out of the ordinary and admirable than what can be attributed to the three historical figures just mentioned.

Such examples show us, I believe, that a high regard for people can be largely based on non-altruistic character or personality traits and to a great extent, therefore, be independent of the sorts of considerations that

utilitarianism treats as the basis of attributions of excellence or admirability. The utilitarian must regard (likely) total contribution to human or
sentient happiness as the sole determinant of greater or lesser personal
admirability, and so for the utilitarian, the comparative judgment respecting the admirability of the above historical figures and that of the
more private persons we also mentioned will turn on how much overall
net happiness each created and will be the opposite of what many or most
of us are inclined to say about such cases, given only that one or another
of the historical figures did slightly less overall for net human happiness.

The same point can be brought out in a slightly different way by
considering some of our counterfactual judgments of admirability as
compared with those utilitarianism would have to be committed to.
Socrates, we know, has had a large and, we hope, beneficial influence on
mankind over the millennia, an influence largely resulting from the way
Plato depicted him in his Dialogues. But in the light of what we believe
we know about Socrates, most of us would say that Socrates would have
been more admirable than almost everyone else, even if he had never
been written about and his life had therefore had consequences less
favorable to overall human happiness (remember the family and friends
his self-chosen death may have made unhappy) than the lives of many
less extraordinary people who are reasonably kind and charitable.

Moreover, direct utilitarianism evaluates not only overall lives and
people, but also the particular traits of given individuals by the criterion
of overall effect on human/sentient happiness or well-being; so it is
committed to evaluating Alexander's single-mindedness and Disraeli's
verve and energy, for example, solely in terms of the effect each had on
total human happiness. But from a common-sense point of view, such a
basis for assessing admirability in a trait or virtue status seems totally
one-sided and absurd: indeed, even more one-sided and absurd than
evaluating total lives or human beings on such a basis.

Let us move next to the differences between utilitarianism and our
ordinary thought that arise in connection with self-regarding and other-
regarding virtues considered together.

Our admiration for people with (outstanding) other-regarding and
other-benefiting virtues is not necessarily higher than what we feel for
people whose virtues are largely of a self-regarding or less other-benefiting kind, and speaking of ordinary intuition now, it is by no means
obvious that we tend to have a higher opinion of mankind's various
*benefactors* than of those whose excellence, as we may say, doesn't
express itself along those precise lines. Do we necessarily have a higher
opinion of Saint Francis, Jonas Salk, or Mother Theresa, who rank

among those who have done most for mankind and whose efforts in that direction we so greatly admire, than of the Alexanders, Samuel Johnsons, Albert Einsteins, Martha Grahams, or Socrateses of this world, whose admirable traits and activities, however extraordinary, didn't mainly or exclusively flow in the direction of efforts to help, and success in helping, mankind? In the case, of Einstein, indeed, we believe that the effect of his theories on mankind may well, through their influence on the development of the atom bomb and atomic power generally, be deleterious or harmful overall and in the long run, but if this stops the utilitarian from regarding Einstein as more admirable than people who simply mind their own business, it doesn't stop most of us from thinking him more admirable and having a greater admiration for his thoughts and deeds, his life, than for lives far less harmful or more beneficial to mankind. And so here as before, our intuitive evaluations are totally out of keeping with those utilitarianism is committed to.[5]

And my own tendency, at this point, is to agree with common-sense virtue-ethical judgment in these matters and disagree, therefore, with utilitarianism. The theoretical benefits of utilitarianism's systematic unifying tendencies should not be underestimated or lightly renounced, but in this area, as in some others already mentioned, I find myself unable to go along with the utilitarian view of things. The gulf between deep-seated intuitions and the deliverances of utilitarianism is enormous and not readily bridged or diminished. And that in fact leaves me at least with a preference for the combination of lesser unification and greater intuitiveness that our virtue ethics embodies over a conceptually and ethically more unified utilitarianism that offers us theoretical and methodological reasons for renouncing our (seemingly coherent and paradox-free) intuitions about a wide range of value matters that includes not only moral issues, but also questions about personal admirability. (Not to mention matters of aesthetic judgment, where, as I have argued elsewhere,[6] the total consistent direct utilitarian seems committed to treating benefits conferred on mankind as the sole criterion of aesthetic excellence.)

Moreover, in the light of what we have been saying in this section, it should be fairly clear how the particular divergence between ordinary and utilitarian judgments about comparative admirability stems at least in part from the different ways in which the two ethical theories interpret and apply the idea of self-other symmetry. Our virtue ethics assents to two principles—representing the virtue-theoretic analogues of imperfect duties—that claim fundamental positive significance for helping others and helping oneself—whether in terms of admirable qualities and attainments or of mere benefits. And as we stated them, those principles expressed an ideal of balance *in sensu composito* between the self and other people. Just above, we explored some of the particular judgments of comparative admirability that a reliance on intuitions can give rise to, and some of those judgments not only are accounted for and partly justified by the way they fit in with the two principles just mentioned, but also serve as some sort of confirmation for those principles. The latter embody the ethical commitments of our virtue ethics very abstractly—in a way so general and overarching as to leave open a wide range of further issues for (intuitive) virtue-ethical specification. But even so, the principles clearly express, as I have said, an ideal of (some degree of) balance as between the self-regarding and the other-regarding, where because of the way the principles are stated and juxtaposed, that balance is clearly to be understood *in sensu composito*. And when we then turn to the particular judgments of comparative admirability that seem plausible to many of us, we find that we are inclined to honor, to admire, both the great benefactors of mankind and individuals who, while not falling into this first category, encompass and exemplify attributes we admire, even marvel at. And it is by no means obvious that our untampered-with judgments of comparative admirability always tend to favor the benefactors over the others. It seems fairer to say, rather, that there is no obvious or generalized direction of preference here, and that our particular beliefs about such matters reflect an emphasis on both self-regarding and other-regarding forms/embodiments of human excellence. And, of course, such a (relative) balance or absence of clearcut universal favoritism toward a particular form of admirability fits in well with the general perspective of virtue ethics as expressed by the above two principles.

Moreover, this particular form of reflective equilibrium favors the admirability judgments of common-sense virtue ethics over those of utilitarianism. For the latter balances the interests of self and other in an *in sensu diviso* fashion that clearly puts a premium on acts and character traits that do a great deal to help large numbers of people. If (for any given assignment) the self counts no more than any single other person, then self-regarding interests and ideals may fairly easily be overwhelmed or outweighed by considerations about the effects one's acts or character will have on the rest of humanity, and on such an ideal vision, the Florence Nightingales and the Mother Theresas—assuming appropriate facts—will rank higher than the Samuel Johnsons, Martha Grahams or Albert Einsteins.

Let us at this point, however, switch over to a brief consideration of negative cases, that is, of how differently utilitarianism and virtue ethics would treat the *criticizability* or *deplorability* of various lives, careers, people. Of course, we tend to think worse or less well of people to the extent they deliberately, or negligently, or even perhaps merely accidentally harm other people and themselves, but a number of other considerations enter into our thinking here, and in some cases we would have lower esteem for someone who did no overall harm to people than for someone who knowingly did more harm than good.

Consider, for example, a family where the father is a hardened criminal involved in extortion, robbery, even murder, and where there are two sons. The first gets himself better educated than his father through hard work and an intense effort of will; he becomes a teller in a bank and at that point starts feeling, for the first time, an inordinate temptation to steal. Although he knows this is wrong, wishes he weren't assailed by such desires, and is in fact horrified by the resemblance to his own despised father, he does steal a small amount. He has his own family, and when he is caught, he is for some reason let off lightly. He is simply fired, but, filled with guilt and anxiety, he finds it hard to find another job. His family suffers, but no one knows what to do. He does, however, find another job. He steals in a petty way again, but this time he is prosecuted and sent to jail. His family suffers worse than before. He eventually gets out, but by this time his wife has decided to raise the children on her own and obliterate him from her life and that of her children. They all suffer as a result, but they keep to this resolution.

Imagine further scenarios of this kind involving petty wrongdoing, more punishment, more guilt and anxiety. The man struggles with his own hated tendencies, comes to realize the effect his father's example has had upon him, tries to free himself from his weakness/compulsion, and finally, despairing of self-help, puts himself in the hands of a social worker who figures out a way of keeping him out of the path of temptation long enough for him to arrive at a better understanding of his problems through intense counseling. Let us imagine the counseling really works, and that he emerges able to overcome any temptation to steal; eventually he leads a fairly normal life, marries again, and is able to maintain a stable relationship with his wife. Overall we can assume the man has done more harm than good, but he has indeed stopped being a destructive and self-destructive person through an extraordinary persistence and effort of will, and a certain luck in finding someone to help him.

Compare this man to his brother. The latter is also traumatized by the criminal father; he develops psychosomatic invalidism and is never put in the way of any temptations to copy his father. He lives with his mother, does some piece work at home to make ends meet, but never goes out, never has any social or emotional life, any life at all, outside his home, where he remains an invalid throughout his life.

The second brother probably does less overall net harm than the first. But because he never gets into life at all, because he, in effect flees life as a way of avoiding his problems, I think I have a lower opinion of him than of his imagined brother, who goes out in to the world, has a life, wrestles with his problems, and in large measure learns to overcome them. I have some admiration for the man we first described, but none for the second, and even if my admiration in the first case is also mingled with criticism, most of us would, I think, have a lower overall estimation of the life led by the invalid brother, a life that seems almost unrelievedly pathetic and redeemed by no really admirable features. Here, then, with lives that make no positive overall contribution to human happiness we can once more see a difference between the utilitarian and the common-sense evaluation of lives or individuals. Most of us, I think, would tend to have a (much) higher opinion of the first brother and his life, but utilitarians will treat as superior or (morally) better the life that does more overall for or less overall against human happiness, and so will disagree with the common-sense or intuitive response many or most of us would have to these two cases.

Utilitarianism therefore both in cases of positive admirability and in cases where there is much to be criticized and/or deplored treats the evaluation of lives and people as a function of net overall resultant (human) happiness. But our common opinions depend on other factors and allow great admiration to exist independently of actual or likely effects on overall happiness. The result is that utilitarianism's judgments about comparative admirability strain our sense of plausibility in a number of directions, and as I have said, I think the unintuitive character of many of its particular judgments gives us reason—some reason—to prefer the virtue-ethical approach in this and other areas of ethics.

But there is another point to be made. As we acknowledged earlier, scalar direct utilitarianism cannot be said to demand too much sacrifice from individuals, since it actually makes no demands, sets no conditions on right action. So this particular route to the charge that utilitarianism downgrades or devalues the moral individual now seems well blocked, but that doesn't mean that there is no other way in which, in the light, for example, of what we have just been saying, a charge of devaluation can be validly brought against utilitarianism. For even scalar utilitarianism puts a premium on what serves mankind as well and as widely as possible, and it allows no other considerations to play a role in its judgments of comparative excellence or admirability. In other words, it consistently idealizes what is instrumentally (most) useful to mankind's happiness, and treats the idea of comparative individual virtue or admirability as having no substance or validity apart from such an instrumental role. By contrast, common-sense thinking about the admirability of people, traits, and lives doesn't so nearly exclusively force us to look to effects upon others as a source of an individual's excellence—some forms of individual excellence will hinge on such extraindividual matters, but others will depend on certain kinds of self-cultivation or individualistic flowering, and to the extent, therefore, that common-sense virtue ethics allows for factors of individual excellence that are largely independent of an individual's (likely) contribution to the larger whole, to mankind generally, it seems to place a greater value on the individual, to show a greater appreciation of genuinely *individual* merit, than utilitarianism does. In some sense, utilitarianism allows each and every individual to be evaluationally submerged in or engulfed by the sea of larger humanity, whereas virtue ethics, while giving considerable weight, in evaluating any given person, to the larger concerns of mankind, also accepts and encourages and values more individualistic forms of excellence. As a result, it precisely doesn't depreciate or deprecate individuals in the way utilitarianism does, and this criticism, along with the wide disparity we have found between utilitarianism's particular judgments and those that seem most intuitive and initially plausible, gives us reason to prefer virtue ethics over utilitarianism.

However, as I suggested at the end of Part III, there is another sort of consideration that looms or can be made to loom large in our critical comparison of these two approaches to ethics. In addition to its implausible implications over a wide range and at differing levels of generality and particularity as well, utilitarianism is multiply underdetermined relative to its own methods and motivations. And even if we go scalar for reasons having to do with the underdetermination of more familiar versions of utilitarianism, two forms of indeterminacy remain that cast doubt on the viability or validity even of the scalar form of utilitarianism we have been working with. It is time to say more about these problems.

# Notes

1. On this point see my "Object-Utilitarianism," *Pacific Philosophical Quarterly* 66, 1985, pp. 111-24.

2. I am assuming here that utilitarians would wish to model judgments of admirability on their judgments of instrumental goodness, rather than on their

judgments of blameworthiness and praiseworthiness. Doing the latter would mean treating the admirability of a thing as a matter of whether it was instrumentally good, that is, morally right, to admire the thing, as a matter, therefore, of whether admiring the thing—as opposed to the thing itself—has good effects, and we could certainly accommodate our discussion to the possibility that admirability should be understood by utilitarians on analogy with praiseworthiness.

Note, however, that utilitarians typically (e.g., Sidgwick in *Methods*) treat desirability in a thing as the (instrumental or intrinsic) goodness of that thing, rather than as the (instrumental) goodness/rightness of desiring the thing, which is a quite different matter. In that case, it would seem most natural for admirability to be understood in similar fashion, and that is how I have understood it here. Since the other potential reading could in any case be accommodated, it needn't concern us further. But cf. *Methods*, pp. 492f., for what seems to amount to inconsistency on this point.

3. For utilitarian evaluation of *persons* see R. M. Adams, "Motive Utilitarianism," *Journal of Philosophy* 73, 1976, pp. 467–81; J. J. C. Smart, "Outline of a System of Utilitarian Ethics" in Smart and Williams, *Utilitarianism: for and against*, Cambridge University Press, 1973; and S. Darwall, "Agent-Centered Restrictions from the Inside Out," *Philosophical Topics* 50, 1986, esp. pp. 309, 313. On the utilitarian evaluation of *objects* see my "Object-Utilitarianism."

4. See W. D. Ross, *The Foundations of Ethics*, Oxford, 1929, and *The Right and the Good*, Oxford, 1930.

5. For such claims and further argument in their favor, see Susan Wolf's important article, "Moral Saints," *Journal of Philosophy* 79, 1982, pp. 419–39.

6. See my "Object-Utilitarianism," *passim*.

# 15

## Utilitarian Underdetermination

### Expectabilism vs. Actualism

In our discussions of utilitarianism, we have so far skirted an important issue about how utilitarianism should be formulated. We have not considered whether utilitarianism in its different direct forms should be thought of as commending acts, motives, etc., whose overall effects or consequences are actually favorable to human happiness or as commending acts, motives, etc., whose overall effects are (from some suitable standpoint) expectably favorable to such happiness. (An analogous and equally difficult problem also arises in connection with consequentialism more generally.) Indeed, this is an issue that both defenders and critics of utilitarianism tend to skirt in one way or another.

Some writers suggest or seem to suggest that it does not matter whether utilitarianism, or consequentialism, is formulated in (what we can call) expectabilist[1] or in (what we can call) actualist terms, and I believe I have seen versions of the principle of utility where such indifference is built into the principle's very formulation—as, for example, when it is said that an act is obligatory if and only if it has *better or expectably better* consequences (for human happiness) than any of its alternatives. Taken literally, this formulation of the principle of utility holds that both having expectably better consequences and having actually better consequences are sufficient for an act to count as obligatory, and this is in fact a position I have never seen anyone explicitly defend. But what really seems to be happening in such vague formulations of the principle of utility is that the defender or critic of act-utilitarianism or act-consequentialism is unsure whether such views are best formulated in actualist or in expectabilist terms and is attempting to evade that issue to get on with other questions concerning utilitarianism.

But the skirting of the issue between actualism and expectabilism is not limited to those who think it doesn't matter whether utilitarianism gets stated in expectabilist or actualist terms. Others take a more or less definite stand on the issue, committing themselves either to an actualist or an expectabilist formulation of the principle of utility, but do so without giving any justification for their particular preference. Since definite positions have been taken on both sides of the issue, one would expect to find discussion and debate about the respective merits of actualism and expectabilism, yet, for all the searching I have done, I haven't yet found any significant discussion of this issue. I hope it becomes clear in what follows that the question of actualism vs. expectabilism is one that both utilitarianism and consequentialism must consider. Until and unless it is answered or resolved, utilitarian and consequentialist views—whether scalar or otherwise—are in a weaker position than has perhaps been realized. Any indeterminacy that may attach to the choice between actualism and expectabilism may open utilitarianism, as well as consequentialism, to a form of criticism that has not previously been recognized, but that, nonetheless, may be damaging to the prospects of formulating an adequate version of utilitarianism or consequentialism.

To get a foothold on this topic, I first describe some of the more or less explicit stands that have been taken regarding the actualist vs. the expectabilist formulation of utilitarianism. Perhaps if I do something to indicate the diversity of opinion on this topic that already exists in the literature of utilitarianism, it will become easier for us to recognize the need for a careful examination of the nature and implications of the question I am raising.

Actualist versions of act-utilitarianism or act-consequentialism are defended in Sidgwick's *The Methods of Ethics*, in Moore's *Principia Ethica* and *Ethics*, and in Smart's "An outline of a system of utilitarian ethics." All three distinguish blameworthiness from wrongness in their efforts to palliate their commitment to the wrongness of actions with unforeseeable bad consequences, but it is worth noting that such a distinction provides us with no reason to *prefer* actualism to expectabilism, and there is precious little in the above-mentioned works that has any bearing on the latter issue.

However, even if Sidgwick and other actualist utilitarians/consequentialists never justify their seeming rejection of expectabilism, I think there may be a fairly reasonable explanation for why these philosophers opted for actualist versions of utilitarianism and consequentialism. They have thought of moral judgment as most properly, validly, or accurately made from a standpoint of total knowledge of the consequences of various alternative actions (or motives) and/or on the basis of a *sub specie aeternitatis* view of things that allows for such total knowledge.[2] They have held, in effect, that the moral assessment of actions is fundamentally a matter of the preferences or attitudes that would be possessed by an impersonally benevolent rational being who viewed those actions from a standpoint free from the usual epistemic limits of time, place, and person.

Now if the rightness or wrongness of acts hinges on the attitude or judgment of an impersonally benevolent, all-knowing rational being,[3] then one can see how a preference for actualism would inevitably arise. The (relevantly) all-knowing being will know about distant consequences of some action that its agent will not be able to foresee, and, given the conditions of impersonality and benevolence, that hypothetical being's attitude toward the action will depend in part on whether such remote consequences are favorable or unfavorable to human happiness. An act like the possible infanticide of Hitler will be seen favorably or more favorably, at least, than it could reasonably have been by anyone actually around during Hitler's infancy, so a gap will open between valid evaluation and evaluations made at the time an action is performed. Correct utilitarian evaluation will be a matter of actual long-term consequences rather than expectable or foreseeable (long-term) consequences, if an impersonally benevolent omniscience is to be the fulcrum for proper utilitarian moral judgments.[4]

However, this still leaves us with an important question that defenders or espousers of actualism have not, to my knowledge, faced. Both expectabilist and actualist versions of the principle of utility require benevolence and impersonality as the foundational conditions of proper moral judgment. But is there any good reason for assuming that the preferred fulcrum of judgment should involve a condition of relevant omniscience or access to a *sub specie aeternitatis* point of view? Just as some direct consequentialists question whether benevolence is a complete enough characterization of the attitude required for proper moral evaluation— holding, for example, that considerations of justice have an independent role in making states of affairs good but are not adequately represented in the psychology of impersonal *benevolence*, so too can an expectabilist claim that judgment of a given agent's act should be made from an epistemic or epistemological position relevantly similar to that of the agent herself. Impersonality and benevolence give us, he says, all the distance we need to make an objectively valid moral assessment of the act freed from the agent's non-moral or anti-moral self-centeredness and bias; but any further departure from the agent's perspective makes it difficult, or more difficult, to regard the consequent evaluation as an evaluation of *the act as done by the agent*, so it is better to make expectable consequences the focus or fulcrum of direct utilitarian or direct consequentialist act-evaluation.

Frankly, I don't quite know what to say in response to this expect-abilist argument. I am not really convinced by it, because it seems to me that if, as direct consequentialists hold, we can properly judge an act in abstraction from its agent's actual motivation, then we may also be able to judge it in abstraction from the agent's epistemic viewpoint. But I have also seen no good argument for *requiring* abstraction of the latter sort as a condition of proper or accurate moral evaluation. Even the obvious argument that it is more consistent, more uniform, and therefore method-ologically better for a utilitarianism that abstracts from agential motiva-tion likewise to abstract from agential epistemic/epistemological limita-tions has its attendant dangers. And, indeed, it may actually backfire, in the present context, because there are other aspects of the agent from which utilitarianism clearly doesn't require us to abstract. Utilitarianism typically applies the epithets "right" and "wrong" only to intentional actions and in effect, therefore, refuses to abstract from the intentional character of the actions it evaluates as wrong or right. And in addition utilitarianism refuses to abstract from the fact that the agent whose act is being evaluated had such-and-such alternative acts within her power—it typically makes such alternatives relevant to act-evaluation and in that sense, therefore, refuses to abstract from the causal powers of the agent. So any argument from consistency here will be a double-edged sword and the issue is perhaps too complex to be effectively dealt with by means of consistency arguments. It is not clear how utilitarianism can defend a preference for its actualist versions or for the *sub specie aeternitatis* standpoint.

However, I should also mention that some philosophers have preferred to *make use* of an expectabilist version of act-utilitarianism.[5] And others have even claimed that expectabilism is the better or more accurate version of utilitarianism—but, disappointingly, have done so without offering any reasons.[6] It is in fact difficult to defend either version of utilitarianism or consequentialism against the other, and yet, as I have said, the fact of this difficulty and its potential for raising problems with particular versions or expressions of utilitarianism or consequentialism have largely been ignored by those advocating actualism, by those advo-cating expectabilism, and by those who have sought to remain neutral on this issue.

I think we have reason at this point to conclude that there is more underdetermination in utilitarian theory than we have realized, under-determination, moreover, that like the forms reckoned with in earlier chapters calls into question familiar versions of utilitarianism and gives us some reason to wonder whether any fairly specific expression or

rendition of utilitarianism—even a scalar one—can be theoretically justified. Clearly, we cannot simply fudge or skirt the issue between actualism and expectabilism in the manner touched on earlier. But the idea that it doesn't matter whether we formulate utilitarianism in actualist or expectabilist terms can in fact be interpreted along lines that may help us with our present difficulties. For just as the underdetermination of optimizing and satisficing versions of utilitarianism (relative to utilitarian foundations and methodology) led us to a scalar version incorporating only what is common to the first two, so too may the apparent underdetermination of actualist and expectabilist forms of utilitarianism lead to a form of utilitarianism that asserts only what is common to actualism and expectabilism.

Both actualism and expectabilism clearly hold that an act with expectably and actually better consequences than some other is better than that other; they disagree only about cases where these two criteria of betterness come apart, and one action has expectably, but not actually, better consequences than some other. And there could be a form of utilitarianism that limited itself to the clear-cut cases in the manner just indicated and in effect, therefore, gave us only sufficient, not necessary, conditions for utilitarian moral superiority or betterness. But just as scalar utilitarianism leaves utilitarianism with a non-comparative-moral-value gap, the formulation just suggested leaves scalar utilitarianism with a sizable comparative-moral-value gap. And with this further erosion of specificity, one may wonder whether, from a theoretical standpoint, it is worth having such an indefinite and, in effect, uncommitted form of utilitarianism. Unless utilitarianism possesses some resources for answering this form of (what at this point can be called) scepticism, its viability as a moral theory seems very much in doubt.

In addition, we musn't lose sight of the earlier discussed difficulty of choosing between standard reductive utilitarianism and eliminative utilitarianism. Our problems in this chapter have concerned the underdetermination of differing forms of reductive utilitarianism, but both actualism and expectabilism represent specific forms of utilitarian reductionism, specific ways in which utilitarianism may propose the reduction of evaluative terms/language to empirical or non-evaluative terms/language. And as I hope was made clear in the final section of Chapter 13, the choice between familiar, reductive utilitarianism (in whatever form) and the sort of eliminative utilitarianism that denies the applicability of a evaluative predicates is also a very difficult one. In fact, it seems just frustratingly underdetermined as the choice between expectabilism a actualism.

These problems of underdetermination may present as great a threat to the utilitarian enterprise as the intuitive implausibilities utilitarianism clearly leads to. The utilitarian can always brazen things out with respect to the latter, but the former problems seem absolutely endemic to the utilitarian's own distinctive point of view. It is not fundamental disagreement with utilitarian assumptions and approaches that leads to the problems of underdetermination we have been discussing. Quite the contrary, the difficulties that have arisen have come up in the course of pursuing the utilitarian approach and utilitarian methodology in as complete and consistent a way as possible. The difficulties brought to light are ones that ought to bother any utilitarian who is thinking of things from within her own philosophical perspective. And until such a utilitarian or someone else shows us how to answer these problems, I think there is reason to regard the utilitarian approach as a self-limiting, self-undercutting failure. That gives us a further reason at this point for preferring a virtue-ethical approach.

However, it has been suggested to me that the utilitarian may go beyond her own utilitarian assumptions and methodology and finally appeal to considerations of common sense or intuitive plausibility to avoid the charge of underdetermination. Perhaps expectabilism is more common-sensical than actualism, and perhaps we can say that reductive utilitarianism is closer to received or common-sense moral opinion than eliminative utilitarianism of the kind discussed briefly in Chapter 13.

But many—even most—direct utilitarians have been unwilling to place much reliance on ordinary thought or intuition (Bentham and, more recently, Hare and Smart are good examples of such an attitude); and it would also seem that if the utilitarian allows himself to place such wholesale reliance on ordinary moral thinking as would be required to elude underdetermination, he creates other difficulties for himself that may be just as threatening, ultimately, to the validity of his overall position. In Chapter 14, I mentioned a large variety of ways in which (direct) utilitarianism differs from common intuitions in what it has to say about the admirability of lives, persons, traits, and human achievements. But just above I said that the utilitarian could perhaps "brazen it out" with respect to the differences between her own view and the deliverances of intuition, and what I had in mind was the typical or frequent utilitarian insistence that ethics needs to rationalize or straighten out our intuitions rather than rely on them.

However, if the utilitarian is for present purposes taken to grant some importance or validity to ethical intuition she cannot simply brazen things out with respect to the conclusions of Chapter 14, and so the price

of overcoming underdetermination is to make the counterintuitive implications of utilitarianism discussed in Chapter 14 loom larger and more
intractably for the utilitarian herself. Either way, utilitarianism seems
deeply problematic in a way that a common-sense virtue-ethical approach
does not.

And similar problems would, I believe, face any non-utilitarian ethical
view that treated the evaluation of acts, traits, and people as some sort of
function of its impersonal/objective assessments of relevant states of
affairs. Pluralistic and/or perfectionistic forms of consequentialism—
views allowing other things than happiness/pleasure to count as personal
goods and/or treating the goodness of states of affairs as more complexly
related to human well-being than direct utilitarianism allows—come
much closer to common-sense thinking about these matters. And one
might therefore think one could look in this direction for an overall view
that can both escape the above problems of underdetermination and
avoid the kinds of unintuitive results described in Chapter 14.

In order to escape underdetermination, one would presumably have to
rely on intuitive considerations to settle the issues of expectabilism vs.
actualism and of reductionism vs. eliminationism. But even having
settled these issues and having accepted a non-utilitarian and therefore
more intuitive theory of personal goods and good states of affairs, a
consequentialism of the kind we are talking about will encounter difficulties—less severe perhaps, but difficulties, nonetheless—along the lines
discussed in Chapter 14.

A perfectionist/pluralistic form of direct consequentialism can avoid
the utilitarian conclusion that (assuming appropriate facts) a great bene-
factor like Mother Theresa or Jonas Salk is automatically more admirable than an Einstein or a Martha Graham, by claiming that the achievements of the latter are just as important as any relevant large-scale relief
of poverty or disease. Perfectionism can say, for example, that it is just as
good a thing that Martha Graham achieved what she did as that Mother
Theresa achieved what she did, and the underlying assumption here
would be that great cultural achievements/advances are just as morally
significant as large-scale improvements in individual welfare or happiness. But I wonder about less world-historical achievements and virtues.
We admire some private individuals' fortitude in the face of tragic loss or
farsightedness in financial affairs even if the fortitude and farsightedness
are not unique and represent no sort of cultural accomplishment or
advance. Yet I would question whether we ordinarily think less highly of
such fortitude or farsightedness than we would of the professionalism or
dutifulness of a doctor who does a great deal of good for her own

patients. As I mentioned earlier, we ordinarily want to allow for individualistic forms of admirability that have little relation to the well-being of (large numbers of) other people. And I believe perfectionistic and pluralistic consequentialism runs into difficulties if it attempts to remain compatible with common-sense or intuitive evaluations of the above traits of character.

Perfectionism (or pluralism) can certainly say that it is good that fortitude or farsightedness should be exemplified. But since it ties its judgments of admirability exclusively to judgments about the goodness of states of affairs, it can say that fortitude, for example, in the face of tragic loss is as admirable as the professionalism/dutifulness of a doctor who helps many patients only if it makes the implausible claim that it is just as important, just as good a thing, that someone should exhibit fortitude as that many people should be saved from serious illness by a doctor. So perfectionism/pluralism must either say that fortitude and the like are less admirable than they seem or make counterintuitive claims about the relative value and importance of various states of affairs. Either way it becomes somewhat implausible.

By contrast, our ordinary thinking about admirability is not so closely tied to what we want to see, or think it is important to see, happen in the world, and even if, like any plausible form of consequentialism I am aware of, we hold it to be more important—objectively a better thing— that many people should be saved from severe illness by a doctor than that some entirely different person should exhibit fortitude in the face of personal loss or be farsighted in personal financial matters, we needn't make the inference that consequentialism seems to be committed to here and conclude that the doctor's dutifulness or professionalism is more admirable than any private example of fortitude or financial farsightedness. Rather, I think we intuitively hold that the latter traits may be just as admirable as, and perhaps are even more admirable than, the doctor's ordinary dutifulness (she doesn't have to be a deep and devoted humanitarian in order to be medically very effective)—even while being willing to grant that it is objectively speaking better or more desirable that many people should be cured of serious illness than that fortitude or financial farsightedness should be exemplified by a given individual.

So non-utilitarian, pluralistic consequentialism must diverge considerably from common sense in the value judgments it makes. The gulf is less wide than we found with respect to utilitarianism, but it is wide enough, I believe, to give our present approach a certain advantage over any form of perfectionist/pluralist consequentialism I am aware of. And since the unintuitive implications we have uncovered arise independently of the issues of expectabilism vs. actualism and of reductionism vs. eliminationism, I think it can be said that the virtue-ethical approach has an advantage over any non-utilitarian view that evaluates exclusively by reference to the goodness of states of affairs.

Of course, non-utilitarian consequentialism has been given short shrift in these pages. Utilitarianism has served as a useful reductive foil to the form of virtue-ethical eliminativism I have proposed, and certainly act-utilitarianism is the most well-known and historically important form of consequentialism. However, various kinds of non-utilitarian consequentialism have been developed both in the past and in recent years, and the few criticisms I have made of such approaches can hardly be said to rule out the possibility of a version of perfectionistic or pluralistic consequentialism that can give common-sense virtue ethics a run for its money. But there is no room to consider these possibilities further here.

## Notes

1. In *Beyond Optimizing* (Harvard, 1989, Ch. 7) I used the less apt term "probabilism" rather than the present "expectabilism" for the view opposed to actualism.

2. In the recent literature of utilitarianism, the idea of evaluation from a position of total (relevant) knowledge—where such knowledge is taken to include imaginative sensitivity to the experience of other people—can be found, e.g., in P. Railton, "Moral Realism," *Philosophical Review* XCV, 1986, pp. 163–207, esp. pp. 190ff. But the notion occurs in many other places and to a large extent is already apparent in Bentham's claim (*An Introduction to the Principles of Morals and Legislation*, London: Methuen, 1982, p. 117) that "The dictates of utility are neither more nor less than the dictates of the most extensive and enlightened (that is, *well-advised*) benevolence." For the idea of utilitarian evaluation from a *sub specie aeternitatis* perspective, see Smart's "An Outline of a System of Utilitarian Ethics" (in Smart and Williams, *Utilitarianism: for and against*, Cambridge, 1972, p. 63); Williams's "A Critique of Utilitarianism" (in Smart and Williams, *op. cit.*, p. 118); and T. Nagel's "Subjective and Objective" (in his *Mortal Questions*, Cambridge 1979, pp. 202ff.).

Rawls (*A Theory of Justice*, Harvard, 1971, pp. 183ff.) portrays the ideal standpoint of utilitarian moral evaluation as involving total knowledge, and he seems to favor an actualist conception of utilitarianism (pp. 22ff.), but his understanding of utilitarianism is in some ways idiosyncratic (p. 182).

3. Alternatively, on the attitude, etc., of a being with all *relevant* knowledge.

4. With consequentialism more generally, matters are more complex and benevolence is not the only possibly relevant attitude, but in the end the issues that arise are similar to those encountered with utilitarianism.

5. See, e.g., Richard Brandt in *Ethical Theory* (Prentice-Hall, 1958, pp. 381ff.). Perhaps I should say that Brandt offers reasons, but doesn't treat them as particularly decisive (and they aren't).

6. See Samuel Scheffler, *The Rejection of Consequentialism*, Oxford, 1982, p. 1n.

# 16

## Forms of Pluralism

Despite all the difficulties described in the last two chapters, some may still want to claim that old-fashioned utilitarianism has a distinct advantage of simplicity over the kind of intuition-based view of virtue and admirability that goes under the name of virtue ethics. Standard utilitarianism ties all its moral/aretaic evaluations to considerations of personal well-being, whereas virtue ethics has proposed no way of unifying all its judgments of admirability under a single such heading or category, and as such it makes judgments of virtue status and admirability depend on what well may be a plurality of considerations requiring delicate weighing against one another. In that respect, virtue ethics, for all its intuitiveness, may be as deeply pluralistic as common-sense morality seems to be, for example, on a Rossian account of prima facie duties. For Ross, duties not to lie, not to harm, to keep promises and the like bear no fixed relation to one another. They are neither all derivable from some single ultimate moral category nor related by any form of lexical priority. On such a view, a consideration outweighed in one situation by some other may outweigh that other in some quite different situation, and delicate intuition is required, therefore, to see when one prima facie principle takes precedence over some other with respect to a particular situation in which they clash.

The pluralism of intuitionist moral views has opened such views to the charges that they make morality subjective and/or that they leave fundamental aspects of morality arbitrary or unmotivated. But as Ross himself and others more recently have noted, non-welfarist non-hedonic versions of act-consequentialism (or direct consequentialism) are open to analogous charges.[1] For if the considerations that make states of affairs good or that fundamentally affect the well-being of individuals are ineluctably plural, then one's theory of the good is just as pluralistic as an intuitionist theory of the right like Ross's.

At this point, utilitarians may step in and argue that they, at least, avoid pluralism regarding personal good and the goodness of states of affairs; and that fact, they may say, favors hedonistic utilitarian conse-quentialism over non-utilitarian versions of these views and over intui-tionism or common-sensism. Hedonism at least reduces personal good to a single factor, to a unity, and welfarism similarly unifies the idea of a good state of affairs, and this, according to some utilitarians, will repre-sent an advantage of utilitarianism, for example, over both intuitionistic moral theory à la Ross and common-sense virtue ethics.

But such a claim on behalf of utilitarianism cannot, I think, be sus-tained. At the very least, and to begin with, hedonism requires us to place pleasure and pain on a single scale. As Rawls, following Santayana, observes:

> [W]e must settle the relative worth of pleasure and pain. When Petrarch says that a thousand pleasures are not worth one pain, he adopts a standard for comparing them that is more basic than either. The person himself must make this decision, taking into account the full range of his inclinations and desires, present and future.[2]

If Rawls is right here, then the relative importance of pleasure and pain is not built into the very notions of pleasure and pain. Far from being pregiven or self-evident, the issue is one that people have to decide for themselves, and even if after careful deliberation, they all came to the same estimate of the relative worth of pleasure and pain, they would nonetheless be relying on common intuition, not on some statable me-chanical procedure or algorithm. By the same token, there is no reason in principle why the application of Ross's prima facie principles or our efforts to judge (relative) admirability couldn't also give rise to (or tend to converge toward) unanimity. Of course, we don't often *expect* unanimity where people have to rely on their sense of intuitive plausibility, but that holds as much for estimates concerning the relative weight of pleasure and pain as for judgments about the situation-relative weight of Rossian principles or about the admirability, for example, of some given mixture of virtues and anti-virtues.[3]

Moreover, the pluralism endemic to hedonistic utilitarianism is not limited to the problem of assigning appropriate relative weight to plea-sure and to pain. For as Rawls also points out:

> [T]here are different sorts of agreeable feelings that are themselves incom-parable, as well as the quantitative dimensions of pleasure: intensity and duration. How are we to balance these when they conflict? Are we to choose a brief but intense pleasant experience of one kind of feeling over a less intense but longer pleasant experience of another? Aristotle says that the good man if necessary lays down his life for his friends, since he prefers

a short period of intense pleasure to a long one of mild enjoyment, a twelvemonth of noble life to many years of humdrum existence. But how does he decide this?[4]

Rawls is here making two important points about the irreducible plurality of hedonism, and thus of utilitarianism understood hedonistically. The first is that, even if what is more pleasurable is automatically better and all assessment of good reduces to issues about pleasure, the various dimensions along which pleasure can be assessed as more or better are not intuitively pregiven or self-evident, and the concept of pleasure itself doesn't simply tell us how to weight those differing positive dimensions. And, second, and more specifically, there is no pregiven or automatic or purely definitional answer to the question of how duration of pleasure weighs against intensity of pleasure. Again, the notion of pleasure (together with those of duration and intensity) cannot by itself resolve this issue, and the delicate weighing involved in doing so may easily fail to result in unanimity among competent judges. It is even possible that the relative weights of intensity and duration could vary from one kind of pleasure to another, so it should at this point be clear that even hedonism cannot evade plurality and the need for delicate intuition.

Of course there are forms of utilitarianism that are not narrowly hedonic, that speak of happiness or the satisfaction of preferences rather than simply of pleasure. But if anything in this area can be said to be self-evident, I would think it self-evident that any plurality involved in hedonism narrowly understood would transfer and be further complicated by the move from pleasure to happiness—in substantial measure, the move itself is largely justified, by those who make it, in terms of the greater flexibility and sensitivity of the latter notion, and this is, among other things, a way of saying that there are more dimensions of happiness than of pleasure. So if anything, happiness is more, rather than less, complex than we have just recognized pleasure to be.

And the accommodation of and to complexity is perhaps even more obvious, and less in need of defense, in the case of a utilitarianism based on the satisfaction of preferences. If we tie human or personal good to the satisfaction of whatever preferences (or considered, consistent preferences) people have, one makes room for many possible bases of preferences, and, most particularly, one may also allow factors not obviously involved in personal pleasure or happiness to play a role in determining someone's preferences and constituting her personal good or well-being.[5]

Utilitarianism may well, therefore, be more complex than some of its defenders and even critics have recognized. Its judgments and comparisons of personal good and bad must take a plurality of factors into account and thus rely on intuition in the same sense, if not to the same degree, that any other ethics must do with respect to such judgments.

In addition—and utilitarians critical of appeals to intuition in deciding moral or other evaluative issues may need to be reminded of this—the utilitarian/hedonist idea that pleasure is good, is not a personal evil, is itself based on strong intuition(s). Bentham in the *Introduction* spends a considerable amount of time discussing a form of asceticism that fundamentally disapproves (all) pleasure and approves (all) pain, and it is difficult to see how a utilitarian or anyone else can reject such a thesis except on an intuitive basis, that is, by considering or appealing to its intuitively repugnant character. No moral view can do without (appeals to) intuition altogether, and the real question, then—as between, for example, utilitarianism and virtue ethics—is whether the relatively greater systematic unity that arises out of an appeal to fewer intuitions can justify the unintuitive consequences that arise from leaving so many other intuitions to the side. Or, perhaps I should say, that would be the real, the most important question as between the two principal approaches we have discussed, if utilitarianism's underdetermination didn't present such a (greater) threat to the viability of utilitarianism.

Given that any specific overall utilitarian view or theory is underdetermined relative to utilitarianism's own stated methodology and foundational assumptions, utilitarianism must either allow itself to be stymied or else rely more freely and substantially on intuition than it previously has as a means to deciding among various possible versions of itself. But in a number of areas, as we have already noted, any such more intuition-friendly utilitarianism would still remain at a considerable distance from common-sense intuition(s), and with its theoretical advantage of unity now recognized as somewhat less than has usually been assumed, I wonder whether such a reworked utilitarian view—and remember we are talking about something that has yet to be actually articulated—can be as plausible as the common-sense virtue ethics defended here.

Clearly, the latter in no way suffers from the underdetermination we have found in utilitarianism. It admits that its principles (as stated in Chapter 6) and its claims about what counts (in general) as a virtue do not by themselves determine every ethical judgment we want to be able to make: for example, judgments about the comparative admirability of various combinations of character traits and judgments about situation-specific actions. But it is insistent that such deficiencies can for the most part be made good by intelligent, sensitive intuition and argument. And although common-sense virtue ethics is self-proclaimedly pluralistic, this is a pluralism with respect to the contents of a single, presumably correct, theory, whereas the underdetermination associated with utilitarianism affects or is a matter of the choice among theories. The virtue ethics defended here allows a plurality of factors into the determination of ethical value, but these are factors operating *within a single overall view*, whereas the threat of utilitarian underdetermination is the threat of being left with a plurality of *different utilitarian views* and no way of deciding among them; such intertheoretic pluralism is far more worrisome and problematic than the sheer or mere fact of intratheoretic complexity. To be sure, it now appears that utilitarianism may be able to avoid under-determination by giving more weight to intuition and possibly allowing for more complexity than it previously has. But it should at this point also be clear that in doing so, such a renewed utilitarian approach would simply be emulating the intratheoretic pluralism and reliance on intuition that common-sense virtue ethics has been completely at home with from the start.

## Notes

1. On these points, see S. Darwall, "Agent-Centered Restrictions from the Inside Out," *Philosophical Studies*, 1986, esp. p. 298.

2. *A Theory of Justice*, Harvard, 1971, p. 557.

3. How much one weighs pain against pleasure may connect with one's attitude toward taking risks. Clearly, in the area of risk-taking there may be differences of opinion even among hedonists and utilitarians. This is just one more topic that must be explored if one wants fully to understand the complexities that underlie and help to determine the various forms of utilitarian evaluation.

4. *Op. cit.*, p. 557. On this whole topic also see Mill's "Utilitarianism"; Amartya Sen's "Plural Utility," *Proc. of the Aristotelian Society* 1980–81, pp. 193–215; and M. Stocker's *Plural and Conflicting Values*, Oxford, 1989.

5. Cf. Derek Parfit's *Reasons and Persons*, Oxford, 1984, esp. Appendices C and I.

# 17

## Conclusion

The present book has to some extent operated at a level of greater abstraction than can be found in most recent work in virtue ethics. But in order to be reckoned with as a genuine theoretical alternative to Kantian, utilitarian, deontological, and other approaches to ethics, virtue ethics must adopt some of the foundational aims of these other views and take into account the structural considerations and issues that have, for example, played such a significant recent role in discussions of common-sense morality vs. utilitarianism (or consequentialism more generally). And it must then prove itself capable of answering foundational questions and of solving difficult problems that other views cannot satisfactorily resolve.

Most of the recent interest in virtue ethics has shown itself in attempts to analyze particular virtues and in descriptions of those aspects of ethics that are unfairly neglected by those who ignore the topic of (the) virtue(s). A utilitarianism that restricts itself to discussing right and wrong action leaves out a great deal that the utilitarian herself should not want to overlook, and until the recent resurgence of interest in motive- and character-utilitarianism, twentieth-century utilitarianism has been far less complete or thorough than what we find in the work of Bentham and Sidgwick. During the period of neglect, of course, the disadvantages and worse of such neglect were not recognized, but in the light of recent developments, it may now be clear—something Bentham and Sidgwick knew, but recent utilitarianism has largely ignored—that everything from functional objects to inner states of character can be systematically evaluated in utilitarian (or in consequentialist) terms.

We have done something here to move utilitarianism in the direction of such greater, self-consistent systematization,[1] but by the same token an ethics of virtue that is content to deal with or define particular virtues or even virtue in general is not a total approach to ethics, but merely a possible supplement to common-sense, Kantian, utilitarian, or other forms of ethics and moral philosophy. Such supplementing developments are very much worthwhile, even if they don't help to establish virtue ethics as a free-standing approach to ethics. Indeed, given the recent history of ethics, the need for an independent virtue ethics may not, perhaps cannot, be appreciated until one recognizes the deep-seated problems of both Kantian and common-sense or intuitive morality. In the light of those problems, Kantian and ordinary morality cannot plausibly (or without great revision) serve as the foundations upon which our (common-sense) understanding of virtue and the virtues can be based, and in this final part of the book, we have seen that a utilitarian treatment of virtue or admirability is also, at least at present, unpromising.

To be sure, a utilitarian approach to virtue or good character gives (the) virtue(s) a role that can be specified independently of its theory of right action. For unlike Kantian and intuitionist morality, utilitarianism characterizes good or admirable character or motivation directly in relation to human happiness and without having to bring in the idea of (causing or leading to) right actions. Thus, again unlike Kantian and ordinary morality, utilitarianism deals with virtue and character on the same level as it deals with right action, rather than treating the former as derivative from or merely supplementary to the latter. But even this enlarged or less secondary role that emerges from a consistently utilitarian ethical approach cannot help a utilitarianism of virtue, for it is in fact partially responsible for the implausible implications of that view that came to light in Chapter 14.

Our present foundational and (fairly) systematic virtue-ethical approach has emerged in part from the felt need to avoid the implausibilities and/or underdetermination of utilitarianism and the paradoxes and other difficulties that plague Kantian and common-sense morality (and common-sense ethics to the extent it includes a moral view as one of its parts or aspects). The idea has been to see whether a distinctively virtue-ethical approach to the evaluation of action and character can go forward surefootedly enough to avoid the pitfalls of the three other major ethical theories we have focused upon. More specifically, if I may talk about the history of the thinking that led to the present book, once I saw, or believed I saw, that the notion of a virtue escaped the difficulties that undermine or at least threaten common-sense and Kantian talk of moral rightness and moral goodness/virtue, I looked for a directly act-characterizing word that would also enable us to escape these difficulties and found what I was looking for in the term "admirable." Indeed, since the notion of *a* virtue is easily confused with that of virtue and since the latter is colloquially interpreted as *moral* virtue, the term "admirable" may serve better than "(is) a virtue" even at the level of characterizing traits rather than particular actions, and so we have frequently spoken of admirable traits (of character) and not just of virtuous traits of character or of virtues or of some trait's being a virtue.

The next step, logically as well as historically, was to consider whether a positive ethics based solely on our intuitive ideas about admirability and virtue-status, and their opposites, could cover enough of the other-regarding facts of moral or ethical life so as to make us not regret our attempt to do ethics without using any specifically moral terminology. And the foregoing chapters—especially of Parts II and III—have attempted to cover just such other-regarding ground and in such a way as to obviate the need for bringing back moral notions. We also saw that the virtue-ethical approach taken here makes self-regarding and other-regarding ethical phenomena seem more of a piece than Kantian and common-sense (and arguably even utilitarianism) allow for. And although this (by me) unanticipated result may not in and of itself be more *intuitive* than other ways of seeing these matters, I think there are clear attractions in such a unifying approach, and I tried to make them visible in the course of expounding the nature and commitments of a generalized virtue-ethical approach, especially in Chapter 8.

Of course, in attempting to deal with foundational and structural problems, I have somewhat skimped on discussion of particular important virtues, and I haven't even tried to say whether or how virtues differ from other admirable personal traits (how character differs, if at all, from personality). So I won't and don't claim that I have tried to say everything that a positive virtue ethics will want or need to say. It will be enough if I have said enough to put virtue ethics squarely on the map of currently competitive approaches to ethical theory—allowing it to be seen as more than derivative from or supplementary to other parts of some different ethical view.

However radical the present approach to virtue ethics may be, it is recognizably much less radical—in relation to the current climate of philosophical opinion—than an egoistic view like those of the Stoics or the Epicureans or Spinoza. But we have not dwelled on egoism as we have on Kantian, common-sense, and utilitarian ethics/morality, because, as I said earlier, at the same time that I was discarding various morality-including forms of ethics, I wanted, for reasons of conservatism and of general appeal and plausibility, to found and formulate a systematic approach to ethics that can cover as much of the same ground as morality does as can be done compatibly with abandoning the forms of morality we have argued against here. If one can formulate a systematic alternative to the approaches criticized here that remains even closer to the latter than our present virtue ethics (much less egoism) allows us to do, then I would say—and it follows from the whole approach of the present work—that one ought to do so and that, in doing so, one will probably be offering us something better than I have come up with here. But until that has been done, the present approach may be our most reasonable or promising possibility. Spinoza's egoism (and, of course, like the Epicureans and Stoics, his view allows for derivative self-interest-serving reasons for being concerned about others) is based on metaphysical ideas that are not very popular at present, and Nietzsche's egoism (if one can accurately characterize his elusive and complex views in a nutshell) rests on assumptions about the underlying psychology of Christian/common-sense morality—assumptions that treat that psychology as largely a matter of aggression and resentment impotently, and poisonously, turned inward—that are not generally regarded as plausible.[2] If one could make them plausible or could do the same for Spinoza's metaphysics, then egoism might be a better intellectual option then it currently is, but failing that, I think a self-other symmetric approach to virtue ethics is the most promising, and that is why I have almost exclusively focused on the kind of approach to virtue ethics that gives ground-floor significance to the well-being, etc., of others, but that, unlike Kant's ethics of virtue, makes room for considerable ground-floor concern for the happiness—and not just the admirability or virtue—of the person whose acts or traits are being evaluated.

In this book, I have also had very little to say about the contractarian tradition of ethics/moral philosophy and about present-day contractarians such as Rawls and Gauthier. In part, that has been because I do not conceive the work of the latter at least as necessarily in competition with or opposition to the various theories we have been exploring here. The idea of an ideal or hypothetical contract, like that of an ideal judge or observer, is in substantial measure a device for generating particular views of morality, and understood most generally, it is unclear whether such a device is necessarily tied to any particular conception of morality. Just as the idea of an ideal observer has played a role not only in deontological theories of morality but also in utilitarianism, so contractarian notions have been used to undergird utilitarianism, just as, differently deployed, they have provided support for anti-utilitarian views.[3] And in fact I see no reason why a virtue theorist shouldn't be able to make use of contractarian ideas in support of her own particular approach.

In addition, Rawls's and Gauthier's respective derivations of morality, however much admired, have been criticized from a number of different perspectives, sometimes with telling effect. There is no room here to rehearse the major criticisms that have been directed at Rawls's use of the contract model, and in regard to Gauthier's argument I would like only to mention what I take to be the particular vulnerability of his attempt to argue from the rationality of certain dispositions to choose to the rationality of acts done from such dispositions. To the extent Gauthier seeks to justify dispositions in terms of their effects on the satisfaction of the agent's desires, but to justify acts in terms of how well they conform to consequentialistically justified dispositions, he raises for himself the problem—familiar from the literature of rule-utilitarianism—of why acts should be justified differently from dispositions. Stephen Darwall has made exactly these points (among others) against Gauthier's contractarian argument, and because I believe Gauthier has no effective answer to this criticism, I very much doubt whether his approach can be made to work.[4] So I don't think we need to consider contractarian views and approaches as any threat to the validity or significance of (a full-blown or systematic) virtue ethics.

In these concluding pages, I would like to mention another facet of the virtue-theoretic approach, an empirical direction in which it may well or may possibly prove useful and interesting. In the wake of Rawls's *A Theory of Justice*, educational psychologists like Lawrence Kohlberg have attempted to apply Rawlsian ideas and categories to the exploration of personality development.[5] And among other things it has been argued that children go through a number of moral stages that culminate in a highest level—to the extent any particular individual develops this far— at which their understanding of morality is Rawlsian or quasi-Rawlsian. This is neither the time nor the place to enter into a discussion of this literature and of the objections that have been made to this enshrining of Rawlsian views at the pinnacle of human moral development. But if the reader thinks about the matter, it should be clear that educational-psychological issues concerning the acquisition of various virtues can be raised along somewhat parallel lines, and I think such issues are well worth pursuing both conceptually and in their empirical ramifications.

For example, both altruism and moderation require cultivation within the individual, and even if very young children display elements of both these traits, parents, teachers, and others have a difficult task on their hands when they attempt to overcome or mitigate children's selfishness and greed. The typical (oversimplified) picture of how children develop (greater) intrinsic moral concern for others involves the assumption that children need to go through (an) intermediate stage(s) where they see certain kinds or levels of concern for others as furthering their own interests, and a similarly simplified picture of the attenuation, say, of childhood demandingness and greediness might well depict the child as having to go through a stage where some forms or levels of moderation are seen (in the Epicurean manner) merely as a means to greater overall satisfaction (the cake will spoil your dinner or give you a tummy ache). But just as the growth of intrinsic concern for others is typically regarded as a form of moral progress, the growth of non-instrumental moderation also strikes most of us as a good thing, a kind of human progress. And this just-mentioned parallelism suggests the more general idea that, on analogy with what Kohlberg and others have done, it may well be worthwhile to study the ways in which both self-regarding and other-regarding virtues develop within the individual. There may or may not turn out to be a relatively fixed series of stages through which any given virtue develops, and there could well be interesting differences to uncover in the multiplicity and order of the stages of development for particular virtues. But at this point we know very little—and I think much less than we should—about these matters.

Of course, since some virtues are other-regarding, previous empirical and conceptual studies of individual moral development may have already in some measure and at least implicitly taken them into account. But I nonetheless think—in fact it seems obvious—that one might well learn interesting new things if one were to study the other-regarding virtues one by one and as virtues; and in any case—and this really is the most important point—previous studies of moral development have had a bias or slant toward the other-regarding that we have seen to be characteristic of our ordinary moral thinking. So work done previously on moral development has largely ignored the development of desirable/admirable self-regarding traits like fortitude, prudence, perseverance, and circumspection. But these traits are, after all and by our common lights, virtues, and if it is worth our while to study other-regarding desirable/admirable moral development, then even apart from any iconoclasm about specifically moral notions, one will presumably also have reason to study the development of self-regardingly admirable traits of character (and personality).

Such studies have been fewer and further between than they should be, and certainly any validity one may see in the approach of the present book should simply add to the reasons one has to hope for or encourage the empirical and conceptual study of self-regarding and other particular virtues, along lines already familiar from the literature of moral development. The lacuna in our understanding is presently enormous, and even if we cannot say that the study of moral development has led to results as firm and as plausible as one might hope for, the study of particular virtues has much in and of itself to recommend it and may even have useful things to teach those working specifically on childhood and adolescent *moral* development.

If, for example, moral development can, among other things, be divided into pre-conventional, conventional, and post-conventional phases or stages, the development of various particular virtues may well turn out also to be chartable (though perhaps with different timing for different virtues) into three such stages. However, the particular contours discovered in the stage-by-stage development of various virtues may also serve to clarify, support, or undermine received or disputed ideas about particularly moral development, so I would think those already engaged in studying the latter have reason to want to pursue or at least encourage the kind of virtue-by-virtue developmental study that has so unfortunately been neglected in the recent literature both of psychology and education. And, just to give you some initial sense of how rich and interesting the studies I am suggesting might prove to be, let me just mention—in no particular or meaningful order—some of the questions that it might occur to one to investigate if one were going to approach the development of the virtues along the above general lines.

With regard to a self-regarding virtue like fortitude, for example, one might be interested in knowing the aspects of family background and individual temperament it correlates positively, or negatively, with, and one might also seek cross-cultural and/or historical information regarding the development of this trait—for example, are peoples who have been persecuted—like the Jews and Armenians—more likely or are they less likely to develop this trait? And from a conceptual standpoint can we make sense of the idea of a pre-conventional or of a conventional stage in the development of fortitude? Or could there be such a thing as instrumental fortitude, and how does it relate, if at all, to the history (ontogeny) of fortitude when the latter is divided up by reference to conventionality? Clearly, this whole set of questions—and many others—could be applied to other primarily self-regarding traits, as well as to other-regarding and mixed virtues like courage, patience, kindness, and generosity.

If studies of the kind just recommended were eventually to accumulate and give us a sense of knowing more than previously about how various virtues develop, those studies might also turn out to be relevant to educational theory and practice. At present, there is much controversy about and interest in questions about the proper division of labor between home and school in regard to the teaching of moral ideals and standards, but that issue, in the light of what has just been suggested, might well be profitably opened up to include issues concerning the teaching of various virtues including self-regarding ones. If it is urged against this suggestion that self-regarding virtues mainly benefit their possessors only, so there is less need to teach them than to teach other-regarding standards and habits that serve to make everyone better off— then the immediate answer ought to be that we can also improve the lot of everyone by making each person better off in self-regarding terms. If one benefits, for example, from being prudent or having fortitude in trying circumstances, then teaching students, or children in general, to have these traits will also tend toward the general good, though it will do so, so to speak, more atomistically, less relationally, than the instilling of moral standards, or of other-regarding virtues, would tend to do.

Moreover, because of our present-day emphasis—not just in philosophy but in society at large—on moral education and moral standards and ideals, most of us tend not to dwell on the self-regarding virtues and on the particular ways in which they are desirable and admirable. And this neglect is perhaps most easily verified or confirmed if one is asked to name a few self-regarding virtues, having been told what the general difference is between self-regarding and other-regarding or moral virtues. Most people are stuck, after naming two or three such traits, for the names of additional traits, but in regard to other-regarding virtues, they find it easier to come up with a substantial or sizable list. One benefit of virtue ethics—considered now *either* merely as supplementary to a morality of rules *or* as the foundation of all ethical thinking—is the way it (re)awakens us to the importance of self-regarding and mixed virtues and makes us aware, probably for the first time, of the sheer variety and number of such admirable traits. And of course both ways of conceiving virtue ethics can lead us (though with different degrees of pressure or urgency) to ask and to investigate whether children are best led into ethical behavior by being taught the importance of particular virtues or whether it is better to teach them moral rules or standards in what I take to be the more usual way.

I am not suggesting that discovering a greater ease or efficiency in teaching people to act in ways we admire, or at least don't deplore, would support the validity of virtue ethics as against other theoretical approaches to ethics. But for obvious practical purposes and as a matter, I think, of general interest, such studies of the comparative effects of the two forms of teaching—whether at home or in school—would be worth having. Am I therefore saying that we should turn children into guinea pigs and ask or bribe schools or parents to focus on the virtues so that we can learn what we might all profit from knowing? Not in the least. There may already, within our society or perhaps among different societies, be relevant differences in parental and school practices in regard to the inculcation of ethical standards. Without in the least tampering with human lives, we might find different parents (in different segments of society or with ethnically different backgrounds) differing with regard to their emphasis on nameable virtues, and these differences might well be enough to give us a better empirical understanding of the relative usefulness or efficiency of virtue-ethical vs. standardly moral modes of moral education.

Also, there may be the possibility of shorter studies that tamper only in the mildest way with people's personalities and that can tell interesting and important things about the efficacy of teaching particular virtues or clusters of such. At a given school, for example, one civics class might be taught about and given illustrations of the virtue of fortitude, and then suddenly, and in seeming disconnection from the content of the civics class, be subjected to some deprivation like going lunchless or having to stay several hours after school, based on some gimicked-up pretext concealing the experimental purpose of the whole set-up. And another, control group might be given totally irrelevant information in civics class and then subjected to the same deprivation, with differences in the patience/fortitude with which the deprivation is faced being the obvious focus of the psychological study in question. Such studies might teach us a good deal about the teachability (at least in a school setting and at a certain age) of various particular virtues and help, therefore, to answer the question whether or how best to teach ethics in school or at home. Clearly, I have been very impressionistic and incomplete in discussing the psychological and educational issues that may be raised by a theoretical study like the present one, in which virtue and/or the virtues assume an importance they have typically lacked in modern ethics. In that sense, this book may have real, substantial, practical implications, but as I have also said, those implications may not so much reflect on the validity of my arguments as on the practical benefits and the intellectual ramifications outside philosophy of taking the virtues seriously.

Of course, it is hardly clear at this point that ethics is best grounded in the sort of virtue-theoretical approach that we have taken in this book. Because Kantianism, utilitarianism, and common-sense morality may be able to find replies to our earlier criticisms and because our specific ethics of virtue is only now just beginning to be examined critically, the claims defended in this book must be regarded as provisional at best. Whether criticisms will emerge that eventually undercut virtue-ethics only time will tell. But the problems of other views and the richness and distinctiveness of an ethics of virtue that discards moral notions without falling into egoism may at least assure us that virtue ethics must be taken seriously as a theoretical option. Its possibilities have been underestimated or ignored in the past, and I hope they are not likely to be in the future.

## Notes

1. Ordinary moral thinking allows for the moral comparison of acts that are not in any ordinary sense alternatives to one another—"it is a far, far better thing that I do than I have done before." And an ethics of virtue can in a similar way say that what Sydney Carton does at the end of *A Tale of Two Cities* is more *admirable* than anything he had done previously. But utilitarianism has never had anything to say about the comparison of non-alternative actions, and it is not easy to develop a good utilitarian way to make transsituational moral comparisons between actions. If we just say that any act with (expectably) good consequences is better than any act with (expectably) less good or bad consequences, we end up, for example, having to say that what is least good in a set of alternatives may be morally better than what is best in some different set of alternatives, and such difficulties may indeed explain why utilitarianism is never formulated in a way that (explicitly) allows for transsituational moral comparisons. The result may be that utilitarianism is in this respect less complete and systematic than common-sense and virtue ethics may rather easily be.

2. For more on such assumptions and on how they stand open to criticism, see my "Morality and Ignorance," *Journal of Philosophy* 74, 1977, esp. pp. 758–63.

3. See, e.g., J. Harsanyi, "Morality and the theory of rational behaviour," in A. Sen and B. A. O. Williams, eds., *Utilitarianism and beyond*, Cambridge Press, 1982.

4. See S. Darwall, "Rational Agent, Rational Act," in *Philosophical Topics* 14, 1986, esp. pp. 50ff.; and, for similar points, though with a different target, my *Beyond Optimizing*, Harvard Press, 1989, pp. 66–70.

5. See Kohlberg, "Moral Stages and Moralization . . ." in Lickona, ed., *Moral Development and Behaviour*, New York, 1976; *Essays in Moral Development*, vol. 1, *The Philosophy of Moral Development*, New York, Harper and Row, 1981, and vol. 2, *The Psychology of Moral Development*, New York, Harper and Row, 1984.

# INDEX

Adams, R. M., 102, 124–25, 238
Adler, A., 201
Agent-neutrality, xvii, 6, 19, 87
Annas, J., 101–2
Aquinas, T., 56
Aretaic vs. deontic concepts, xiv–xvii, xix, 89–90, 93–96, 102, 110, 113–15, 136, 147, 157, 159–68, 223
Aristotle, xx, 33, 54, 65, 89–93, 102, 128, 132, 143, 167, 212–14, 216, 224, 250
Asymmetry. *See* Symmetry/asymmetry

Baier, A., 54
Ball, S., 182
Baron, M., 101
Beck, L. W., 30, 197
Bentham, J., 30, 73, 77, 82, 178, 183, 185, 195, 223, 244, 247, 252, 254
Berkeley, G., 208
Blum, L., 125, 146–47, 149–50, 157–58
Brandt, R., 196, 248
Butler, J., 41, 48, 55

Categorical Imperative(s), 46–51, 56
Clarke, S., 196
Common-sense morality, xiii–xvi, xix–xx, 3–21, 22–24, 26–27, 31, 35–52, 54–55, 59, 76, 81, 83–84, 87–88, 93, 96–97, 112–13, 126, 134, 138, 140, 144, 167, 171–73, 254–57, 262–63
Consequentialism, xvii, xix, 6–7, 12–14, 19, 27, 53–54, 73–75, 77–78, 83–84, 88, 141, 195, 223, 239–42, 245–48, 249–50, 254
Contractarianism, xx, 257–58
Cooper, J., 213, 224

Darwall, S., 56, 238, 253, 258, 263
Davidson, D., 128, 143, 175
Deontic. *See* Aretaic vs. deontic concepts
Deontology, xv, 37–39, 46–52, 54–55, 66, 83–84, 140–42, 144, 171, 254

Egoism, xviii, xx, 7, 10, 12, 23–25, 63, 74, 92, 121–22, 167, 201, 203, 214, 229, 256–57
Elevation(ism), xviii, 201–18, 221–22, 224, 229
Elimination(ism), xvii–xviii, 171–76, 180–82, 186, 191–95, 200, 217–22, 243–45, 247
Epicureanism, xviii, 11, 89, 92, 132, 134, 167, 185, 201–10, 223, 256–57, 259

Foot, P., 8, 19–21, 30, 82, 102, 157
Frege, G., 34
Freud, S., 201

Gauthier, D., xx, 56, 257–58
Goodman, N., 43, 55, 99–100, 103
Green, T. H., 106–7, 115
Gregor, M., 56
Grice, H. P., 183

Hare, R. M., 159, 244
Harsanyi, J., 253